BASIC in Business

BASIC in Business

Arnold Handley
TEng (CEI), MIMI

Newnes Technical Books

Newnes Technical Books
is an imprint of the Butterworth Group
which has principal offices in
London, Boston, Durban, Singapore, Sydney, Toronto, Wellington

First published in 1984

© **Butterworth & Co (Publishers) Ltd, 1984**
Borough Green, Sevenoaks, Kent TN15 8PH, England

British Library Cataloguing in Publication Data
Handley, Arnold
  BASIC in business
  1. Business – Data processing
  2. Basic (Computer program language)
  651.8'424   HF5548.2

  ISBN 0-408-01472-5

Library of Congress Cataloging in Publication Data
Handley, Arnold
  BASIC in business
  Includes index
  1. Basic (Computer program language)
  2. Business – Data processing
  I. Title. II. Title: B.A.S.I.C. in business
  HF5548.5.B3H36 1984   650'.028'5424   83-23714

  ISBN 0-408-01472-5

Photoset by Butterworths Litho Preparation Department
Printed in England by The Thetford Press Limited, Thetford, Norfolk

Contents

1

You are in business

Officially it's Beginners' All Purpose Symbolic Instruction Code, but everybody calls it BASIC. Learn the language and you can talk to computers and they will talk right back to you. Professional programmers try to sneer at that word 'beginners', but you can bet that the majority of business programs sold today are written in BASIC.

It has become the world's most widely used computer language because it is so adaptable, so friendly, so much like English. And it is improving: new, faster commands are being added every year.

How long will you take to learn it? Knock off work in the evening, have a meal, sit in front of the computer, neglect your family . . . six months.

How long before you can exploit the full capabilities of your computer?

Never.

There is so much power in that combination of computer and BASIC that you'll soon realise that you will never be smart enough to reach the end.

To run a business you need a computer, a couple of disk drives and a printer. That's the working minimum. That's what this book prepares you for.

But don't knock the cheap, Sinclair-style, personal computers that plug into your TV screen and store data on a cassette recorder. Running a business on one would be like trying to play Beethoven on a mouth organ yet they are incredible value. They are even cheaper than a weekend seminar on computing.

If you can spend a small fortune on a mainframe, then lucky you. Just mind that you don't get ripped off. There is nothing wrong with the machinery: it is just that some of the prices are exorbitant. The best advice is to find an accounts program or a stock control program or a payroll that ideally suits your own business . . . then buy the computer to run it.

1

Nobody ever takes this advice; everybody is so machinery oriented. So you are landed with an under-used computer and an awkward program that is nearly, but not quite, fitted to your firm.

This book is going to tell you how to patch up that BASIC program. And you will learn how to write programs of your own.

Compare a computer with yourself

When you were born, you could breathe, suck, cry. You could see, but you didn't understand what you were seeing. You couldn't walk, but the ability to learn was there.

A new computer can look out for messages coming through its keyboard and send signals to the video screen – the equivalents of the simple animal functions in a human. And, like a baby, it has a big, empty memory, ready to accept information.

Fig. 1.1 The Commodore Vic 20 microcomputer

Some machines have the BASIC language built into them. Switch on and, with no cassette recorder or disk drives, you can type commands straight to their screen. Others need to be fed BASIC from tape or disk.

A disk containing, say, a commercial payroll program consists of four parts. It starts with the Disk Operating System, the DOS (pronounced 'doss'). This tells the computer to start up, to operate the drives at the right time, even how to read the disk. The technical phrase is to 'boot up', which comes from pulling itself up by its bootstraps. Secondly, that disk feeds in the language. In our case, BASIC. Third, it transmits the payroll program.

At this point, most of the information from the disk is in two places. It is permanently on that disk and it is temporarily in that once-empty memory. You could take the disk away and, unless it needed to refer to other sub-programs on the disk, the payroll program would work.

It is like when a human uses a telephone directory; (1) without the directory you have no idea of the telephone numbers; (2) you have been taught to read English; (3) you carry the necessary number in your head only long enough to dial it. Tonight you will have forgotten it, but that doesn't matter because the information is still written in the book.

The fourth part of the store-bought payroll disk is blank. That is for you to write the details of your employees on. In human terms it is the notepad. You can scribble on it, cross things out, start again.

To sum up

A new computer
>   Can operate itself and send signals to the video screen.
>   Some can understand BASIC.
>   Others can't understand your commands yet.

You put a programmed disk in the drive
>   It reads the Disk Operating System and learns how to READ, WRITE and SAVE information.
>   It can't speak English yet.

The disk tells the computer about BASIC
>   It stores BASIC into its once-blank memory.
>   You can now type words and it will understand them.

No disks?
>   Use magnetic tape.
>   There is not a tape operating system, so tapes are simpler than disks.

It won't do anything interesting
  Until you give it a program.
So either: there is a business program on the disk or tape
  It reads this, stores it in memory then works from memory.
Or: you invent a program
  And type it straight into the computer memory.
  It runs this.
  You may or may not SAVE the program on disk or tape later.

2

Backup

Before even thinking about BASIC you have to buy a box of ten floppy disks or a box of tapes. On them you are going to make copies of the master disk (to save words, can we miss out 'or tape' every time 'disk' is mentioned?) that the shop sold you with your computer.

Buying this box of disks has given you insurance. You can make mistakes, erase them, rewrite them. Apart from bending, burning, spilling coffee on them, writing labels with hard ballpoint pens, getting dust or cigarette smoke inside, putting fingerprints on the exposed surface . . . apart from these it's hard to physically ruin a floppy disk.

But the data is very ephemeral.

Tapes won't load unless the cassette recorder's volume is exactly right. And a spike of electricity travelling through the mains as, in another part of the building, a fridge switches off, can make a floppy disk unreadable. So install a mains suppressor between the wall socket and the computer so that you no longer lose a day's work when a thunderstorm or the workshop compressor causes the power to fluctuate.

You learn to avoid magnetism as a photographic technician shuns light. Things on your desk that you had never thought about can wipe data off a disk: the fancy paperclip holder with a magnetic top, the magnetic paperweight, the executive magnetic toy. The Hoovers that your cleaning staff push around emit a magnetic field from their motors; so do electric fans, the telephone, your electric typewriter, even the computer peripherals themselves. If the disk drives are not built into the computer, where the designers would have taken care of stray magnetic fields, place them at least four or five inches away from the video screen.

If you have a printer, try to plug it into a separate power supply. And if it is a high speed printer, run an earth, ground, wire to take away static electricity as the paper feeds through fast.

With a very sensitive set-up, where you are forced to use a rough power supply, you can discipline yourself to SAVE (that's in capital letters because it is a computer command) your work every hour or so instead of waiting until the end of the morning and then saving the lot. That way, if a power fault occurs, you have only lost an hour's typing at worst. The drill is to BREAK (another command word) off typing, put in a BACKUP (some computers use this word, some don't) disk, think up a temporary name for your hour's work, SAVE the information and then remove the backup disk to safety.

Fig. 2.1 The Atari 800 personal computer

It is analogous to your being asked, say, when your firm's vehicles were last taxed. You don't know but you know where to find out. Neither does the computer know but it came from the store with a built-in ability to know where to find out. You look in the filing cabinet for 'Vehicle Taxes'; it would look on the floppy disk. Don't forget, too, that somebody would have to write all that information about the vehicles and they would have had to put the information physically into the right place in the filing cabinet. Similarly, somebody has to record the data on to disks. If you were to look in the wrong filing cabinet or if the wrong disk were in the disk drive, then neither you nor the computer would find what you wanted.

With everything right, you might find that your vehicles had been taxed on March 23 and you could walk back to your desk remembering this. At that moment the information is in two places: temporarily in your head yet still permanently written in the file; your memorising it hasn't destroyed it. If you forgot half-way back to your desk, you could still walk back and read it again. Tomorrow, when you will certainly have forgotten, that information will still be written there. Unless somebody were to take it out of the filing cabinet and spill ink all over it. If there were any risk of that, or if you have a bad memory, you would jot down 'March 23' on a bit of paper. That is similar to making a backup disk.

Write-protect

The disk containing your main program, the one that you paid so much money for, has to be rigorously protected.

On one edge of the sleeve there is a rectangular notch, about a quarter of an inch deep. That is the 'write-protect notch'. A tag should have been provided to stick over that but if not, a small piece of sticky tape will do. With the tag in place on a 5¼ inch disk, one danger is gone: the computer cannot write new stuff over this and so wipe out the expensive program. The computer can read the disk but not write on it; the 'write-protect notch' is equivalent to the cassette tag that you have to knock out to stop people recording over your favourite tunes.

Eight-inch disks are write-protected if the notch is left uncovered.

So, before you do anything else, stick that protective tag over the notch on your 5¼ inch disks or take it off your 8 inch disks.

Powering up

Small computers have BASIC built in, but most have the language on a disk that has to be fed in.

BASIC usually comes on a disk, free with your computer. To give you value for money, that disk will be crowded with other programs that are a sort of toolkit for repairing and examining the memory of the computer. Heading the programs will be a Disk Operating System . . . DOS.

When you power up with this DOS (is the disk safely write-protected?) in the first disk drive it will automatically instruct the computer on how to SAVE files, how to KILL programs and how to give ERROR messages . . . all the general housekeeping chores of computing.

With computers that already have a built-in BASIC, the disk will add bonus commands like FREE to tell how much space is left and DIR for a directory of the contents. You don't usually get these on tape.

There is no universal DOS. The best-selling computers not only have their own operating systems but also independent firms have produced improved systems. So although you get a free disk containing TRSDOS (pronounced 'Triss-doss') when you buy a Tandy, there are other firms offering NEWDOS and LDOS with more facilities to run your disk drives. Apple has DOS 3.3 and DOS Plus, while Commodore has PETDOS. The nearest to a standard is CP/M, a disk operating system used on computers that individually do not sell in such volume as the brand leaders. Even CP/M has its variants.

And there's no universal BASIC. They all differ, not so much in words but in tiny colons and commas and spaces. Operating someone else's computer is like driving a strange car . . . sure, you can drive it: but where's the ashtray?

Disk operating systems have their own vocabulary. Though some of the words like KILL, PRINT, LOAD and LIST are in BASIC too, and although they'll be used sensibly and not indiscriminately in this book . . . to be pedantic, they are not BASIC.

To get BASIC you must load the DOS disk and wait while computer absorbs its new instructions. Sometimes you have to type the date as an irritating initialisation routine, but more usually the computer chugs and clicks until a prompt comes up on screen for you. This prompt could be a flashing cursor block on the screen, a > sign, the words DOS READY, or, in CP/M, A> which indicates that the first disk drive, A, is ready for work.

Making a copy

Once a copy is made, you can lock your expensive master program disk away in a safe place and can play around with the copy, make mistakes, screw it up; confident that if the worst happens you can always make another copy.

You will have to go to the computer manual to find out how to copy disks. There are several methods and in most of them the protocol, the grammar, the punctuation, are critical. One space or one comma missing and the computer refuses to understand you. Here are some of the main methods.

Backup

You answer the DOS READY prompt by typing BACKUP and the computer should then prompt you with (the words may differ) 'INSERT SOURCE DISK'. It is talking about the master program disk that you want to copy and that should already be in the first disk drive . . . with, and this can't be too often emphasised, proper protection against being written on. You tell the computer it is in place by pressing the ENTER key or RETURN key.

The screen then shows 'INSERT DESTINATION DISK'. This is one of the blank disks you have just bought. This goes in your second disk drive. When you press ENTER or RETURN the computer will take over. It will FORMAT the blank disc, laying down the tracks and marking off the sectors. It will read the first few tracks of your program disk and hold them in memory for a few seconds before copying them on to the new disk. Then it will read a few more tracks and copy them over.

If you own only one disk drive, you will be prompted when to take the original disk out and when to put the new one in while all this is proceeding. When it is over, you have a duplicate of your valuable program disk.

The snags? Some computers will BACKUP only on to a brand new disk; they will reject old disks with information on them. So they prevent you from reusing old disks unless you buy an electro-magnetic eraser to wipe clean the old disk. A better alternative is to talk to other users and find a different disk operating system. For instance, the TRS-80 will not BACKUP old disks under TRSDOS but it will COPY them under NEWDOS.

COPY

This is an extension of the COPY command that copies single programs from disk to disk; it copies the entire disk. The computer manual is essential for this one since the words you type can vary from:

```
COPY
COPY :0 TO :1          (the spaces are essential)
COPY :0 :1
COPY :0 :1 05/12/84 (includes the date)
COPY,0,1              (with commas instead of colons)
```

going on to complexities like:

```
COPY,:0=35,TO,:1,05/12/84,NFMT,PASSWORD,KDD
```

which is useful only to advanced users.

In some computers, COPY is identical to BACKUP: they will FORMAT the virgin disk before going on to COPY track after track.

At the same time they will give you prompts about which disk to insert and where. In others, you have to FORMAT the new disk separately first.

The snags? Most often the computers will blindly COPY on the top of any data that happens to be on the destination disk: that is one advantage that COPY has over certain BACKUPs. The disadvantage is that you could have put the wrong disk in and a valuable program could be wiped out. This is why write-protect tags are so essential. The best COPY facilities first check on the destination disk then pause while they ask; 'DISK CONTAINS DATA. DO YOU WANT IT OVERWRITTEN?' and you have time to say yes or no.

PIP

This is the CP/M version of COPY although some versions of CP/M do have BACKUP as well. Like COPY, PIP can be used for transfering selected programs from disk to disk. It has a wild card, the '*', which means copy everything without bothering about individual program names.

The procedure is first to type PIP, then when the prompt reappears, to have a previously formatted new disk in your second drive and to type:

   B:=A:*.*

which asks for the disk on Drive B to be given all the information that is on Drive A.

Format

This isn't a BACKUP. To give an analogy, when you take a new disk it is as if you had bought a blank notebook and intended to turn it into, say, an address book. Formatting is the equivalent to ruling lines through the pages. And CP/M has another facility: SYSGEN. The 'SYS' comes from SYSTEM, because it writes a minimum disk operating system on to the new disk. This, in your address book, might be equivalent to cutting a thumb index into the edges of the pages and labelling them A, B, C, etc.

Notice, though, that there are as yet no names and addresses written in your book . . . and neither are there any programs written on a formatted disk. The procedure is to answer the DOS READY prompt by typing:

   FORMAT

or with some computers:

   FORMAT 1, NAME, 05/12/84, PASSWORD

Check with your operator's manual.

After pressing ENTER, you may be asked: 'DISKETTE NAME?' so you answer this with any name containing no more than eight letters, like ACCOUNTS or BASIC or TESTDISK or anything you like.

On pressing ENTER again, the screen may ask: 'PASSWORD?' At this stage of experimenting, you are not likely to want to secure your data from prying eyes, so try just pressing ENTER to give a password of nothing. If the computer insists and repeats the question, then answer 'PASSWORD', which is easy enough to remember.

Most FORMATs will wipe out any previous data on the disk, including the operating system you've just put on the disk. The better ones will warn you with: 'DISKETTE CONTAINS DATA, FORMAT OR NOT?' and give you chance to answer yes or no.

Until the formatted disk has the DOS printed on to it – and you do this with the COPY or PIP facility – it won't run on its own in the first disk drive. Depending upon the make of computer, this first drive is either numbered 0 with subsequent drives being 1, 2, 3 and so on, or it is called Drive 1 with the others being 2, 3, 4. In CP/M systems, the first drive is named A with the others being B, C, and so on. No matter how they are numbered or how many drives you own, that first drive has to be powered by a disk containing the DOS, the operating system. But secondary drives don't usually need a DOS.

By not having DOS on a formatted disk, you leave more space for data. Disks aren't endless: they are like notebooks; you can soon fill them. A typical example would be when you had on the first drive a disk so crowded with the DOS and BASIC plus a complex stock control program that there would be hardly any space left on it for your list of stock. Yet you could store thousands of stock items in the empty space on formatted disks in the second and third drives.

Copying problems

If your master disk will not duplicate itself even though you have tried BACKUP, COPY or PIP then there might be a reason for it. A major one is that the people who invented the program may be so annoyed at being ripped off that they have made the disk hard to copy.

Your precaution in making a BACKUP so that the original master disk doesn't get damaged is fine: it is so sensible that you are encouraged to make two or three copies. But it doesn't take some users long to work out that they could make dozens of free copies and sell them to their friends and keep the profit. That sort of thing became quite an industry with music tapes and video cassettes.

If you are in business, you too would be annoyed if moonlighters were taking away your trade or back-street plagiarists were imitating your products; so you can understand how program-authors hate to lose money from bootleg copying of their disks. So the rule is: make extra copies for your own peace of mind . . . but no copies for so-called friends.

Despite the authors' ingenuity, very few programs are uncopiable. Talk to other users or the the firm who sold you your computer and ask about programs that copy other programs. They are called Utilities, Toolkits or Monitors or have the word 'Zap' somewhere in their title.

Copy the copy
When you have made a copy lock the master disk away. Write a label for your once-blank-now-usable floppy disk and stick it on. Don't stick the label on first and then write on it with a ballpen or it will damage the disk surface.

Take another new disk and make a copy of the copy. That is the one you are going to play with.

Now you can relax.

Getting BASIC

With the new copy in the first disk drive, press the RESET button, which is usually hidden at the back of the computer keyboard. The machinery will whirr, then show on the screen its READY prompt.

You type BASIC then press the key marked ENTER, RETURN or CR, which stands for 'Carriage Return' from the old typewriter terminology. Computers have different names for it, but it should be larger than the other keys and possibly a different colour. To save repetition, from now on this book will use the word ENTER.

And what happens now? You may go straight into BASIC with the screen showing a READY prompt. Or you may be asked MEMORY SIZE? then HOW MANY FILES? Ignore these and answer by just pressing ENTER. The kinds of BASIC programs you are about to write do not need to define memory and numbers of files.

A last precaution
Now you have finished this chapter, and before you switch the computer off, take the disk out of the drive. That spike of electricity as you switch off can damage the data on the disk. Even the write-protect notch won't protect it.

The disk isn't permanently ruined: you can FORMAT it again but that's a chore. You can COPY fresh data over it, but what happens if you haven't got an unmarked copy?

So, to be safe, get into the habit of checking that the drives are empty before switching off.

To sum up

Data in the computer memory is only held there as long as the electricity is flowing. So if you are worried about losing it, transfer it to more permanent storage on disk or tape. Read about the command **SAVE** in Chapter 16.

Data on disk is permanent so long as it isn't affected by an electro-magnetic field, either while in the disk drives or in storage. Make several backup copies, never use the master disk as the working disk, fit a filter to the mains, and take the disks out before switching off.

3

Basic BASIC

It is stocktaking time and you say to the new apprentice, 'Go to the stockroom, find the box of screws . . .'. You are holding up three fingers and ticking off the instructions as you tell him. '. . . And count them.'

Then you remember something else. 'Oh, not the ones in the brown box, we already counted those.' You ought to hold up another finger to tell him that.

Two hours later, you go into the stockroom to see if he's finished. 'How many are there, then?'

'I don't know,' he says. 'You only asked me to count them: you didn't tell me to remember how many there were.'

That's how computers work. You have to tell them, in strict order, what to do. Then they do just that. Nothing more, nothing less.

You can try it. Power up, put in one of the copy disks and call up BASIC. With ten floppy disks, two or three with BASIC on, the rest still unused in their box, the master disk safely stored away . . . there is nothing you can break, no matter how little you know about computing. That BASIC language is now in the computer's memory as well as on the disk: you could even take the disk away and the memory would still work in BASIC.

Type something like FRED. It is a handy name to type because all the letters are next to one another on the keyboard. Sure, the word comes on the screen but that's all. The computer doesn't react in any way. Worse, if you press ENTER, it may even say SYNTAX ERROR, which means that you have made a grammatical error in this language of BASIC.

It is as if somebody came up to you and said, 'Fred'. What are you supposed to do about it? Is his name Fred? Does he think that you are Fred? Is it a secret code? Best thing to do is ignore him and maybe he'll go away.

But if you were handed pen and paper and told, 'Print "Fred" ', with a significant emphasis on the word Fred, you would know what to do.

So type PRINT "FRED" and don't forget the inverted commas, the speech-marks, round "FRED". Now press ENTER.

Quicker than you can take your finger off the keyboard, the screen shows:

    READY > PRINT "FRED"   (as you typed it in)
    FRED   (the computer obeys you)
    READY >   (and is ready for more)

So type nonsense: type PRINT "DERF". The screen shows:

    READY > PRINT "DERF"   (the new command)
    DERF   (it obeys)
    READY >   (and is ready for work again)

Why did it print a nonsense word like "Derf"? Because surrounding a word in inverted commas means, 'Never mind what this is: print it regardless.' In fact, if you don't put inverted commas round the words you want printing, the computer will refuse to obey you.

And what has happened to Fred? It has forgotten about him. As the apprentice might say: you only told the computer to print FRED, you didn't tell it to remember who he was.

The way to stick commands into memory so that they are not forgotten as subsequent commands are carried out is to number them. So type:

    1 PRINT "FRED"   (press ENTER)
    2 PRINT "DERF"   (and press ENTER again)

Now type the BASIC word RUN, which tells the computer to start work, then press ENTER.

The screen will show, after your two lines of instruction:

    FRED
    DERF
    READY >

Type RUN and Press ENTER again.

    FRED
    DERF
    READY >

Type RUN and press ENTER again and again and again. The screen will scroll up Freds and Derfs as the computer obeys this first program you have ever written.

To turn this into something more useful to your business, get rid of the Freds by typing NEW. NEW means 'wipe out any existing program and get ready for a new one.' Indeed if you try RUN and ENTER again, all you will get will be the READY prompt. Fred and Derf have been killed.

This time, instruct the computer to print your name and address. For example:

```
1 PRINT "ALLSTOP GARAGE"        (press ENTER)
2 PRINT "LANGHAM"               (press ENTER)
3 PRINT "COLCHESTER, ESSOX"
```

Oh, no, that should be ESSEX. So press the back-spacing arrow on the keyboard to wipe out the mistake and retype those last two letters. Now press ENTER.

Still another mistake: I forgot to put my name. There is no room to write it. The whole program will have to be wiped out with NEW and started again.

Except that there is a programming trick to save this: instead of numbering the lines 1, 2, 3, 4 and so on, you number in tens, or even in hundreds and thousands. The computer doesn't care about this, all it wants is a numbered sequence of instructions. So with:

```
10 PRINT "ALLSTOP GARAGE"
20 PRINT "LANGHAM"
30 PRINT "COLCHESTER, ESSEX"
```

you are allowed the afterthought of:

```
5 PRINT "ARNOLD HANDLEY"
```

Nicer still: the computer will shuffle these into order in its own memory. If you ask it to list the program lines (type LIST and press ENTER) it will show on screen the revised program, neatly set out:

```
5 PRINT "ARNOLD HANDLEY"
10 PRINT "ALLSTOP GARAGE"
20 PRINT "LANGHAM"
30 PRINT "COLCHESTER, ESSEX"
```

So try it with your own name and address: number in tens, forget a line and add it at the end with an in-between number like 5 or 25. Forget two lines and add them as 25 and 27. Make the last line 9999 if you like. Just remember though that every line, when it is completed, has to be logged in by pressing ENTER.

Finally, the whole program is run by typing RUN then pressing ENTER. The screen will show something like:

```
ARNOLD HANDLEY
ALLSTOP GARAGE
LANGHAM
COLCHESTER, ESSEX
```

No line numbers are shown, no print instructions. They are only there if you use the command LIST.

It is often funny to read professionally produced programs. They start off authoritatively with line numbers going 10, 20, 30, 40, 50, 60, and on to awesome lines numbered 2240, 2250, 2260, 2270. And then you can see the point where the programmer has said, 'Aw, dammit: I've forgotten the whatsaname,' as the lines run 2272, 2273, 2274, 2275, 2276 before reverting to the cool 2280, 2290, 2300, 2310.

So, to write a program, you start every line with a line number; you can correct spelling mistakes by backspacing with the left-pointing arrow; and you end every line by pressing ENTER. The numbers don't need to be consecutive, they don't need to go up in even steps; you can add lines out of sequence and the computer sorts them into order. To look at your program, you type LIST and press ENTER. To make ready for a new program, you type NEW and press ENTER.

There are three ways of deleting a whole line. Usually it is enough to type that line number again and write nothing: just press ENTER. In the address programs:

```
5 PRINT "ARNOLD HANDLEY"          (ENTER)
10 PRINT "ALLSTOP GARAGE"         (ENTER)
20 PRINT "LANGHAM"                (ENTER)
30 PRINT "COLCHESTER, ESSEX"      (ENTER)
20 (ENTER)
```

would give result:

```
ARNOLD HANDLEY
ALLSTOP GARAGE
COLCHESTER, ESSEX
```

if it were RUN. The word LANGHAM would be missing and if you LIST the program, there would be no sign of line 20.

The trouble is that, too easily, you can absent-mindedly delete a line by keying in the line number and hitting ENTER. So some newer dialects of BASIC insist that you type either:

```
DELETE 20   or   D20
```

Of course, they have no objection to your rewriting a line. This program has as line 10, PRINT "ALLSTOP GARAGE". If you were now to type at the end 10 PRINT "ENGINE WORKSHOP" and then look at the program by LISTing it, Allstop Garage would have gone forever and the new line 10 would be in its place.

Programs are not written on tablets of stone; they are just electronic impulses that you can change, add to, delete, edit. In fact you will have to, because hardly any program runs properly the first time. For every hour spent composing the program, you can expect to spend three hours ironing out the bugs.

GOTO

Normally the computer chugs, inexorably, line by line through the program. But you can make it jump, go back and go into loops by using words like GO TO. This is usually spelled as one word: GOTO.

What follows is an artificial example, but try adding lines 2 and 40 to your address program so that it looks like this:

```
2 GOTO 30
5 PRINT "ARNOLD HANDLEY"
10 PRINT "ENGINE WORKSHOP"
30 PRINT "COLCHESTER, ESSEX"
40 PRINT "LOOK, IT HAS JUMPED OVER 5 AND 10"
```

The result when you RUN it?

```
COLCHESTER, ESSEX
LOOK, IT HAS JUMPED OVER 5 AND 10
```

There are more practical uses for GOTO commands. Suppose the computer were running through your stock list and adding 15 per cent VAT on to most, but not all, of the items. You could program it so that when it came to an item that was tax-free, it would GOTO a different line. If it were printing a mailing shot and normally starting every letter to Mr Smith with 'Dear Sir,' you would want it to jump those lines and GOTO the line reading PRINT "DEAR MADAM," if it came to a customer called Mrs Smith.

Not only can it GO TO, it can also go back. Add line 35:

```
2 GOTO 30
5 PRINT "ARNOLD HANDLEY"
10 PRINT "ENGINE WORKSHOP"
30 PRINT "COLCHESTER, ESSEX"
35 GOTO 10
40 PRINT "LOOK, IT HAS JUMPED 5 AND 10"
```

But, before you type RUN, read the next few lines . . . the result is going to be crazy but it can't harm your computer. To stop the run, look for the BREAK key and press that. If you can't find BREAK, take your disk out of the disk drive and either press the RESET button or switch off completely. BREAK, though, is best (CONTROL-C on CP/M).

First of all, that continuous loop as the computer runs from line 35 to line 10 shows the sort of speed and power that you can tap if needed. It runs so fast that you can't read the words until you stop it with BREAK. Then you see a screen full of:

```
ENGINE WORKSHOP
COLCHESTER, ESSEX
ENGINE WORKSHOP
COLCHESTER, ESSEX
ENGINE WORKSHOP
COLCHESTER, ESSEX
BREAK AT LINE 30
```

The significant thing is that now it will never print line 40 "Look it has jumped 5 and 10" because line 35 will always command it to go back to line 10.

There is a use for lines that are never reached: they can trap errors. No matter how careful a programmer you are, there is always the exceptional instance that catches you out. Take that mailing list detail: it works fine when you tell it that if the name begins with 'Mrs' it should GOTO the line that prints 'Dear Madam' and if not, it should carry on normally to print 'Dear Sir'. Suppose though there is a Duchess or a Ms or a Lady hidden in the list and the idea had never occurred to you. Their title doesn't begin with 'Mrs' so they are going to get a 'Dear Sir' letter unless you add a line that is never normally reached, like PRINT "SOMETHING WRONG HERE".

The usual use of GOTO is where the keyboard operator is given a choice. As the program starts, the screen may show a menu:

```
IF YOU WANT TO SEE THE    ACCOUNTS     TYPE 'A'
                          BOOKS        TYPE 'B'
                          CUSTOMERS    TYPE 'C'
```

and if they type A the program will GOTO the accounts section starting on, say, line 2000. If they type B the program will GOTO line 3000 and on C it will jump to the customer list starting on line 7000.

Notice how those large line numbers have no comma to mark the thousands. It is 7000 not 7,000 all the time in computing, whether dealing with line numbers or real numbers. A comma has a special significance, nothing to do with thousands.

No line numbers

There are three occasions when you don't need a line number. The first is with the direct commands such as RUN, NEW, LIST and others like them. You just type the word and press ENTER.

The second is if your computer can handle multi-statement lines. These are lines with several instructions on them. So far you have only written one statement per line because that makes for clarity and, if a problem crops up, then it is easier to find the line with the error. Most computers though will treat multi-statement lines just as if they were two separate lines.

Test your computer: get rid of the remains of the address program with NEW and then type this line:

10 PRINT "ONE" : PRINT "TWO"

with that colon in the middle to signal that this is the equivalent to a two-line program. Some older computers may use a back-slash \ instead of the colon.

Tell it to RUN and you should see:

ONE
TWO

Remember though that this is treated as two lines and that the command PRINT has to be repeated. It wouldn't work if you typed 10 PRINT "ONE" : "TWO" because you haven't told the computer what to do with that word 'TWO'.

You could extend the line to read:

10 PRINT "ONE" : PRINT "TWO" : PRINT "THREE" : PRINT "FOUR"

and so on, as far as your computer will allow.

Multi-statement lines are used to save memory, because every line number takes up memory; so the more efficiently the lines are used, the more memory is free for running the program. At this stage you won't need multi-statement lines, but when a long program is crammed into a small computer every memory-saving trick is needed.

The third occasion when a line number isn't needed happens when you interrupt the computer to ask a simple question. All you do is stop the program with the BREAK button and type your question:

? 2 + 2

and expensive electronics give the same answer as a cheap, hand-held calculator. It can be more elaborate:

? 2.002 + 22.22 / 999.9

As long as you preface the question with a '?' the answer will come. It is handy for back-of-an-envelope arithmetic when you can't be bothered to get your calculator out.

Handier still is the chance to BREAK into a troubled program to find out what is bugging it. Maybe you have been using X to represent the amount of money that is supposed to be in the bank, yet the complicated accounts program has had to GOTO this line then go back to that line and GOTO the other line, until nobody knows where it is supposed to be. What is X at this particular moment?

Press BREAK, then type ?X and it will tell you. Similarly, it will answer questions like ?X : ? (A+B)/Z if the computer can accept multi-statement lines.

To sum up

Programs are written in lines. Most machines accept several statements on a line if they are separated by a colon and contain proper commands like PRINT. Lines start with numbers except when there is only one of them, as in ? 2 + 2. Lines are completed by pressing ENTER or RETURN. The orderly run through the lines can be diverted by GOTO.

Read more about **PRINT** in Chapter 4. Learn the significance of **commas** in Chapter 4. There is more about **GOTO** and **GOSUB** in Chapter 10. **Multi-statement** lines with **IF** are dealt with in Chapter 8.

Exercises

1. This program won't work:

    10 X = 2 + 2

Type it in, type RUN, and nothing happens. Why not?
    Make it work.

2. How does your computer handle speech marks, inverted commas? Test it with:

    10 PRINT "FRED SAID, "HELLO"."

And if it doesn't work, don't worry.

4

Address labels

TAB

The last chapter's address program will type your address on the left-hand side of the screen every time you ask it to RUN. But maybe you want the address to be on the right. There are several ways of doing this. That's the beauty of BASIC: there are alternative ways of doing most jobs.

Retype the program using long spaces before your name and address. Something like:

```
5 PRINT"                    ARNOLD HANDLEY"
10 PRINT"                   ALLSTOP GARAGE"
30 PRINT"                   COLCHESTER, ESSEX"
```

hitting the SPACEBAR at the bottom of the keyboard to get lots of spaces. Then RUN it to see the result.

Most computers have a TAB facility just like typewriters. You set the TAB and the printing starts there. There are differences that you will have to check with your manual. Most use the layout:

```
PRINT TAB(30);"ARNOLD HANDLEY"
```

Others use PRINT TAB(30) "ARNOLD HANDLEY" with no semicolon, and yet others, PRINT TAB 30 "ARNOLD HANDLEY" with neither semicolon nor brackets. The punctuation is essential: that's one snag with BASIC. And if you haven't got TAB look for some command that lets you print spaces.

Before you compose the new program, tap the RIGHT ARROW key to find out how many letters will fit across your video screen. Sometimes it is 80, but some screens are only 64 characters wide so, since an invisible blank takes up the same space as a letter, then a line like:

```
5 PRINT TAB(60); "ARNOLD HANDLEY"
```

would result in this:

                                                                                    ARNO
   LD HANDLEY

The object of the new program therefore is for you to set the TAB so finely that your name and address fit hard against the right-hand edge of the screen.

Commas

The third method of moving across the screen is by using commas. These act like permanent TABs set every 16 spaces (but it depends upon your screen).
   To see the effect of commas, add more lines to your address:

   50 PRINT "ARNOLD HANDLEY",   (notice the extra comma)
   60 PRINT "ALLSTOP GARAGE",
   70 PRINT "LANGHAM",
   80 PRINT "COLCHESTER, ESSEX"

When this is RUN, the screen will show your address tabbed hard against the right-hand side as instructed in lines 5, 10 and 30. Then, below that, will be the result of the new lines:

ARNOLD HANDLEY ALLSTOP GARAGE LANGHAM   COLCHESTER, ESSE
X

This example is on a screen width of 64 and, though you can't see the four divisions that the comma commands have made, they are there. The A of Arnold, the A of Allstop, the L of Langham and the C of Colchester start there. Also, because there are 17 characters in 'Colchester, Essex' if you include that comma and space between the two words, there is no room for it in the 16-space final zone. So the 'X' is pushed on to the next line.
   Why doesn't the comma after 'Colchester' force a new zone? Because it is inside the inverted commas of the PRINT statement. Those inverted commas are interpreted as 'don't bother about the meaning: just print regardless'.
   For instance, if you typed PRINT 2 + 2 you would get the answer 4. But type PRINT "2 + 2" and the screen will show just that, 2 + 2, because of the inverted commas.
   Notice, though, how the real commas at the end of every line affected the way the following line was printed. Instead of the address being screened on separate lines, it all tried to come on the same line.

If you rewrote the program as one multi-statement line, it would give very different results with:

10 PRINT "ARNOLD HANDLEY" : PRINT "ALLSTOP GARAGE" : PRINT "COLCHESTER, ESSEX" .

compared with:

10 PRINT "ARNOLD HANDLEY", : PRINT "ALLSTOP GARAGE", : PRINT "COLCHESTER, ESSEX"

even though they look superficially the same. In fact that last example could be written with no dividing colons and only the first PRINT command:

10 PRINT "ARNOLD HANDLEY", "ALLSTOP GARAGE", "COLCHES-TER, ESSEX"

and it would still work. But put the colons back in and you would get an error message because, thinking that anything after a colon was the equivalent to another line, the computer would be looking for, and not finding, a PRINT command. Leave the colons out and put PRINTs in – and you would get another error message, this time because you were trying to give three PRINT commands in one line.

The effect of a semicolon is just as significant. No matter how you wrote your address program, (a) as three separate lines 10, 20, 30, or (b) as a multi-statement line separated by colons, or (c) as one line, if you have semicolons like this:

10 PRINT "ARNOLD HANDLEY"; "ALLSTOP GARAGE"; COLCHES-TER, ESSEX"

the result will run as:

ARNOLD HANDLEYALLSTOP GARAGECOLCHESTER, ESSEX

because while a colon indicates a multi-statement line and a comma means 'move to the next zone', a semicolon means 'join together'. Thus punctuation has a far greater significance in computing than in written English.

So, if you were lost in the middle of a long program and wanted to be reminded of the values of X and Y and Z, it would be no use asking:

? X Y Z

The computer might know the value of X and Y and Z but it has never heard of a variable called 'X Y Z'.

Nor would it help much if you asked:

? X; Y; Z

because if their values were, say 5, 35 and 12, the screen would answer:

53512

joining them together, as instructed by the semicolons. Instead you ask:

? X, Y, Z

and get a nicely spaced-out reply:

5 35 12

Printing nothing

There are many times when you want to print nothing. The blank line between the section title above and these words is a typical example: it makes the title stand out better. Yet it didn't come there automatically. The printer had to be specially instructed to leave that space.

So it is in computing. And the special instruction is in line 15:

```
10 PRINT "NAME"
15 PRINT
20 PRINT "ADDRESS"
```

Most computers will RUN this to give:

```
NAME
(blank line)
ADDRESS
```

Maybe your computer is a bit more pedantic and needs line 15 to be:

```
15 PRINT ""
```

or even 15 PRINT " " with one space in between the inverted commas.   However it goes, you can space the printing out just as you want by using a multi-statement line:

```
15 PRINT : PRINT : PRINT
```

would leave three blank lines.

Hard copy

For your business, you will want to print on paper. The command is usually LPRINT where the L stands for Line printer. That's the golfball typewriter, daisywheel or dot matrix printer that is coupled to your computer.

Some computers pass instructions to this with PRINT P or PRINT/P. There is one computer that uses DISP (meaning Display) to put words on its screen and saves the word PRINT to mean 'print on paper'. We'll use LPRINT.

All there is to do is to recompose your address program, line numbers, TAB details, commas, colons and all, except that the word PRINT becomes LPRINT.

But before you RUN, check that there is paper in your printer and that it is switched on. Otherwise the frustrated computer finds itself sending signals to a dead printer and, infinitely obedient, it will continue signalling until the world runs out of electricity. There is no way you can stop it; no way of breaking into its persistent dialogue, short of switching everything off and losing your program.

Another warning: slip the BASIC disk out of your disk drive for a minute while you switch your printer on, and more especially, off. You may be lucky enough to own a well-buffered printer but, with many machines, that spike of electricity as they go on and off can travel through the system and damage the data on the disk. The disk won't work but it is not permanently ruined. You can re-FORMAT it later, though this wipes off the programs that were on it.

After your address program has run and after it has printed your name and address neatly on the paper, check that it has obeyed the 'print blank line' commands, which should be like line 15:

```
10 LPRINT TAB(30); "NAME"
15 LPRINT
20 LPRINT TAB(45); "ADDRESS"
```

There are some printers that ask for something more than a plain LPRINT, even though the computer does a blank line after a simple PRINT. If this has happened, try:

```
15 LPRINT ""
```

or else:

```
15 LPRINT " "
```

with a space between the inverted commas.

Once this is sorted out, and maybe you have tuned things up by altering the TAB numbers, then you can have your address heading on as many sheets of paper as you want: just by typing RUN.

An LPRINT bug
A common abbreviation for PRINT is '?' and if you type something like:

```
20 ? A * B
```

and then later LIST it, the computer spells it in full as:

```
20 PRINT A * B
```

This is a great time-saver, and you may have been using PRINT instead of LPRINT or PRINT"P" in the trial version of your program so that you can clear the bugs before putting anything on paper. You later change all those PRINTs to LPRINTS by going into EDIT and quickly inserting 'L'.

Watch out for a bug in certain computers: they don't take this. They come across 'L?' and wonder what it means. If you intend to use LPRINT then spell it out letter by letter.

To sum up

All the time you are using PRINT, you have to bear in mind: Do I want the stuff on separate lines? . . . if so, do nothing. Do I want it run together? . . . use semicolons. Do I want it spaced in zones? . . . use commas. Do I want it spaced exactly? . . use TAB(3).

There is no reason why these shouldn't be used in combination in lines like:

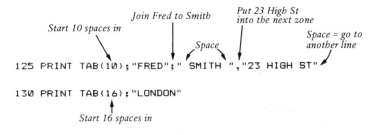

```
125 PRINT TAB(10);"FRED";" SMITH ","23 HIGH ST"

130 PRINT TAB(16);"LONDON"
```
Start 16 spaces in

You have read about **multi-statement lines** in Chapter 3. Read more about **PRINT AT** in Chapter 11. Read about **PRINT STRING$(50,32)** in Chapter 18.

Exercises

The wording in these is not important. You can change it to suit your own use. But test yourself by producing a similar format.

1. Make your computer print forms, headed like this:

```
-----------------------------------------------------------
          ! LAST YEARS ! THIS YEARS ! FORECAST FOR
          !   RESULTS  !   RESULTS  !   FUTURE
          !            !            !   TRADING
-----------------------------------------------------------
     !             !            !
     !             !            !
```

2. Print weekly timetables:

```
-----------------------------------------------------------
              WORK SCHEDULE FOR WEEK
.........................................................
              MAINTENANCE   !  PAINTWORK   !  OTHER WORK
.........................................................

MON      !                  !                  !
.........................................................

TUE      !                  !                  !
.......................... and so on
```

5

Variables

If you own a shop, open seven days a week, and last week's takings were £3456.78, what was the average day's takings? The answer is £493.82, which is 3456.78 divided by 7. If this week's takings are £3004.05 the average day's takings would have been £429.15.

Then, if that is too easy, what will next week's daily takings be? The reason why you don't know is that the weeks' takings vary. You can't divide the money by 7 because you don't know what the money is going to be.

That's why computers use *variables* so much. You don't know the number – because it varies – so you represent it by a letter. You don't know the answer either, so that is called by another letter.

The daily average then becomes $D = W \div 7$. There is no $\div$ sign on the computer keyboard so it uses /, the same symbol that is used in fractions like 22/7. Then at the end of the week when you count the money you know the value of W, and after a bit of arithmetic you know D. The beauty of this is that while 3456.78/7 only gave the answer for last week $D = W/7$ works every week.

People who were not so hot at algebra at school tend to shy away from variables. They can't get rid of the idea that B ought to be bigger than A, and C should be bigger than B, just because C comes after B in the alphabet.

The alphabet has got nothing to do with it. It is only convenience that makes mathematicians choose letters to represent variable numbers. Squiggle = Splat/7 would still work if you gave Splat the value of the week's money. Most computers would accept that. Try it on yours:

```
10 SPLAT = 3004.05
20 SQUIGGLE = SPLAT/7
30 PRINT SQUIGGLE
```

then type RUN to see if you get 429.15.

The simpler computers are going to baulk at the problem because they are only capable of handling single-letter variables like A, B, C and so on. Therefore SPLAT is too much for them.

One or two computers are so smart that they can accept whole words as variables. This makes program reading easy when, instead of mysterious Xs and Zs, you can see recognisable words like TOTAL or AVERAGE.

Most computers cheat though. They give the impression that they are accepting whole words yet really they are only remembering the first two letters. They will run the Daily Average program all right because they think of it as:

```
10 SP = 3004.05
20 SQ = SP/7
30 PRINT SQ
```

But if you use words that start the same, like DATE and DAY or STOCK and STEREOPHONIC, they get mixed up.

Two-character variables give you enough choice. First there are the 26 single letters of the alphabet. Then there are most of the combinations of AA AB AC AD . . . BA BB BC . . . up to ZX ZY ZZ. Then there are letter/number combinations that can be used to name variables: A0 A1 A2 . . . B0 B1 B2 . . . up to Z9.

They are not related in any way. Nor is there any relationship even with variables like C3 and C4. The second needn't be bigger than the first: C3 could have the value of 302.007 and C4 could be the tangent of an angle, e.g. TAN(AF + NZ).

There are a couple of restrictions. While A3 is fine, 3A can't be used. The computer thinks of it as a number and wonders what the letter means. So variables beginning with a number are out. You are also banned from every combination. IE is all right but IF is a word in BASIC so it can't be used to label a variable. Forbidden too are ON, OR, TO, FN and a whole list of 'reserved words' that will be found in your operator's manual. That SQ in the last program is acceptable but SQR would be on the reserved list because it means 'square root'.

It is no big worry. You are still left with some 900 legal combinations with which to label your variables.

A nuisance

Some professional programmers have an annoying habit of using the letters O and I which, though they are legal, makes their programs hard to read. You find yourself puzzling over badly printed lines like:

```
10 I = O : O = 1
```

Does that mean that I is zero or letter O? Is O the same as I or is O valued at one? If you have copied a program from a book and it doesn't RUN, then look again at the lines containing O and I, 0 and 1.

On a typewriter you often type capital O for zero and small letter I for one. This does not work at all on a computer keyboard. O is O, 0 is 0, 1 is 1 and I is I.

'Becomes'

People who were clever at school might have skipped over the first part of this chapter as trivial. All their lives they have had no difficulty in thinking in algebra. To them, the area of a circle is πr^2 and they have solved problems by saying, 'Let X be the unknown quantity.'

But even they find it hard to realise the speed at which computer variables vary. In simple school algebra if N = 4 then it stayed as 4 right to the end of the sum. Not so in computing. The expression:

N = N + 1

is very common. Now that looks crazy if you substitute the value of 4 for N.

4 = 4+ 1
4 = 5

which can't be true.

It needs a change in thinking. You have to throw off years of conditioning and stop calling the '=' sign 'equals'.

Think of '=' as meaning 'becomes'. Now N = N + 1 can make sense. It means: 'A fraction of a second ago, N was 4, now it becomes 5.'

The word 'becomes' works so well that it is a pity it wasn't used years ago when arithmetic was first taught in schools so that kids would have been drilled into chanting, '12 × 2 becomes 24.'

There are a couple of other conventions to be cast away. X is used as a letter in computing so it can't also be used as the multiplication sign. The new symbol is * and 12 × 2 changes to 12 * 2. The + and − stay the same though, and you know about the new division sign, the /.

Also in school algebra, the multiplication sign could be missed out. To indicate 'Y times Z' you could write YZ and to double this, you wrote 2YZ. As you have seen, a combination of letters in computing is the name of a variable, so now you have to think of things like YZ as being just one number and if you want to multiply them, you must write Y * Z.

This isn't difficult to get used to. Where you might slip up is in the use of brackets. In algebra N(F+T) meant 'add F to T then multiply the answer by N'.

This won't work in BASIC. The computer has to be told what to do with N. There has to be a multiplication sign:

N * (F+T)

In BASIC the brackets have the same effect: the computer first works out what is inside them before it works out what is on the outside of the brackets. The reason for that, in computing and in algebra, is that you would get confusion over a sum like 9 − 4 + 3. Is the answer 8, which comes from 9 − 4 (that's 5) + 3? Or is it 2, which is 9 − 7 (the answer to 4 + 3)? Adding brackets, making the problem 9 − (4 + 3), will resolve the ambiguity.

BASIC works with these priorities: first it sorts out the brackets, starting at the inside in complexities like PQ + N * (P − (A + B)). Then it multiplies and divides; finally, it adds and subtracts.

A small snag
Look again at exactly how the Squiggle and Splat example was written:

20 SQ = SP/7

It wouldn't be accepted if you wrote:

SP/7 = SQ

No, the rule is: the new variable first (SQ), then immediately the '=' sign, and finally the definition (SP/7).

It doesn't take long to remember this, because in front of the '=' is a single variable and after the '=' comes a bit of arithmetic. The trouble happens when, in the middle of a complicated program, you want a new variable (call it NV) to take the value of an old variable (say, OV). Maybe OV has been tallying up the number of people going through a turnstile and you still want to keep it going but you also want to multiply NV by the admission money to find out what the takings are. So you put a line:

250 OV = NV

and not only is it *wrong* but it wipes out OV, the number of people through the turnstile.

Ask: PRINT OV and instead of getting 4234 or so, you get 0. This is because the new NV, like all unused variables, has a zero value. Ask your own computer: tell it to PRINT Z or D3 or XF or any *new* combination and it will put 0 on the screen.

So, although in school algebra A = B means exactly the same as B = A, this can't be done in computing. The correct line 250 should be:

    250 NV = OV

New variable = old variable.

To sum up

All this may give the impression that BASIC is mathematical. That is not so. But it is about logic. It is about varying situations. If you know the numbers – if you know, for instance, that for one particular week your takings are £5678.90 – then it is quicker to use a calculator. But if you don't know, or if you want hundreds of calculations, then work out the general formula by substituting variables for numbers . . . and hand the work over to your computer.

Read more about **variables** in Chapters 6 and 7. Read about **arrays** in Chapter 14.

Exercises

1. This book doesn't bother, but does your computer insist on having the word LET before you define a variable? If it insists on:

    10 LET B = 25

then that's an added chore. You have our sympathy. Test it first with the word LET and then without.

2. Or maybe you are lucky and own a machine that doesn't care whether there are spaces between the commands or not. This may look confusing to read at first but when you get used to it, it saves a lot of typing time. Test your computer with:

    10 B=25
    20 C=4:VG=100   (notice, no spaces)
    30 PRINTC*B+VG
    RUN

3. Why doesn't the following program give the answer 17?

    10 GF = 5
    20 HJ = 2(GF + 1)
    30 HJ = OT
    40 PRINT (OT + GF)

There are two mistakes in it.

6

Strings

Computing isn't just numbers. Every word in this book was typed at a computer keyboard and only a bit of it is about arithmetic.

BASIC can label anything in inverted commas as a *string* variable, presumably because words are strings of characters. The symbol is $ and it can be shown working in this trivial example:

```
10 A$ = " WAS VERY TOUGH ": Z$ = "THE "
20 ZH$ = "IN" : B$ = " BUS" : G3$ = "ESS"
30 DA$ = "1984"
40 S$ = " "
50 PRINT Z$; B$; S$; B$; ZH$;
60 PRINT G3$
70 PRINT A$; ZH$; S$; DA$
```

If you could accept numeric variables in the last chapter, and happily write things like A = 5, then there is no reason why A$ (some people pronounce it 'A dollars' but it has nothing to do with money; you pronounce it 'A string') shouldn't represent the string of characters "WAS VERY TOUGH".

Secondly, the variables have been deliberately mixed up to remind you that there is no relationship between them and the words in the inverted commas. Once you have lost that preconception, you can safely use sensible mnemonics like B$ = " BUS" and DA$ = the date.

Notice line 40, where S$ is nothing more than a tap of the spacebar. Some of the strings inside the inverted commas have spaces, some haven't. BASIC doesn't care about our convention of having spaces between words, it just prints what it is told. So when you RUN the program, you should get:

THE BUS BUSINESS
WAS VERY TOUGH IN 1984

34

because the semicolons and ends of lines operate just the same when printing variables as they did when printing your name in Chapter 4. If there had been commas rather than semicolons, they would have put the strings into tabbed zones and it would have worked like this:

Consider that "1984". It is treated as a string, not as a number. In real life, a date like 1984 is not always a number on which you can do arithmetic. Certainly you can subtract 1984 − 1974 and say that there were 10 years' difference. But 1984 * 7 doesn't make sense.

There are plenty of 'numbers' like that: a house number is a place rather than an arithmetical number; a 972 fanbelt may or may not be larger than a 903 fanbelt; Size 8 isn't twice as big as Size 4.

If you confuse numbers with strings you get error messages: N$ = 25 is wrong because, without inverted commas, that 25 is a real number. And K = "FRED" is wrong because variable K, without the $, can only be allocated to a number.

Concatenation

Get it right though, and you can manipulate strings. The old joke, 'What's 2 + 2? Answer: twenty-two', really does work in BASIC as long as you put inverted commas round those 2s and treat them as strings. Try:

```
10 T = 2
20 T$ = "2"
30 PRINT T + T
40 PRINT T$ + T$
```

This will RUN to give two answers, 4 and 22, as line 30 does the correct arithmetic to produce 4 and line 40 joins the strings together to give 22. The operation in line 40 is called *concatenation* and the command is +.

Look again, though, at those answers, 4 and 22. The 4 is a true number but the "22" is still a string. Test this with two more lines:

```
50 PRINT (T + T) * 3
```

which will RUN to give the expected 12, but

    60 PRINT (T$ + T$) * 3

will be thrown out with an error message TYPE MISMATCH because you have tried to multiply the string "22" with a true number, 3.

VAL

There is a way to turn strings back into real numbers. The command is VAL ( ), short for 'value', and the string is written inside the brackets. So:

    60 PRINT VAL(T$ + T$) * 3

really would give an answer 66.

    Running through that slowly: (a) the computer looked in its memory for the meaning of T$ and found "2"; (b) it concatenated (joined) the "2" + "2" to make "22"; (c) the VAL command translated that into a real number, 22; and (d) it multiplied by 3.

    This also works with strings that are a mixture of numeric characters and words:

    10 EX$ = "25 DECEMBER"
    20 PRINT VAL(EX$)

would answer 25, and you could do arithmetic on that 25. But:

    10 EX$ = "JOE 90"
    20 PRINT VAL(EX$)

wouldn't work, unless you own an exceptional computer, because that 90 isn't at the beginning of a string.

    Beware of this because it may not throw up an error message to show you that you are going wrong. It may quietly look at "JOE 90" and think, 'I can't see a number at the beginning so I'll call it zero.' And in a long program you are hopefully imagining that the computer is multiplying later variables by 90 while really it will be multiplying by a 0 and screwing up your totals.

    The rule for most machines is that as soon as VAL ( ) meets anything that is not a number, it will give up its search. So VAL("10 COMMANDMENTS") gives 10 because it finds the numbers; VAL("2 + 2") only gives 2 because it is stopped by the + sign; and VAL("JANUARY 1985") gives 0 as soon as it meets the J in "JANUARY".

    Some further examples: VAL(T$ + T$) where T$ = "2", gives 22 because it first concatenates into a string, "22", under the Do Brackets First rule; VAL(T$ + "." + T$) surprisingly gives the real number 2.2, with that "." turned into a genuine decimal point; but VAL("2 15 TRAIN") breaks the rules. Many BASICs would ignore the blank between 2 and 15 and, unfortunately, give 215.

And, equally awkward for doing books, VAL("$35.97") will give a 0 because it doesn't consider $ to be part of a number. You have to work the money out in straight numbers and then PRINT the total as a string variable plus numeric variable. Something like this:

```
100 MO = 20.90          (Monday's money)
110 TU = 5.00           (Tuesday's money)
120 WE = 10.07          (Wednesday's money)
130 T = MO + TU + WE    (total)
140 D$ = "$ "
150 PRINT D$; T
```

String bugs

In the early days of computing, a live bug once crawled into the works, died across the circuitry and caused days of mysterious errors. So errors are now called 'bugs'.

You can concatenate yourself into a bug. Most BASICs limit the length of any one string to 255 characters. That's no problem: if you want to write FREDERICK H ROBINSON, 233 SYCAMORE AVENUE, SOUTH MORESFIELD, CLEVELAND – TYPE OF MOTORCYCLE: SECONDHAND 1983 KAWASAKI KH125 EX. BOUGHT 23 FEBRUARY 1984, there's room.

But if you join (concatenate) this to the next string in your filing system, you hit a STRING TOO LONG error message.

To sum up

A 'string' is a string of characters. It can be labelled just like numeric variables but with a $ sign added . . . A$, AB$. It can be concatenated (joined) and, as you'll see later in this book, it can be split up. VAL(A$) extracts the number from it.

Read more about **strings** in the next chapter. Read about **arrays** in Chapter 14. Read about **splitting strings** in Chapter 17. Read about **STR$** – the opposite to VAL – in Chapter 18.

Exercises

1. In the example where you were adding up Monday's money, Tuesday's money and Wednesday's money the variables were MO, TU and WE. How come the Total variable was T and not TO?

2. Here are some words and numbers:

   34   FRED   BOEING 747   12/04/84   12.0484

Fit them to these variables:

   A1 A1$ 2B 2B$ C3 C3$ D2 D2$ E E$

Sorry: there seem to be too many variables. Throw out the two wrong ones and ignore any surplus.

3. Some small computers can't handle more than 16 characters in a string. Test yours:

   10 TE$ = "THIS IS A TEST TO SEE HOW MANY CHARACTERS MY COMPUTER CAN HANDLE."
   20 PRINT TE$

Does it RUN all right?

7

INPUT

Putting something into a computer is called INPUT, but try to avoid the word in ordinary speech. If the screen were to show a newcomer to your staff a pretentious:

INPUT NAME?

it would put them off computing. Whereas:

WHAT'S YOUR NAME?

is a lot friendlier. If you feed this into your programs:

10 PRINT "WHAT'S YOUR NAME?"
20 INPUT N$
30 PRINT "HELLO " N$

it RUNs to ask:

WHAT'S YOUR NAME ?
?

then waits for an answer. That second ? on the lower line belongs to the INPUT statement.

It will wait forever until someone (perhaps Fred again) types in their name and completes the answer by pressing ENTER. Only then does the screen show:

HELLO FRED

There is an improvement on this in some computers. They will do it this way with a PRINT line followed by the INPUT line, but they will also allow the words and the INPUT to be on the same line, so that there is no need for a separate PRINT line:

10 INPUT "WHAT'S YOUR NAME "; N$
30 PRINT "HELLO " N$

In this version, notice how there is need for a semicolon before the N$. Notice also that there is no need for you to type a question mark: the INPUT statement provides its own. Notice the inverted commas: they are around "WHAT'S YOUR NAME " in this just as they were with PRINT. Yet no inverted commas are needed for the answer, even though "FRED" must be a string.

Obviously this little program will accept somebody's name, but because the N$ variable is a string, it will accept anything. You can answer RUBBISH and still get the polite reply:

HELLO RUBBISH

You can also answer with a number and get:

HELLO 5

That 'number', though, is stored as a string. Somewhere in memory is a note that N$ = "5". You would get an error message if you tried to multiply or divide it.

In business you are likely to need numeric input: the day's takings, the percentage tax, the amount of stock, all need numeric variables like N, ZX, F3, and so on. (But remember that stock numbers are strings: a 57577332 wiper blade would be INPUT under N$.) So for numbers the program is:

```
10 INPUT "HOW MANY ITEMS "; G
20 INPUT "WHAT IS THE PRICE "; PR
30 PRINT "TOTAL COST = " PR * G
```

The screen would ask:

HOW MANY ITEMS?

then it would wait for somebody to type 15, say, because that '?' wasn't put in by you: it is an INPUT prompt.

After ENTER, the screen would ask:

WHAT IS THE PRICE ?

and wait again for your answer, perhaps 7.34. This time there would be no wait after ENTER; the screen would immediately flash:

TOTAL COST = 110.1

There is no compromise allowed with numeric variables. If you answered HOW MANY ITEMS? with the word FIFTEEN or, more likely, answered WHAT IS THE PRICE? with a £ or $ sign in $7.34, there would be a TYPE MISMATCH error message and the program would halt. That's because you tried to give the computer a string of letters when it wanted a number.

Sometimes you want error messages to happen so that they prevent untrained staff from putting garbage into your computer. More often you want the program to be kind enough to accept people's natural mistakes. The problem of the date is typical. Christmas Day 1983 could be written 25 December 1983, 25 December 83, 25 December '83, 25 Dec 83, December 25 1983, Sunday Dec. 25 '83, 25/12/1983 in Europe, 12/25/1983 in America, 12.25.83, 25–12–83 . . . there must be dozens of perfectly valid ways. A later chapter in the book looks at the way round this confusion.

Your immediate solution, though, is:

10 INPUT "WHAT IS TODAY'S DATE "; DA$

and have the answer come in as a string. All right, you won't be able to do arithmetic on it because even VAL(DA$) will give some funny results: but at least your staff can type their own versions of the date without causing a program crash.

Nor does it matter much. In an invoice program you could have, later:

250 LPRINT TAB(40); DA$

and your customers wouldn't care whether that printed THUR 3 MARCH or 03/03/83 on their bills.

INPUT a lot

Several items of data can be collected with one INPUT statement. They can be a mixture of numbers and words if needed:

10 PRINT "TYPE THE QUANTITY, NAME, CODE AND PRICE"
20 INPUT QA, NA$, CO$, PR

See how QA is asking for a number, NA$ asks for a word, CO$ asks for a string even though the Code for the item might be a 'number', and PR asks for a number.

The screen responds with '?' as it waits for your input, and some computers display '??' after the first prompt. This is what the screen might look like half-way through the run:

TYPE THE QUANTITY, NAME, CODE AND PRICE
? 7
?? SOLVENT
??

There is no problem over your answer to the current prompt, the CODE for the item. Because CO$ is a string you can enter words like QUICK DRYING, or numbers like 5564432, or a mixture like S23-BB77. Just remember that no arithmetic can be performed on that 5564432 until it is changed to a real number by VAL(CO$).

There could be trouble over the next input, the PRICE. Because PR is a numeric variable, it will only accept true numbers. Certainly not TEN PENCE, and it would even refuse $73 because of the dollar sign. Anything except a straight 73 or some other number would halt the program with a REDO error message. Depending on your computer, you would have to re-do that line or, more likely, have to re-do the entire INPUT, right back to entering the Quantity again.

The above dialect of BASIC is pretty good: it puts the '??' prompts line by line and forces you to answer correctly. Other dialects have you answering all on the same line. They say:

    10 INPUT A, B, C

and expect you to answer:

    22, 3, 18

which leads to the problem of what happens if you (a) put in too much data, or (b) don't put in enough data.

With too many answers, some BASICS chop off the extra and carry on working; others halt with an error message TOO MUCH DATA, RETYPE LINE. With not enough answers – if in the above instance you answered just 22, 3 – the BASIC might keep on prompting '?' until you did what you were told or it might give a NOT ENOUGH DATA, RETYPE LINE message.

The BASIC of the 'QUANTITY, NAME, CODE AND PRICE' example allowed a space between words in the strings. It allowed, for instance, QUICK DRYING. Yours may not like that: you may have to fool it into thinking that it is receiving one word, by hyphenating QUICK-DRYING style answers. Or maybe put the words into inverted commas as "QUICK DRYING".

The fascination of being a programmer is in being aware of these idiosyncrasies of the BASICs and then overcoming them so that whoever uses your program never has any problems.

GET INKEY$

People not used to computing need constant reminders to press ENTER. The program might have: INPUT "WHAT'S YOUR NAME";N$ and they have no difficulty in typing in FRED but as the letters go up on the video screen, they just sit watching, fascinated by the miracle of modern electronics, not realising that they have another key to press. Your job as a programmer is to overcome this.

There is a BASIC work, INKEY$, that responds as soon as any key is touched. In theory, it should be included in the program as follows (but don't type it out because it doesn't work):

```
10 PRINT "IF YOU WANT TO SEE THE STOCK LIST, PRESS 'S'"
20 PRINT "    . .  . .  . .  . .      THE ORDERS    . .      'O'"
30 A$ = INKEY$
```

There can be a variation in this. Many BASICs use the word GET so that line becomes:

```
30 GET A$
```

One computer uses 'CALL KEY'. We shall continue with INKEY$.

So, returning to the example, if the operator pressed S the program would GOTO the line with the Stock List. Or O to GOTO the Order section.

The trouble is that computers work so fantastically fast that line 30 A$ = INKEY$ has been and gone and the computer is somewhere working out line 200 by the time your operator has chance to hit a key. The trick is to hold it back by putting it into a loop.

The following example is done in two lines (30 and 40) for clarity: the usual method is to have one multi-statement line.

```
10 PRINT (stocklist and all that)
20 PRINT (for Orders press 'O')
30 A$ = INKEY$
40 IF A$ = "" THEN GOTO 30
```

Translating lines 30 and 40: in line 30 the computer is told, 'Whatever key is hit, then label that as A$'. That instruction is just the same as INPUT so the computer says, 'OK I'll do that,' but dashes straight on to line 40 before anybody has chance to hit the keyboard. Line 40 says 'If A$ is nothing (denoted by the closed-up inverted commas) that is, if no key is struck, THEN go back to line 30 again'.

You can imagine it going from 30 to 40, 40 back to 30, 30 to 40, flash, flash, flash, flash. In the time that a clumsy human is pressing letter S or letter O the computer will grab hold of the answer, label it as A$, and go on to line 40. And this time, the condition in line 40 will not be fulfilled: A$ is no longer nothing, A$ is now S.

So the program then passes to line 50, which will be something like:

```
50 IF A$ = "S" THEN GOTO 5000
```

5000 being the line where you have the Stock List.

You can see, since the program is going nowhere until a key is struck, how convenient it is to put the command on a multi-statement line:

```
30 A$ = INKEY$ : IF A$ = "" THEN 30
```

or in other dialects of BASIC:

    30 GET A$: IF A$ = "" THEN 30

Notice how there is no need for the GOTO. You can put it in or
leave it out, the computer still understands.

There is a need for the previous line to PRINT the question
because INKEY$ doesn't provide a '?' to prompt the typist. INKEY$
on its own just gives a blank screen and inexperienced operators
would have no clue what to do next without that PRINT.

This INKEY$ (pronounced 'in-key string') speeds up operations.
With it you can have slick menu selection. The Stock/Order
example earlier just gave two choices but you could have 20
selections. With it you need no longer have lines as slow as:

    10 INPUT "ANSWER 'YES' OR 'NO'"; Y$

and have to wait for your operator to type Y - E - S and then to press
ENTER. With:

    10 PRINT "ANSWER 'Y' OR 'N'"
    20 Y$ = INKEY$: IF Y$ = "" THEN 20
    30 IF Y$ = "Y" THEN GOTO 5000
    40 IF Y$ = "N" THEN END

as soon as the Y or N key is touched the computer goes into action.

Press any key when ready
Maybe your operator has to put paper in the printer or put a backup
disk in Drive 2; maybe they have to read a screenful of instructions.
Then they have to indicate that they are ready. So, first we have
lines of program telling them what to do, and then:

    100 PRINT "PRESS ANY KEY WHEN READY"
    110 A$ = INKEY$: IF A$ = "" THEN 110

and the computer will wait at line 110 until they hit any key.

INKEY$ bug
The big snag is that INKEY$ only works for one-character answers:

    10 PRINT "HOW BIG IS THE DIAMETER?"
    20 DI$ = INKEY$: IF DI$ = "" THEN 20

would grab hold of the first number you pressed. If the diameter was
894, then DI$ would just become 8 – and to hell with the rest.

The emphasis is on 'string'. INKEY$ will accept a number but
once it has it, it is no longer an arithmetical number. You have to
change it back with the VAL( ) function before you can add,
multiply, subtract or divide it.

Exercises

1. Here is a program to convert Centigrade temperatures to Fahrenheit:

```
10 PRINT "WHAT IS THE TEMPERATURE IN CENTIGRADE ?"
20 INPUT C
30 F = 9/5 * C +32
40 PRINT C;" DEGREES CENTIGRADE IS "; F ; "DEGREES
   FAHRENHEIT"
```

Rewrite this to work out a calculation that you are constantly doing at work.

2. What happens to the INPUT question mark prompt if you put a semicolon at the end of line 10 in question 1?

Can your computer handle a straight INPUT "WHAT IS THE TEMPERATURE "; C ?

3. Adapt your program so that, after giving the right answer, it doesn't stop with a READY prompt but instead goes to (there's a clue!) line 10 and asks the question again and again.

And, finally, here's an idea. Turn your computer into an electric typewriter. Make it operate your printer with a little program using LPRINT and its version of INKEY$.

But how does it stop at the end of a line? You'll have to read the next chapter to find out.

8

IF and OR

IF—THEN

A prime difference between a computer and a calculator is the former's ability to wonder IF.

You can set the computer to run hours of calculations, looking for the right answer, and there is no need for you to sit monitoring the results: it can check for itself using the word IF.

IF is always followed by THEN because when the right condition occurs . . . IF the Price is right, IF the Stock falls below reordering point, IF Mr Black comes before Mr Brown . . . THEN you want the computer to do something about it.

Suppose you were a wholesaler buying oil at £1.75 per litre and selling it for the best price you could get. You could have a neat little Sales program, with Q for the quantities and C for the cost, to give your salesmen some idea of what to charge the customers:

```
10 INPUT "QUANTITY – IN LITRES "; Q
40 C = Q * 1.75
50 PRINT "TOTAL COST = " C
```

and that had been working fine for months until you got a new salesman who didn't realise that you had a minimum order of 25 litres to keep retail customers away. The IF—THEN statement can handle him.

You set up warning lines somewhere else in the program:

```
600 PRINT "SORRY – WE HAVE A MINIMUM ORDER OF 25"
610 GOTO 10
```

Then you direct the program towards line 600 if, and only if, he makes an error:

```
10 INPUT "QUANTITY – IN LITRES "; Q
20 IF Q < 25 THEN 600
```

That '<' sign means 'smaller than'. The '>' means 'larger than'.
Remember them by the smaller side of the '<' pointing to the
smaller number. You know the meaning of '=' sign? Well, '< >'
means 'not equal'. Combined with IF, these are called logical
operators, and a few computers need brackets round them so that
line 20 would become:

    20 IF (Q < 25) THEN 600

Now if the salesman books down 150 litres , that's fine: 150 is not
smaller than 25 so the program progresses to PRINT the price. But if
he tries to sell 5 litres, the program goes to (in some BASICs you
have to write GOTO in line 20) line 600 where it tells him about the
Minimum Order. Line 610 goes back to the beginning to make him
explain all that to the customer.

Multi-statement lines
You could rewrite that Sales Invoice program, so that it didn't have
to go all the way to line 600, by turning line 20 into:

    10 INPUT "QUANTITY– IN LITRES "; Q
    20 IF Q < 25 THEN PRINT "SORRY – WE HAVE A MINIMUM ORDER
       OF 25" : GOTO 10
    40 C = Q * 1.75
    50 PRINT "TOTAL COST = " C

It seems as if computers do as little work as they can get away
with. Yours will accept an input of, say, 150 litres in line 10. Then it
will start to read line 20 'If Q < 25' and that's as far as it will go. It
will know that 150 is not less that 25 so it won't bother to read the
rest, the 'THEN PRINT "SORRY – MINIMUM ORDER"' bit. So it
won't read the ' : GOTO 10' at the end of the line. It won't go to 10;
it will travel on to line 40 and work out the C for Total Cost.

Beware of a bug here. Earlier you may have got the impression
that the parts of a multi-statement line were always just like separate
lines:

    10 A = 1 : B = 7 : C = 4

behaving exactly the same as:

    10 A = 1
    20 B = 7
    30 C = 4

and so they do . . . normally. But in an IF line, on most machines
the extra parts only operate if the IF condition comes true.

In your own programs you know about this and rely on it, but if
you are debugging someone else's program – using that common
technique of breaking up multi-statement lines in order to pinpoint

the error – don't split the IF lines or you will get a different meaning from what their author intended. For example in:

10 A = 1: B = 7: C = 4

then C always becomes 4.
But in:

10 IF A = 1 THEN B = 7: C = 4

then C is not 4 if A isn't 1.

IF bugs
Take care in using 'equal to' (=) and 'not equal to' (< >) when talking to a precise computer.

Suppose you insist on a 33% mark-up on all your goods and you want the computer to check that. Agreed, there are big arguments about the arithmetic of profits, so suppose you use the formula:

Total profit = selling price − cost price

$$\text{Percentage profit} = \frac{\text{selling price} - \text{cost price}}{\text{selling price}} \times 100$$

and put that somewhere into your program:

70 P = (S − C)/ S * 100

and then the check if the profit is not 33 per cent:

80 IF P < > 33 THEN PRINT P "% IS NOT ENOUGH PROFIT"

The bug is that P very rarely will be 33. Nor can you fix it by saying that since one-third profit is 33.33 per cent the line could be altered to:

80 IF P < > 33.33 THEN etc.

Ask your computer what one-third is in decimal, give it retail and cost prices that, for all practical purposes, give a one-third profit . . . and the computer answer will be something like 33.333333. Which, to its finicky mind, is certainly not 33.33.

The cure? In this example: to use the 'less than' (<) symbol.

80 IF P < 33.33 THEN etc.

In other cases you might give the computer some leeway in the IF condition by using < = or > =, meaning 'less than or equal to' and 'greater than or equal to'.

IF – THEN – ELSE

It is a bonus if you have ELSE in your BASIC vocabulary. Not all computers have it.

You use it when you want one of two different sets of actions to take place, depending on how the results so far are working out. As a simple example, you could add to line 80 of the Sales Invoice program, where it complains if you don't make enough profit:

```
80 IF P < 33 THEN PRINT P; "% IS NOT ENOUGH PROFIT"
ELSE PRINT "GOOD, YOU HAVE MADE "; P "% PROFIT"
```

No ELSE on your computer? Then use two lines:

```
80 IF P < 33 THEN PRINT P; "% IS NOT ENOUGH PROFIT"
90 IF P = > 33 THEN PRINT "GOOD, YOU HAVE MADE "; P "%
   PROFIT"
```

In fact, that 'IF P = > 33 THEN' in line 90 is superfluous. If line 80 finds that P is not less than 33 then P *must* be 33 or more than 33.

AND – OR

In the last chapter there was an IF line coupled to INKEY$. It went something like:

```
100 PRINT "ANSWER 'Y' OR 'N'
110 Y$ = INKEY$ : IF Y$ = "" THEN 110
```

and you can imagine that the next lines might be:

```
120 IF Y$ = "Y" THEN . . . do something interesting
130 IF Y$ = "N" THEN . . . do something else
```

(Notice the important inverted commas round Y and N.)

But suppose somebody answered Z ? People do that. They hit the most unlikely keys. A good BASIC can handle that. Check your operator's manual for the word AND: then you might be able to use:

```
140 IF Y$ < > "Y" AND Y$ < > "N" THEN PRINT "SORRY, YOU
    MUST ANSWER ONLY 'Y' OR 'N'": GOTO 100
```

Translated, this means 'if the answer is not Y and the answer is not N then print "Sorry, you must answer only Y or N" and then go back to line 100 to put the question again.'

But look: BASIC can use =, > and < on strings. It can recognise that B comes after A in the alphabet. Try it.

If your BASIC has the word AND, it might well have OR also. With these you can write programs to consider: IF the stock of red paint AND the stock of blue paint is greater than the stock of white paint THEN order more white; and, IF the temperature of the wine vat falls below 18 degrees Centigrade OR the temperature rises above 28 degrees THEN ring the alarm bell.

So in the earlier sales invoice program you can build in check lines like:

> 20 IF Q < 25 OR Q > 9999 THEN PRINT "WE DON'T USUALLY SELL THESE QUANTITIES"

The computer treats these IF—AND—OR lines on a 'do as little work as possible' basis, too. When it meets AND, it will check out the first condition and if that is true, it will check the second condition

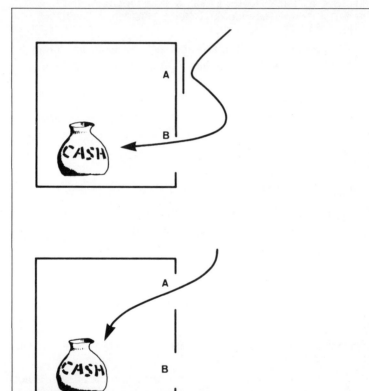

Fig. 8.1 The OR logic. Consider a burglar alarm, wired to the doors so that:

> IF A$ = "OPEN" *OR* B$ = "OPEN" THEN PRINT "TROUBLE"

(1) A thief would check door A and, if it were not open, would check door B. (2) If door A is open, it doesn't matter what the state of B is: there would be trouble

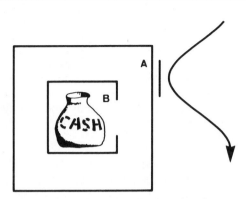

Fig. 8.2 The AND logic. This burglar alarm is set so that:

IF A$ = "OPEN" *AND* B$ = "OPEN" THEN PRINT "TROUBLE"

A thief gets to check door B only if door A is open. If A is not open, no matter what state B is in, there's no trouble

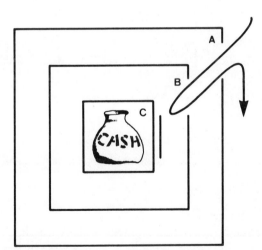

Fig. 8.3 The AND AND logic. Wire the alarm so that:

IF A$ = "OPEN" *AND* B$ = "OPEN" *AND* C$ = "OPEN" THEN PRINT "TROUBLE"

Only if doors A, B and C are open together will there be trouble

to decide whether to take action or – if either of the conditions is untrue – pass on to the next line.

When it meets OR it will check the first value and, if that is true, it will rush off to do what the THEN command tells it, not caring about the value after the OR. It will only check the second value if the first value proves untrue. With OR, only if both the conditions are untrue will it pass on to the next line.

Think of ANDs and ORs as gates. Imagine that around your firm you have a perimeter fence with two gates, A$ and B$:

IF A$ = "OPEN" OR B$ = "OPEN" THEN PRINT "TROUBLE"

because if one gate OR the other is open, a thief can get in. If the first gate he comes to is open, he is not going to check whether the second gate is open or not: there's no point, he is in. Figure 8.1 shows the OR logic in diagram form.

Now imagine the security fence to have only one gate, A$. There is an inner fence with only one gate, B$.

IF A$ = "OPEN" AND B$ = "OPEN" THEN PRINT "TROUBLE"

because only if both gates are open can the thief get in. Figure 8.2 shows this logic and Figs 8.3, 8.4 and 8.5 illustrate the AND AND, the AND OR, and the OR AND situations.

IF–AND–OR bugs

The first two are not real bugs: you just have to be careful, that's all. First, notice the pedantic way of writing AND–OR lines. You can try your particular dialect of BASIC with:

IF A$ AND B$ = "OPEN" THEN PRINT "TROUBLE"

but it is doubtful that it will work. You have to spell out:

IF A$ = "OPEN" AND B$ = "OPEN" THEN and so on.

Secondly, there is an unfortunate mathematical notation which gives

    * for AND
    + for OR

Somebody introduced this years ago, and we are stuck with it. You need constantly to remind yourself that the '+' meaning OR is *not* the same as the '+' in '2 and 2 makes 4'.

The real bugs come when your own logic gets lost in the convolutions of the lines. See if you can forecast these:

IF A = 7 AND B = 9 AND C = 3 THEN jump somewhere

What will trigger off a jump?

Answer: only when A and B and C are correct . . . it jumps. When even one is not true . . . no jump.

IF A = 7 AND B = 9 OR C = 3 THEN jump somewhere

What will trigger off a jump?

Answers: A = 7 AND B = 9 when C = anything . . . it jumps. C = 3 when A and B = anything . . . it jumps. When A < > 7 even if B = 9, if C < > 3 . . . no jump.

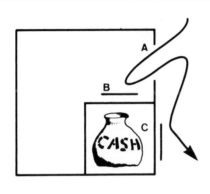

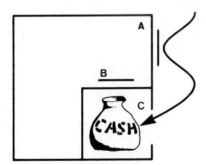

Fig. 8.4 The AND OR logic. With the alarm at:

IF A$ = "OPEN" *AND* B$ = "OPEN" *OR* C$ = "OPEN" THEN PRINT "TROUBLE"

(1) If A is open, B is checked then C. (2) If A is not open it doesn't matter what B is: C is checked and if it is open there's trouble

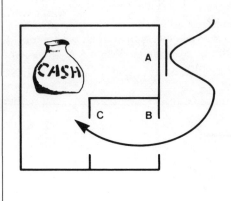

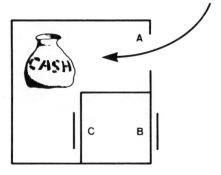

Fig. 8.5 The OR AND logic. The alarm will go off:

IF A$ = "OPEN" *OR* B$ = "OPEN" *AND* C$ = "OPEN" THEN PRINT "TROUBLE"

(1) A is checked then B is checked. If neither were open the thief would pass on. Since B is open, C is checked and if it is open there's trouble. (2) A is checked. If it is open, no matter what B and C are, there's trouble.

The secret is to put imaginary brackets round the AND conditions: to slur these words together and say the last situation as 'If A is open or BandCareopen then trouble'

So far it is logical, but here comes the bug:

IF A = 7 OR B = 9 AND C = 3 THEN jump somewhere

There is no syntax error in that line so the computer won't warn you. What will trigger off a jump?

Answers: When A < > 7 but B is a correct 9, yet C < > 3 . . . no jump. As you might expect. When C = 3, provided either A = 7 or B = 9 . . . it jumps. As you might expect. You have stumbled into the right answer even though you have the wrong logic, and you are going to be surprised at the next answer: when A = 7, no matter what B and C are . . . it jumps.

If this puzzles you, it is because your logic is not the same as the computer. You are in the same situation as in arithmetic when you meet $7 + 9 \times 3$. You could add first and then multiply: $16 \times 3 = 48$, but convention has decided that you would be wrong. Mathematicians long ago came to an agreement to do the multiplication first: $7 + 27 = 34$.

Perhaps you can now see how, in logical operations, + became the symbol for OR and * meant AND. They get the same priorities: the * is done first. Because, remember, the computer can't understand the subtleties of the English words AND and OR, it thinks only in arithmetic.

The line becomes:

IF A = 7 + B = 9 * C = 3

Using this convention of the * priority, the computer splits the statement into:

IF A = 7 OR   (B = 9 AND C = 3)   THEN jump

. . . thinking of the 'B=9ANDC=3' statement as one lump. So if 'A=7' is true, it will jump. Or if both 'B=9ANDC=3' is true, it will jump.

Does yours do the same? Set up a simple test program:

```
10 INPUT A, B, C
20 IF A = 7 OR B = 9 AND C = 3 THEN GOTO 100
30 PRINT "NO – IT DIDN'T JUMP."
40 END
100 PRINT "IT JUMPED – THIS IS LINE 100"
```

Make a chart on a scrap of paper, listing the permutations of A being 7 or not 7, B being 9 or not 9, C being 3 or not 3. Guess what the results will be and then feed the figures through the computer. Then make other programs by just rewriting line 20 with the AND and OR shuffled about.

A cure for the OR-AND bug

Maybe you want the logic of the line to mean: 'If C = 3 and either A = 7 or B = 9 then do something' (if it is a Ford part and the stock number is neither above 1999 nor below 100; if the customer lives less than 50 miles away and he works either Saturdays or Sundays) then you have to override the * priority.

Try putting brackets round the OR section:

IF (A = 7 OR B = 9) AND C = 3 THEN do something

You might have a computer that accepts that.

More reliable is to fix things so that the computer only looks at A and B so long as C is true. Do this by skipping over A and B if C is untrue:

100 IF C < > 3 THEN 200
110 IF A = 7 OR B = 9 THEN do something
200 carry on with the rest of the program

Finally, here's the Sales program in full:

```
10 INPUT "QUANTITY IN LITRES "; Q
20 IF Q < 25 OR Q > 999 THEN PRINT "WE DON'T USUALLY SELL THESE
   QUANTITIES" : GOTO 10
30 IF Q =100 THEN PRINT "SORRY, NO 100 LITRE CANS": GOTO 10

40 C = Q * 1.75
50 PRINT "TOTAL COST = " C
60 INPUT "HOW MUCH ARE YOU SELLING IT FOR ";S
70 P = (S - C)/ S * 100
80 IF P < 33 THEN PRINT P; "% IS NOT ENOUGH PROFIT" ELSE PRINT
   "GOOD, YOU HAVE MADE ";P "% PROFIT"

90 PRINT "DO YOU WANT ANOTHER ?"
100 PRINT "ANSWER 'Y' OR 'N'"
110 Y$ = INKEY$: IF Y$ = "" THEN 110
120 IF Y$ = "Y" THEN 10
130 IF Y$ = "N" THEN END
140 IF Y$ <> "Y" AND Y$ <> "N" THEN PRINT " SORRY ... YOU MUST
    ANSWER ONLY 'Y' OR 'N'": GOTO 90
```

To sum up

With IF–THEN you can make the computer choose to do a piece of work only IF certain conditions are right. With IF–THEN–ELSE it will do one job if conditions are right and another job if conditions are different.

AND can be symbolized (on paper if not in your computer) by *
while OR is +. They take the same priority as in maths, with the
AND * operation being worked out first.

If you are attracted by the science of logic find a textbook about
Boolean algebra.

Read more about **IF–AND–OR** in Chapter 24 on error trapping.
Read again about **multi-statement** lines in Chapter 3.

Exercises

1. What's your job? Rewrite the Selling Oil program to help your
own work . . . and have some IF–THEN–ELSE lines in it.

2. To pass an exam, students need at least 60 per cent marks in any
two of the three subjects: computing, mathematics or programming. But they must have over 50 per cent in English or they fail
completely. Write a program so that when a student's name and
grades are INPUTted, it tells if they pass or fail.

3. How far can your computer check strings? Write a program so
that, if you INPUT two words like PROGRAM and PROTEST it will
say that PROTEST COMES AFTER PROGRAM IN THE DIC-
TIONARY.

9

The FOR-TO loop

Think about a kid's multiplication tables . . . and the kind of chant that used to drift from schoolroom windows. One three is three. Two threes are six. Three threes are nine. Dah dee are dum. They follow a rhythm. You could take any line at random and it would be

First-number times Second-number = Answer
    F   ×   S   = A

Sure, you could write a program to do this but it would be a chore:

```
100 F = 1
130 S = 3
140 A = F * S
150 PRINT F "X" S "=" A
```

Notice how the strings "X" and "=" are in inverted commas to tell the computer not to bother what they mean but to print them regardless. This would print out '1 X 3 = 3' all right but then you have to alter line 100 to read F = 2 to get the next bit of the three-times table.

How many times would you have to do this? Twelve times. FOR F goes from 1 TO 12 in school multiplication tables.

And this is the valuable FOR–TO loop (also called the FOR–NEXT loop) that takes the hardship out of so much repetitive work. Your computer will understand if you change line 100 to read:

```
100 FOR F = 1 TO 12
```

and it will run through the program thinking of F as being 1. So it will still print out '1 X 3 = 3'.

Now put in line 170 to tell it to take the next F:

```
170 NEXT F
```

It will go back to the beginning, it will see that the next value of F will be 2, it will obey line 140 and line 150 and print out:

2 X 3 = 6

Line 170 will send it back again for the next F which will be 3, then go for 4, then 5, right up to 12. The computer will loop through the program, printing out the three-times table just as if you had typed out the full range in line 100. Figure 9.1 shows the sequence.

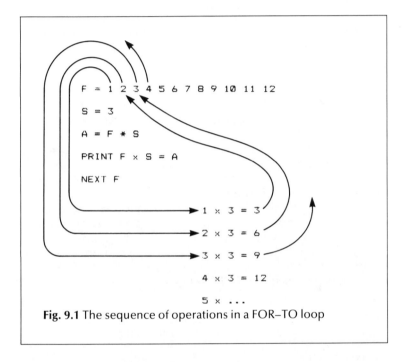

Fig. 9.1 The sequence of operations in a FOR–TO loop

This can be adapted to print out a price list for your business. Let F be the number of pounds or litres or tonnes or boxes of whatever you are selling, and let S be the price for one of them. Line 100 goes TO the highest number that a customer is likely to buy. Something like this:

```
40 CLS                          (clear the screen)
100 FOR F = 1 TO 60             (or 90 or 20 or whatever)
130 S = 3.35                    (if that's the price)
140 A = F * S
150 PRINT F "BOXES COST " A
170 NEXT F
```

You can improve this. That 'BOXES COST' for every calculation is a confusing mass of printing, so just hit the spacebar a few times to put blank spaces instead of words between the inverted commas on line 150. You can't see them but the computer will print them. Or, if you like, you could put dots in there.

Do you want a title? Then put it outside the FOR–TO loop or you will get 60 of them. But even if you squeeze in a new line 20:

20 PRINT "PRICE LIST"

you will still have a problem. This will flash on to the screen so fast that nobody will have time to read it before line 40 clears the screen. So you put in another FOR–TO loop:

30 FOR D = 1 TO 1000 : NEXT D

This one doesn't produce anything on the screen so there is no reason why you shouldn't put the two commands, FOR–TO and NEXT on the same, multi-statement line. It is a delaying tactic. It is the computing equivalent of telling a kid to close her eyes and count to a hundred . . . but, since the microchip works so fast, you tell it to count to 1000 or more. You can imagine that D shuttling backwards and forwards to the next D, a thousand times, while all the time the screen still shows PRICE LIST.

There are many times when you will want a title or a set of instructions to remain on the screen while somebody reads them. Or maybe you compose an examination program that tests apprentices and it gives them only so many seconds to answer the questions. It is handy to know how long your own computer takes to run through a delaying FOR–TO loop.

Get a stop-watch and time this program:

```
1 PRINT "GO"
2 FOR D = 1 TO 20000   (make this number large)
3 NEXT D
4 PRINT "STOP"
```

Hit the stop-watch on GO and check the time before the screen prints STOP then calculate how many thousand loops will delay the computer for one second. That is the figure that you can build into future programs.

Similarly, if you have bought a proprietary program and the title stays on the screen for an inordinate amount of time because it was designed for slow readers, you can BREAK into the program, LIST it, look for that title and the following FOR–TO delay and then you can reduce that number to speed things up (but only mess about with a backup copy, never ruin the original program). It might look something like this:

```
2550 PRINT(TAB20) "PROGRAM TITLE"
2560 FORX=1TO10000:NEXTX
```

and if you retype line 2560 to read:

```
2560 FORX=1TO5000:NEXTX
```

then press ENTER (or RETURN or CR or whatever your keyboard calls that key), the computer will accept the line and you will have halved the time that PROGRAM TITLE stays on screen.

Back to your Price List, which has now got a title: but there are still more improvements possible. Do you sell your products in five-litre measure or in boxes of a dozen? Then the computer will understand if you want to list prices in STEPs. There is just a little problem:

```
100 FOR F = 1 TO 60 STEP 5
```

will make the list run 1, 6, 11, 16 and so on, up to 56, with every STEP being five greater than the last number. You can change this to:

```
100 FOR F = 0 TO 60 STEP 5
```

because there is no reason why the number before TO has to be 1. This will give a list of 0, 5, 10, 15, 20, 25, 30 up to 60 all right, but your first price is going to look stupid, saying '0 litres costs 0'.

You could miss that first price out by starting at 5 with:

```
100 FOR F = 5 TO 60 STEP 5
```

and get a list of 5, 10, 15, 20 up to 60. Or you could even list the prices backwards with:

```
100 FOR F = 60 TO 1 STEP − 5
```

meaning that every STEP will become the previous number minus five. This will run: 60, 55, 50, 45, 40, 35 down to 5. Notice that it still won't print the 1 because 5 − 5 is zero.

Really, even with the simple FOR–TO statement, you are saying FOR F = 1 TO 60 STEP 1 but you can miss out the STEP 1 because, unless told otherwise, the computer assumes that's what you mean.

There are hardly any restrictions on the first line of a FOR–TO loop. You can use variables, as in FOR F = 1 TO N and FOR F = X TO N. You can have arithmetic, as in FOR F = 1 TO (X/N + Z). You just need to remember to call up the NEXT F and not mix it up with the NEXT N because then the computer wouldn't know what you were talking about.

The value of using a variable would come if you intended this Price List program to be used time and time again for different products. There could be a line in it asking:

```
50 INPUT "HOW MANY BOXES DO CUSTOMERS BUY"; M
100 FOR F = 1 TO M
```

and so on.

In the original school multiplication tables program, there was another variable, S, that was valued at 3. There is no reason to stick to this; when kids chant their tables they go all the way to 'twelve twelves are a hundred and forty-four'. That S can change from 1 TO 12 just as the F did. The program could be expanded to look like:

```
100 FOR F = 1 TO 12
130 FOR S = TO 12
140 A = F * S
150 PRINT F "X" S "=" A
160 NEXT S
170 NEXT F
```

and that would show all the tables from 1 × 1 = 1 through all the hard bits, the 7 × 8 = 56, up to 12 × 12 = 144.

But it is important to notice how the FOR S – NEXT S is nested inside the FOR F – NEXT F. You can have as many FOR–TO loops as you like: as long as they are nested inside one another. If FOR F is the first one, then NEXT F is the last one. IF S is the second one, then S must be the second from last one. If X is the third one, then X must come out of its loop before S and before F.

In practice, you can just type NEXT without bothering about the F or the S but this is a dangerous habit. In a complex program there might be a stray 'FOR Z' or something, drifting along, looking for a NEXT. When this old variable, which you had long forgotten about, meets the plain NEXT it will trigger off the NEXT Z instead of the variable that you wanted and so cause hard-to-trace chaos in your program.

But there is no harm in being lazy over a quick delaying loop, as in:

```
30 FOR D = 1 TO 1000 : NEXT
```

because there is no room for a stray variable to squeeze in there.

So your Price List, with its title and delay loop and its 5-litre STEPs, can now cope with price variations.

Suppose you sell three grades of your product: Cheap, Middle Grade and Best. Maybe 2-star, 3-star and 4-star petrol or 9-carat, 18-carat and 22-carat gold. And suppose there is an equal price difference of, say, 50 pence or 50 cents between the grades. That would be in STEPs of £0.50 or $0.50. Line 130 could now become:

```
130 FOR S = 3.35 TO 4.35 STEP .50
```

Better still, you could turn it into a program to be used every time there is a price change by adding a few INPUT lines asking for the latest information. These are lines 50, 60, 70, 80 and 90 in the program below. You can write your own words inside the inverted commas.

```
10 CLS
20 PRINT "PRICE LIST"
30 FOR D = 1 TO 1000: NEXT
40 CLS
50 INPUT"HOW MANY THINGS ON THE LIST ";M
60 INPUT"ARE THEY IN BATCHES OF 5 OR 12 OR WHATEVER ";B
70 INPUT"WHAT IS THE PRICE OF THE CHEAPEST GRADE ";C
80 INPUT"WHAT IS THE PRICE OF THE DEAREST GRADE ";E
90 INPUT"WHAT IS THE DIFFERENCE IN PRICE BETWEEN THE GRADES ";P
100 FOR F = B TO M STEP B
110 LPRINT" "
120 LPRINT F,
130 FOR S = C TO E STEP P
140 A = F * S
150 LPRINT"..... "A,
160 NEXT S
170 NEXT F
```

Some BASICs don't handle INPUT in one line like that. You may need to split the lines into a PRINT then an INPUT, like:

    50 PRINT "HOW MANY THINGS ON THE LIST ?"
    55 INPUT M

It's no problem; it means the same thing.

Your biggest problem will come with the printout. This program makes a very neat job of setting out three price ranges for the Cheap, Medium and Best products. But if you sell more than three grades of the same stuff, if line 130 goes in more than three STEPs, then the printed columns go all over the place.

It pays to type just PRINT instead of LPRINT until you have tuned the program. Then all your confused columns will be on screen instead of wasting paper in the printer. The bits to alter are those commas at the end of lines 120 and 150 (refer to Chapter 4 on PRINT TAB for help). And you can line things up by changing the number of dots in line 150.

Bugs: jumping into loops

In more complex programs, your troubles come when the computer jumps into and out of loops. Everything works well with an orderly program but there are plenty of times when you have chopped lines

out or added sections, until the FOR–TO and the NEXT are
separated by dozens of lines. You might even have chopped the
FOR–TO line out, deciding that it wasn't necessary, and forgot to
delete the NEXT. More likely you'd have the variables mixed up by
having the nesting wrong, as in:

```
┌─100 FOR F = 1 TO 12
│┌─130 FOR S = 1 TO 12
│└─160 NEXT F   (wrong)
└──170 NEXT S   (wrong)
```

The computer will have made a note of the value of F and S in its
memory. But as it passes line 130 it will be concentrating on the S,
looking for a matching NEXT S. Instead, when it reaches line 160,
you have presented it with the wrong variable.

Its defence is to halt the program with an error message 'NEXT
WITHOUT FOR ERROR'. Prevent this by keeping all loops neatly
nested inside one another and never letting their paths cross.

Another 'NEXT WITHOUT FOR' error happens when you tell the
computer to GOTO a line, forgetting that that line is in the middle
of a loop. Imagine that last example with the addition of a line
earlier in the program saying: GOTO 160. The computer will read
160 NEXT F, it will look in its memory banks for F but at that time it
has never heard of F. Avoid this bug by being cautious over
GOTOs.

A stupid little bug happens when you hit the wrong key and type
NEXT G instead of NEXT F. Remember that as the computer is
chugging through all its multiplications and addings and printings it
is carrying in its memory the current value of the FOR variables. In a
big program there could be a lot of these and it would remember
them for a long time.

But, just as you remember half-a-dozen key telephone numbers
and if somebody asked you for another number it would throw you,
so the computer is confused if, despite knowing about F and S, it
unexpectedly comes across a line that asks it what the NEXT G is.

It will reply by halting the program and throwing up a 'NEXT
WITHOUT FOR ERROR' message. The cure is to hunt out the
offending loop, which can take a long time when you are playing
with someone else's program, and to make sure that the NEXT
variable agrees with the FOR.

There is no 'FOR WITHOUT NEXT' error message, unfortunately.
If you have a line:

10 FOR A = 1 TO 50

and forget the NEXT A later, the computer will accept this, leaving you to run blindly through your program, multiplying by A, dividing by A, expecting it to be increasing all the time. Instead it will remain as 1 (well you said, didn't you, 'FOR A = 1') and all your calculations will be false.

Jumping out of loops

This is quite legitimate and reasonably bug-free. Some programmers think of it as a 'till–when' loop or a 'do–until' loop, because the computer is asked to do the loop until it discovers something.

Suppose you wanted a warning built into your Price List when the price got over £100 or $100 because you couldn't afford to pay so much. A line:

    145 IF A > 100 THEN GOTO 500

would do the trick. The computer would jump out of the loop and GO TO line 500 where you might have:

    500 PRINT "CAN'T AFFORD IT"

It wouldn't mind about having unsatisfied NEXTs on lines 160 and 170 and in most cases you don't need to worry either. Your problems come in long programs.

In these there are so many variables that you tend to run out of the alphabet, so programmers get into the habit of using the same variables time and time again. In your Price List, that D of the delay loop in line 30 has done its job and could quite happily be used in a later section. Indeed, it is handy to know that D will always indicate a delay. People make a collection of their favourite variables and use them all the time for routine jobs, which is fine.

However, if you have jumped out of a loop, those FOR–TO variables are still in memory. If your Price List were part of a long program that you had been working on for weeks, you would be choosing variables like Z and X and Y in full confidence that, when you choose them from nowhere, the computer would give them a value of zero. But use an F or an S and it would still be carrying the value it had when the computer jumped out of the loop. That could foul up some later calculation and it would screw it so subtly that you might take hours to trace the bug.

The cure is either to zero the FOR–TO variables or to give them their final values:

    500 F = 0: S = 0: PRINT "CAN'T AFFORD IT"

or

    500 F = M: S = E: PRINT "CAN'T AFFORD IT"

After the loop

Even when the computer runs normally through a loop, there is still a doubt about the value of the FOR–TO variable. BASICs vary, so type in this test:

```
1 FOR A = 1 TO 5
2 PRINT A,
3 NEXT A
```

and obviously this should print out 1, 2, 3, 4, 5. But when it has finished, what is the value of A ? Is it still 5 ? Or has the computer gone on to the NEXT A which will be 6 ? So add:

```
4 PRINT A
```

to see what your computer does.

You need to know this. Just to take one example, suppose you wanted another line on your Price List saying something like:

```
180 PRINT "THE MOST A CUSTOMER WILL BUY IS" F "BOXES"
```

Will that print out 60 BOXES if you had said FOR F = 1 TO 60 or will it print 61 ?

It's nothing to worry about, it's just a little quirk of the BASIC. If your computer insists on memorising the next value then the cure is to make line 180 into:

```
180 PRINT "THE MOST A CUSTOMER WILL BUY IS" (F − 1) "BOXES"
```

Don't mess about with the variables

Expect problems if you alter the variable in a loop.

Suppose you wanted a monthly schedule, broken down into weeks. You might design a little FOR 1 TO 30 loop because there are 30 days in the month and perhaps use D for Day. Then add an 'After the seventh day of the week, start again at Day 1' clause . . . and it could be as bug-ridden as this:

```
10 FOR D = 1 TO 30
20 IF D = 8 THEN D = 1
30 PRINT "THE DAY IS " D
40 NEXT D
```

which is wrong!

Left on its own the computer would have chugged faithfully round the loop 30 times. As it is, with that line 20, every time D reaches 8 it has to go back to 1 again. It will never reach 30. It will never stop.

You have discovered the endless loop. The screen goes blank as if nothing is happening, yet, in the darkness of the microchip, the poor 'D' variable is flipping backwards and forwards millions of times. If you are renting time on a mainframe terminal, this is costing you money.

Fig. 9.2 The ACT 1 Sirius 16-bit business microcomputer

The only way to get out of it is to hit BREAK or the RESET button. This modification would work:

```
10 FOR D = 1 TO 30
15 Z = Z + 1
20 IF Z = 8 THEN Z = 1
30 PRINT "THE DAY IS " Z
40 NEXT D
```

The choice of letter Z for the seven-day-counting variable doesn't matter. What is important is that the 'D' is left unhindered to get on with its 1–TO–30 loop.

There is one other error that you are not likely to make; but in computing, anything can happen . . . don't use the same variable twice inside the loop:

```
10 FOR A = 1 TO 10
20 PRINT A
30 FOR A = 1 TO 5   (wrong)
40 PRINT A
50 NEXT A
60 NEXT A
```

is nonsense. Instead, change those variables to A and AB or A1 and A2 or AA and A . . . anything so long as they are different.

Final reassurance

After all this talk about bugs and programs coming to a halt, be reassured that the worst that can happen if you screw up a FOR–TO loop is that you will have to spend a few more hours puzzling out where your program has gone wrong.

None of the bugs can damage the computer, none of them can damage a disk.

To sum up

Loops can be set out in the form:

```
FOR Z = 1 TO 100
NEXT Z
```

implying that they go up in steps of 1. Or as:

```
FOR Z = 1 TO 100 STEP 5
```

looping in steps of 5 or any other number, including decimals like .02. Or downwards:

```
FOR Z = 100 TO 1 STEP −2
```

They can use variables and expressions:

```
FOR Z = A TO B STEP (C * F + 1)
```

You can nest loops, provided the NEXTs are in the right order:

```
FOR Z = 1 TO 10
FOR Q = 1 TO 50 STEP 2
NEXT Q
NEXT Z
```

You can jump *out of* loops with:

```
IF Z = (A/B) THEN GOTO 2000
```

provided you tidy up the variables. But it causes errors if you jump *into* a loop.

You have read about **GOTO** in Chapter 3 and about **variables** in Chapter 5. Read about **IF** in Chapter 8. Read about the **alternative to FOR–TO** in the next chapter.

Exercises

1. Put a roll of blank sticky labels into your printer . . . all right then: pretend! Tell the printer to churn out 100 labels with your name and address on.

2. Make your computer print on the screen a countdown of 10−9−8 etc. to zero. If it has a voice chip, make it say the words. Get the delay loop right because these have to be in exactly one-second intervals.

3. Look at line 130 of the program early in the chapter:

    130 S = 3.35

then read about the go-faster tricks in Chapter 19.

10

GOSUB

You are totalling up your sales figures and you haven't got a pocket calculator handy. Here is a little routine to let you use the computer. S is the variable for the amount of money taken on every sale. T is the total:

```
60 INPUT "SALE "; S
110 T = T + S
130 PRINT "TOTAL MONEY " T
140 GOTO 60
```

Don't worry about these odd line numbers: the computer doesn't; it just takes them in order. Type RUN and the line 60 will ask:

SALE ?

and wait for you to put in your first amount of money. Just a 123.45 style straight number remember, no £ or $ sign, or the computer will think of it as a string and refuse to accept it as the S numeric variable.

Line 110 might be hard to understand if you have had a formal mathematical education where variables are invariable and don't change their values as fast as in computing. Translated into English, line 110 says: 'T ? I've never heard of T so I'll give it the value of zero. Now T becomes its last value 0 plus S, which I've just been told is 123.45.'

Line 130 prints TOTAL MONEY 123.45, which is the sum of 0 + 123.45. Line 140 sends the computer back to line 60 to ask for the next amount of money on your list. Let's suppose you input 99.99.

This time round, T starts with the value of 123.45 so in line 110 it becomes 123.45 + 99.99. The third time round T has the value of 223.44 and so on and so on, because this is a program that never stops. That GOTO 60 in line 140 has turned it into an endless loop. When you have finished adding your list of sales, you have to stop it by hitting the BREAK key.

A counting routine

Maybe you want to know how many sales you have added up: it is no problem to get the computer to count. Just incorporate:

    100 N = N + 1

and the first time your program runs, N, like the T, will be zero. Immediately, line 100 will turn it to 0 + 1. When it loops, N = 1 + 1. When it loops again, N = 2 + 1.

The beauty of this little routine is that you, the operator, are not doing any work in counting the sales. It is not like line 60, which really demands you to count every time that you hit the keyboard to input S. Instead, both N and T are happily ticking up totals, untouched by human hand.

The FOR–TO alternative

BASIC is tolerant enough to accept several ways of doing the same job. In Chapter 9 the FOR–TO loop was used to build a price list. Here is an alternative. It is neither better nor quicker, just different.

Suppose you want a price list to look like this:

    1 KILOGRAM OF STUFF COSTS $ 4.55
    2 KILOGRAM OF STUFF COSTS $ 9.10

and so on. By choosing N to represent the Number of kilograms, you could use FOR N = 1 TO 20, or you could try this method:

    10 N = N + 1
    20 PRINT N " KILOGRAM OF STUFF COSTS $ " N * 4.55
    30 GOTO 10

You have deliberately created an endless loop where N increases every time it goes round. How do you stop it?

As always, there are alternatives. To stop it permanently, switch off or hit the RESET button. To stop and then RUN again, hit the BREAK key. To halt the inexorable flow of figures, try pressing SHIFT and @ simultaneously and then restart by tapping any other key. If all else fails, as they say, read the manual.

You can program a stop by altering line 30:

    30 IF N < 21 THEN 10

using the IF statement from Chapter 8.

Bugs in N = N + 1

Bug Number One comes from your blind assumption that the computer will allocate the first value of 0 to the N or T or whatever variable you are using in your counting or adding routine. Some machines complain about an UNDEFINED VARIABLE or in a long, convoluted program there could be an old N drifting around with a value of its own. The cure? Write N = 0 or T = 0 before the computer enters the counting process.

Bug Number Two comes when you are so damn careful to do this that you write the 'N = 0' *inside* the loop. Then every time the program goes to the routine, instead of the variable carrying its increased value, it gets zeroed. The cure? Write N = 0 in the right place.

Subroutines

'N = N + 1' and 'T = T + S' are trivial. But take a collection of trivial routines, merge them together and they form a powerful programming aid.

You don't have to be programming long before you realise that, every day, you are re-inventing the wheel. Little chores are cropping up in every program you write: you need a nicely set out title; you want the operator to type in the date; there has to be a check to stop people answering with a number when the program demands a string; you want the accounts to end with neatly tabulated rows of money.

So what experienced programmers do is collect a heap of tried and tested subroutines. It is called 'modular programming'. Then when they are commissioned to write, say, a Wages program, they already have an old title that says:

```
2000 CLS
2010 PRINT TAB(10)"********************************"
2020 PRINT TAB(15) "GEAR RATIO CALCULATIONS"
2030 PRINT TAB(10)"********************************"
```

and another bit that says:

```
5000 INPUT "WHAT IS THE DATE " etc.
```

They MERGE these together with the word 'MERGE' or 'CHAIN' so all they have to do is to edit a few words in that line 2020 then concentrate on the core of the program, the Wages arithmetic.

You already have a program from Chapter 8 to check on Sales invoices at an oil wholesalers. Here it is with an extra line 30 added:

```
10 INPUT "QUANTITY IN LITRES "; Q
20 IF Q < 25 OR Q > 999 THEN PRINT "WE DON'T USUALLY SELL
   THESE QUANTITIES" : GOTO 10
30 IF Q =100 THEN PRINT "SORRY, NO 100 LITRE CANS": GOTO 10
```

```
40 C = Q * 1.75
50 PRINT "TOTAL COST = " C
60 INPUT "HOW MUCH ARE YOU SELLING IT FOR ";S
70 P = (S − C)/ S * 100
80 IF P < 33 THEN PRINT P; "% IS NOT ENOUGH PROFIT" ELSE
   PRINT "GOOD, YOU HAVE MADE ";P "% PROFIT"
```

The story is that, as well as discouraging in line 20 retail customers who want less than 25 litres, you don't have any 100 litre sizes: so the program throws those out too.

It works. Then you get worried about lost sales. How many customers are asking for 100 litres? Would it be worth your while stocking that size? So you count the number of requests by adding an 'N = N + 1' subroutine:

```
100 N = N + 1
110 PRINT N "CUSTOMERS HAVE ASKED FOR 100 LITRE CANS"
```

and you aim the computer towards it with the command 'GOSUB', which means 'go to the subroutine'.

Alter line 30 to:

```
30 IF Q =100 THEN PRINT "SORRY, NO 100 LITRE CANS": GOSUB
   100
```

You remember from Chapter 8 that after IF, the section of a multi-statement line following the colon is only obeyed provided the IF condition is true. In this case, the program will only jump to the subroutine on line 100 if Q = 100. If Q is not 100 then the program will continue in its normal way to line 40.

Return

While GOTO is a very dictatorial command meaning 'go there and stay and work there', GOSUB means 'go there, do the job and then come back again to carry on with the main program'. So it is combined with another command: RETURN. You can't have one without the other.

Bring the 'Count the 100 litres' subroutine back with a line:

```
120 RETURN
```

This returns the computer to the command after the GOSUB. In this Sales program it would be to line 40 and we don't want that. We don't want to waste time working out the cost of 100 litres, because we haven't got any 100 litres. We want it to go back to line 10 and start again.

So add a bit more to line 30:

30 IF Q =100 THEN PRINT "SORRY, NO 100 LITRE CANS": GOSUB
    100 : GOTO 10

This works: if your salesman takes an order for, say, 75 litres the
program calculates the cost and bawls him out if he sells at too low
a profit. If he orders 100 litres it jumps to the subroutine, makes a
note that here is yet another customer wanting this awkward
amount, then returns to the main program at line 30, only to be told
to go to line 10 and take another order.

It shows that RETURN will go back to a multi-statement line. It
will treat the bit after the colon as a separate line – even when the
multi-statement line starts with an IF.

There is one small quirk in this: if line 30 had read '. . . GOSUB
100 ELSE 40 : GOTO 10' it would have returned to the 'ELSE 40'. It
returns to the next *command*, not necessarily the next *line*.

ON GOSUB

One of the nice things about a computer is its ability to surprise.
    Suppose you start a program by giving people a choice:

```
10 PRINT "WHAT DO YOU WANT TO DO? "
20 PRINT TAB(10) "LOOK AT THE BOOKS . . . 1"
30 PRINT TAB(10) "WRITE AN INVOICE . . . 2"
40 PRINT TAB(10) "ALTER THE BOOKS . . . 3"
50 PRINT TAB(10) "QUIT . . . 4"
60 INPUT W
```

then you could carry on with a lot of:

```
70 IF W = 1 THEN GOTO 5000
80 IF W = 2 THEN GOTO 6000
90 IF W = 3 THEN GOTO 7000
100 IF W = 4 THEN END
```

but the more helpful computers have a facility:

```
70 ON W GOTO 5000, 6000, 7000, 8000
```

They look at W and direct you to the appropriate part of the
program.
    There is usually an ON–GOSUB facility too.

GOSUB bugs
The best way to see a GOSUB bug is to run this program as it is so
far:

```
10 INPUT "QUANTITY IN LITRES "; Q
20 IF Q < 25 OR Q > 999 THEN PRINT "WE DON'T USUALLY SELL THESE
   QUANTITIES" : GOTO 10
30 IF Q =100 THEN PRINT "SORRY, NO 100 LITRE CANS": GOSUB 100 :
   GOTO 10
40 C = Q * 1.75
50 PRINT "TOTAL COST = " C
60 INPUT "HOW MUCH ARE YOU SELLING IT FOR ";S
70 P = (S - C)/ S * 100
80 IF P < 33 THEN PRINT P; "% IS NOT ENOUGH PROFIT" ELSE PRINT
   "GOOD, YOU HAVE MADE ";P "% PROFIT"

100 N = N + 1
110 PRINT N " CUSTOMERS HAVE ASKED FOR 100 LITRE CANS"
120 RETURN
```

Feed in 100 when it asks for the QUANTITY and it works fine. It goes to subroutine 100 and it tells you that 1 CUSTOMERS HAVE ASKED FOR 100 LITRE CANS. The grammar isn't too good but it returns all right to ask you for the next QUANTITY. Answer 100 again, for the pride of watching it say 2 CUSTOMERS HAVE ASKED FOR 100 LITRE CANS.

The next time, answer something like 55. The screen shows:

TOTAL COST = 96.25   (right)
HOW MUCH ARE YOU SELLING IT FOR?   (you answer 123.45)

22.03% IS NOT ENOUGH PROFIT   (right)
3 CUSTOMERS HAVE ASKED FOR 100 LITRE CANS   (wrong)
*** ERROR IN LINE 120 – RETURN WITHOUT GOSUB ***

Where did that '3 CUSTOMERS' line come from? Can you spot the bug? What's wrong with line 120?

Plod through the program, line by line. You can forget about line 30 because the QUANTITY wasn't 100. Go on to line 40, line 50, 60, 70, 80 and then, quite conscientiously because nobody has told you otherwise, carry on with line 100, line 110 and pick up an error message in line 120.

The real error was in going on to line 100, crashing into the subroutine that was designed only to be used if QUANTITY = 100. That's the bug: there is no error in line 120.

All right: the computer met a RETURN without first meeting a GOSUB; the reason for that was that it read the first bit of line 30, saw that Q was not 100 and never bothered to read any more of that line.

The cure? To write some sort of STOP or END just before the subroutine, to stop the main program crashing through. Normally:

90 END

would cure the problem. But, in this program, if you typed RUN to restart for another sales invoice you would zero all the variables. And you don't want to zero N because that is being used to count the customers. In this program:

90 GOTO 10

would send the computer back to the start, ready for another input. It would always loop, never crash into the subroutine, and N would be left undisturbed.

So the debugged program would look like this:

```
10 INPUT "QUANTITY IN LITRES "; Q
20 IF Q < 25 OR Q > 999 THEN PRINT "WE DON'T USUALLY SELL THESE
   QUANTITIES" : GOTO 10
30 IF Q =100 THEN PRINT "SORRY, NO 100 LITRE CANS": GOSUB 100
   ELSE 40

35 GOTO 10

40 C = Q * 1.75
50 PRINT "TOTAL COST = " C
60 INPUT "HOW MUCH ARE YOU SELLING IT FOR ";S
70 P = (S - C)/ S * 100
80 IF P < 33 THEN PRINT P; "%  IS NOT ENOUGH PROFIT"  ELSE PRINT
"GOOD, YOU HAVE MADE ";P "% PROFIT"

90 GOTO 10

100 N = N + 1
110 PRINT N " CUSTOMERS HAVE ASKED FOR 100 LITRE CANS"
120 RETURN
```

REM

It's handy to stick subroutines under memorable line numbers like 5000, 90000, 2000. You can do this because they don't have to be in order: the computer can GOSUB 8000 one minute and GOSUB 7000 the next minute.

You can then make sure that they are safe from being crashed into by the main program by putting the protective 'END' line just before them, as in:

4990 END
5000 . . . subroutine

It is useful to label them because BASIC is like shorthand: you can't understand it a couple of weeks after you have written it. You label sections of the program with the word 'REM', standing for

'Remark' and often given the abbreviation ' (a *single* quotation mark).

When the computer meets a line:

95 REM *** COUNTING SUBROUTINE ***

it ignores it.

The line will show up in LISTings so, if you want to share programs with your friends, you liberally label them with REM lines to show what the variables mean, program notes and subtitles. This Sales program could have these extra lines:

1 REM *** SALES INVOICE PROGRAM ***
2 REM IT CHECKS WHETHER THE SALESMAN IS SELLING
3 REM AMOUNTS BELOW 25 LITRES

15 REM * Q = QUANTITY, C = COST TO US,
16 REM * S = SELLING PRICE, P = % PROFIT,
17 REM * N = "100 LITRE CUSTOMERS"

Notice how in 2 and 3 if your sentence is broken into two lines, you must still put REM. Notice in 15, 16 and 17 how commas and inverted commas are ignored and the stars are treated as just decoration, not as multiplication signs.

You can GOSUB and GOTO remark lines but this can lead to . . .

REM bugs
There is a programming technique called 'packing'. It takes a massive program that has been using up a lot of memory and packs it down to just the essentials. Lines like:

150 FOR A = 1 TO F
160 T = B * A + 7
170 NEXT A

become a cramped multi-statement:

150 FORA=1TOF:T=B*A+7:NEXTA

with all the memory-wasting spaces cut out.

Cut out too are the redundant REM lines because, although they are nice for you, the computer doesn't need them. Packing is a great technique for the working copy of your program.

Suppose, though, you have gone to a REM line? Suppose your program has:

30 GOSUB 1000

and 1000 is neatly labelled:

1000 REM *** COUNTING ROUTINE ***

When the REM lines are deleted for the sake of economy, the computer isn't going to find a line 1000. It will flash up an UNDEFINED LINE ERROR complaint.

The cure? With your subroutines on lines 1000, 2000, 8000 and so on, put the REM labels on the nearby lines 999, 1999, 7999 so that they can be packed away without anybody missing them.

Don't let this minor bug inhibit you from using as many REMarks as possible. They turn unintelligible programs into interesting reading.

To sum up

Where something needs to be called up several times in a program you save typing it every time by putting it into a subroutine.

The command is GOSUB and, after finishing the subroutine, the computer returns to the next part of the main program on the word RETURN.

You take precautions against the main program crashing through into the subroutine and you label the subroutine. The program looks like:

```
(Main program)
150 GOSUB 8000
160 (More main program)
  :
7990 END                        (to stop any crashing through)
7999 REM *** LABEL ***          (to remind you what it is)
8000 (Subroutine)
  :
8720 RETURN                     (to line 160)
```

You have read about **FOR—TO** in Chapter 9. You'll meet **GOSUB** in later chapters.

Exercises

1. You work in a clinic, weighing babies and typing the results into the computer. It's simple enough to write a program that gives a printout under the headings: BABY'S NAME, LAST WEIGHT, TODAY'S WEIGHT, GAIN/LOSS. Now add subroutines that (a) ask if you've made a typing error if the weight is over . . . what's a reasonable figure? 17 lbs? (b) print warning exclamation marks if there is a weight loss.

2. Add another subroutine that counts the number of babies and gives the average percentage weight gain.

3. If you knew there were going to be exactly 50 babies per session you could set up a FOR N = 1 TO 50 : INPUT "WHAT'S THE BABY'S NAME ";B$: NEXT N loop. Since you can't be sure, you've probably used the N = N + 1 technique. But which is the quicker? Race these programs with a stopwatch:

```
                        10 PRINT "GO!"
                                       20 N = 0
30 FOR N = 1 TO 5000                   30 N = N + 1
40 GOSUB 100                           40 GOSUB 100
50 NEXT N                              50 IF N < 5000 THEN 30
                        60 PRINT "STOP!"
                        70 END
                        99 REM . . . MEANINGLESS ARITHMETIC
                        100 PRINT SQR(N * N * 7 + 99999.99)
                        110 RETURN
```

11

PRINT AT

You are a wall-protection contractor. Your operators spray a decorative, waterproof coating over house walls. To estimate the cost of materials and the time, you need to know how big the walls are.

Here's a routine that draws a rough rectangle on the screen to represent the house wall. First you clear the screen:

```
10 CLS
20 PRINT TAB(20) "!––––––––––––––––––!"
30 PRINT TAB(20) "!"; : PRINT TAB(40) "!"
40 PRINT TAB(20) "!"; : PRINT TAB(40) "!"
50 PRINT TAB(20) "!"; : PRINT TAB(40) "!"
60 PRINT TAB(20) "!––––––––––––––––––!"
```

This must be the worst way of drawing a rectangle, but it will have to do in a book about BASIC. Modern micros have high-resolution graphics (see Fig. 11.1) with commands like DRAW, which draws a perfect line from any point X on the screen to any point Y. If you own one, replace lines 20 to 60 with what the computer manual tells you.

To ask your operator how high the wall is needs a PRINTed question followed by an INPUT statement later:

```
70 PRINT : PRINT "HOW HIGH IS THE SIDE 'H' ?"
```

Why PRINT : PRINT? To put a blank line underneath the drawing so that the words don't crowd it.

Your operator is going to ask: 'Which is Side 'H' ?' and there's your problem. To type in PRINT "H" or even PRINT TAB(42) "H" won't put the "H" where you want it: up, midway beside the right-hand wall of the diagram. These PRINT commands continue on the next line down the screen.

The word to use is:

80 PRINT AT 170, "H" ;

It means 'Print an H at position 170 on the screen'. Some computers say "PRINT@", a few say 'SCREEN', some use PRINT AT 12,5 indicating Row 12, Position 5 on the screen . . . you will have to check on yours.

The screen is usually mapped out into 16 lines, as you can see when you type. The width of the lines could be 64 characters. This is what you are calling up when you ask for TAB(20) . . . the printing will start at position 20.

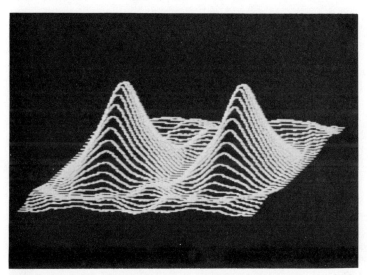

Fig. 11.1 High-resolution graphics (courtesy Strathand)

So with 16 lines of 64 characters there are 16 × 64 = 1024 potential positions on the screen. The first one is counted as 0 so the last one on the first line is number 63. And they go up in 64s until the bottom right-hand corner of ths screen is called 1023.

Does your computer differ from this by having a screen width of 80 or 72 characters? Then alter the arithmetic of the last paragraph. And, unfortunately, the PRINT AT numbers in the following program.

```
10 CLS
20 PRINT TAB(20)  "!-------------------!"
30 PRINT TAB(20)  "!"; : PRINT TAB(40)  "!"
40 PRINT TAB(20)  "!"; : PRINT TAB(40)  "!"
50 PRINT TAB(20)  "!"; : PRINT TAB(40)  "!"
60 PRINT TAB(20)  "!-------------------!"
70 PRINT : PRINT "HOW HIGH IS THE SIDE 'H' ?"
80 PRINT@ 170, "H";
90 INPUT H
100 PRINT@ 384, "HOW LONG IS THE SIDE 'L' ?"
110 PRINT@ 348, "L";
120 INPUT L
200 PRINT@ 662, "YOU NEED " INT((L * H /15) + 1) "CANS"
```

There might even be a video display chart in the computer manual to help you visualise this. To get that letter H in the proper place beside the right-hand wall, you can be scientific about it and work out that the position is about 2 or 3 further than the TAB(40) of the third line. So it is at 63 + 64 + 40 + 3 = 170. Or you can make a reasonable guess, RUN the program and then adjust line 80 backwards or forwards a bit.

Notice, though, the comma after the number 170. Notice too the semicolon at the end of line 80. Without it, and you can try if you like, the PRINT AT command throws up a new line straight after itself. If you allowed this new line it would blank out part of the diagram. Hence the semicolon.

This makes the next line of the program

90 INPUT H

put its question mark right after the H because the semicolon acts as semicolons usually do: it makes printing continuous.

You know by now that the program will wait at line 90 until your operator types in the height of the wall. Next you need the length before you can do the length × height = area calculation.

PRINT "HOW LONG IS THE SIDE 'L' ?" is no good because it would print right after the INPUT of H and ruin the diagram. You want the question to come underneath the bottom of the drawing. That's six lines down on the screen and 6 × 64 = 384, so:

100 PRINT AT 384, "HOW LONG IS SIDE 'L' ?"

Now mark the bottom side of the diagram:

110 PRINT AT 348, "L "

Now ask for input:

120 INPUT L

And this is magic: in both cases the INPUT comes exactly in the right place beside the drawing so your operators can't be in any doubt over which side they are measuring.

There are some enhanced BASICs with the facility to INPUT AT so that owners can set their screen layout neatly. This program gives the same result without INPUT AT.

Of course, this is a trivial program. If calculating wall sizes were as easy as this, everybody would be in the business. You need to repeat these lines for the four walls of a house: then what about the triangular bits up to the roof? You are going to be asked to do a more comprehensive program in the Exercises at the end of this chapter, so here is a hint: make this into a subroutine and GOSUB for every wall, then add up all the L1s, L2s, H3s and even T4s if you can work out the area of triangles.

PRINT AT bugs

The invisible bug is with BASICs that accept PRINT@. A lot of them will baulk if the shifted @ is typed, even though the two characters look exactly the same on screen. Maybe you have disciplined yourself to keep your left finger off the shift key as your right hits the @ but if you have borrowed a program that was typed in by another operator and if it works on their machine but not on yours then check all the @ symbols.

To sum up

PRINT AT, PRINT@ or SCREEN place your words at any position on the screen. The form is:

PRINT AT 234, "EXAMPLE"

with or without a semicolon at the end.

The number can be replaced by a mathematical expression:

PRINT AT X * (Y/2), "EXAMPLE"

should work.

Unless you own a printer designed to wind the paper back, there is no equivalent LPRINT AT command. However, there are commands, different in every BASIC dialect, that allow you to transfer the contents of the screen to your printer.

You learned about **TAB** in Chapter 4 and **INPUT** in Chapter 7.

Read how to translate the area of these walls into cans of waterproofing compound in the next chapter.

Exercises

1. Extend the program so that it covers all the walls of a house. Take into account the windows and odd wall protrusions. If your computer can draw a better picture, then do so.

2. Add what programmers call 'bells and whistles' to the program by making the L and H marks flash on and off. (Hint: try a FOR–TO loop with a blank space being alternately printed over the L and H positions.)

12

INT

You are still in the wall-coating business and after working out the area of a house wall there still comes the calculation to work out the number of cans of compound needed to cover so many square feet of wall.

It is expensive stuff: one can only covers 15 square feet. The calculation should be L * H / 15, the area in feet divided by the 15 square feet that one can covers. But, in practice, you can't go to the store and buy 7.80435 cans: they have to be in whole numbers.

A whole number is called an INTeger, and the BASIC function would be INT(L * H /15). If the result came to 7.80435 the screen would show just the whole number 7. Which means that you would run out of compound towards the end of the last wall. What you need is one more can. So add one:

INT((L * H/15) + 1)

Notice the brackets inside the brackets. Or will your machine accept INT(L * H/15) + 1 ?

To place this neatly on screen, use PRINT AT. And it would come after all the extra lines you composed in the last chapter to handle the four walls and the tricky triangular bits:

200 PRINT AT 662, "YOU NEED " INT((L * H/15) + 1) " CANS"

This technique of adding something before you get the integer is pretty common. You did it yourself in pre-computer days when you made a rough total of numbers. The sum of:

5.6	rounded up to	6
3.2	rounded down to	3
2.8		3
6.1		6
gives 17.7	which is near enough	18

The rule, then, is to go up to the next number if the decimal is .5 or over.

In BASIC you add an extra .5 inside the brackets. INT(N + .5), with N varying through the above table from 5.6 to 6.1, will give the reasonably right whole numbers. Even INT(17.7 + .5) = 18.

There could be two more integer-finding commands in your computer. FIX (7.80435) simply chops off the figures after the decimal and gives 7. CINT (7.80435) won't give a whole number bigger than the one in the brackets. It will give 7 all right but CINT (− 7.80435) would give −8 since minus seven would be too big.

All of these have practical use to a business. Just as you don't go into a store for 7.80435 cans, you don't saw wood into 3.33333333 metre strips and it is hard to ride 0.75 of a horse. So use INT, especially when your calculations use division, otherwise people are going to take the mickey out of your results.

Strangely enough there are occasions when you need INT to produce decimals . . . in money calculations.   What's one-ninth of £10? One pound eleven pence? Oh no it isn't. The real answer is £1.11111111111 etc., though you would have to file metal off a penny to cover those last decimals. It is the sort of result that would screw up the neat totals at the end of your accounts program.

The computer cure is to: multiply by 100, giving 111.11111; then add .5 to round up (not needed in this case), giving 111.61111. Take the integer, leaving 111, and then divide by 100, giving 1.11; a sensible answer for your accounts books.

The statement is:

INT(N * 100 + .5) /100

where N is the long decimal number that you want to cut down to pounds and pence, or dollars and cents.

PRINT USING

There is another way. You can make a pattern of how you want the decimals to look, then tell the computer to print using that pattern.

Suppose you have been feeding money into a program – wages, turnover, stock costs – then doing arithmetic . . . it is possible that the result will come out as 75663.34242102 when really you want it to look like $75,663.34. Then you insist on a pattern of $##,###.## with the dollar sign, the 'thousands comma' and only a couple of figures after the decimal point.

In some BASICs the pattern takes an entire line:

260 : $ ##,###.##
270 PRINT USING 260, N

where N is the 77663.34242102 style number.

In other BASICs the pattern is set as a string:

```
280 U$ = "$$#,##.##"
290 PRINT USING U$; N
```

Check your manual because the punctuation is tricky. Notice the colon starting line 260. Then the $ sign, the thousands comma and the decimal point in its right place. Then look at the comma before the N on line 270. The official Standard BASIC says that this ought to be a colon, but nobody seems to own a computer that uses a colon.

In the second style of PRINT USING on line 280, there are quote marks around the string as you would expect. But, in Microsoft BASIC, notice the two $$ signs and notice that it doesn't matter where you put the thousands comma. Notice that this time a semicolon comes before the N in line 290.

Here are the INT and the PRINT USING in action . . . You have been in business for a few weeks. What's it going to be like at the end of a year? Let's count the money for the weeks so far:

```
10 INPUT "HOW LONG HAVE YOU BEEN IN BUSINESS "; N
20 FOR W = 1 TO N
30 PRINT "IN WEEK " W " WHAT WERE THE ";
40 INPUT "TAKINGS "; T
50 PRINT TAB(22) "COST OF MATERIALS "; : INPUT M
60 PRINT TAB(22) "COST OF LABOUR "; : INPUT L
70 PRINT TAB(22) "RENT & RATES "; : INPUT R
80 PRINT TAB(22) "VEHICLE COSTS "; : INPUT V
90 PRINT TAB(22) "INSURANCES "; : INPUT I
100 PRINT TAB(22) "OTHER COSTS "; : INPUT O
```

where N = the total number of weeks, W = week number, T = takings, M = materials, L = labour, R = rent, V = vehicles, I = insurance and O = other things.

Now a routine for adding last week's money to this week's:

```
110 TT = TT + T
120 TM = TM + M
130 TL = TL + L
140 TR = TR + R
150 TV = TV + V
160 TI = TI + I
170 TQ = TQ + O
180 NEXT W
```

Translated, line 110 reads, 'The current Total Takings = last week's Total plus this week's Takings.' You could have used any letters: it is just that putting T in front of the Ms and Ls makes it easier to remember that TM = Total Materials.

But in line 170 why does TQ = Total Other ? Why not TO ? Because TO is reserved for the command FOR–TO; it is forbidden to use it as a variable. Neither can you use variables like IF or ON.

Once the N number of weeks' money has been counted (and when you do a dummy run of this program, don't let N be higher than 3 or 4, else you'll be INPUTing all night) the screen is cleared and the title line of the summary is laid out:

```
190 CLS
200 PRINT TAB(20) "TO WEEK " W ;
210 PRINT TAB(35) "AVERAGE " ;
220 PRINT TAB(50) "A YEAR "
```

Notice the semicolons to keep TO WEEK 3 AVERAGE A YEAR all on the same line. No semicolon after A YEAR so that the TURNOVER figures will come on the next line:

```
230 PRINT "TURNOVER ";
240 PRINT TAB(20) TT ;
```

That puts the total takings right underneath the TO WEEK 3 heading.

The arithmetic to get the AVERAGE is to divide the turnover by the number of weeks (TT/N) and, to keep it to dollars and cents, to do the multiplying by 100, rounding up with .5 then dividing by 100 routine. To forecast for the year, you find this average week and multiply by 52:

```
250 PRINT TAB(35) "$" INT((TT /N * 100 + .5) /100);
260 PRINT TAB(50) "$" INT((TT /N * 52 * 100 + .5) /100)
```

The TABs place the results right under their correct headings.

The arithmetic to find how much you spend on materials is exactly the same. But this time, use PRINT USING to cut any decimals down to two:

```
270 PRINT "COST OF MATERIALS ";
280 U$ = "$$#,###.##"
290 PRINT TAB(20) USING U$; TM ;
```

The program isn't finished, but do a dummy RUN. Pretend you have done 2 weeks' trading so that N = 2. And keep your Cost of Materials to whole numbers: no decimals.

Even if your Total Materials is, say, 123, that line 290 will print it as $123.00. It will write a dollar sign, realise that there is no need for a thousand comma, and put two zeros after the decimal point. Note, then, that there is no harm in making your $$#,###.## pattern too big: the BASIC accommodates that. What if you make it too small? If you dictate ##.## when the number comes to 123,456.789?

Some BASICs happily handle it. Some come to a halt with an error message. Some do their best to print as many numbers as possible but they signal their distress with a % symbol. So be generous with your patterns.

```
300 PRINT TAB(33) USING U$; TM /N ;
310 PRINT TAB(48) USING U$; TM /N * 52
320 PRINT "EXPENSES ";
330 PRINT TAB(20) USING U$; TL + TR + TV + TI + TQ ;
340 PRINT TAB(33) USING U$; (TL + TR + TV + TI + TQ) /N;
```

The logic is correct here. Certainly the average week's expenses is the total of all the Labour plus Rent and Rates plus Vehicles plus Insurance plus Other stuff. But it is a chore to type it out every time.

You can miss out the spaces: they are only in this book to make it readable. This could be perfectly acceptable:

```
350 PRINTTAB(48)USINGU$;(TL+TR+TV+TI+TQ)/N*52
```

An easier method would have been to lump the lot under one fresh variable, TE, standing for Total Expenses:

```
360 TE = TL+TR+TV+TI+TQ
```

and your business Profit will be Takings minus the Cost of Materials and Expenses:

```
370 P = TT − TM − TE
```

Print an empty line to make the table look neater, then put the Profit figures underneath their proper headings:

```
380 PRINT
390 PRINT "PROFIT " ;
400 PRINT TAB(20) USING U$; P ;
410 PRINT TAB(33) USING U$; P /N ;
420 PRINT TAB(48) USING U$; P /N * 52
```

And here is the complete program:

```
10 INPUT "HOW LONG HAVE YOU BEEN IN BUSINESS "; N
20 FOR W = 1 TO N
30 PRINT "IN WEEK " W " WHAT WERE THE ";
40 INPUT "TAKINGS "; T
50 PRINT TAB(22) "COST OF MATERIALS "; : INPUT M
60 PRINT TAB(22) "COST OF LABOUR "; : INPUT L
70 PRINT TAB(22) "RENT & RATES "; : INPUT R
80 PRINT TAB(22) "VEHICLE COSTS "; : INPUT V
90 PRINT TAB(22) "INSURANCES "; : INPUT I
100 PRINT TAB(22) "OTHER COSTS "; : INPUT O
110 TT = TT + T                              continued
```

```
120 TM = TM + M
130 TL = TL + L
140 TR = TR + R
150 TV = TV + V
160 TI = TI + I
170 TQ = TQ + Q
180 NEXT W

190 CLS
200 PRINT TAB(20) "TO WEEK " W ;
210 PRINT TAB(35) "AVERAGE " ;
220 PRINT TAB(50) "A YEAR "
230 PRINT "TURNOVER ";
240 PRINT TAB(20) TT ;
250 PRINT TAB(35) "$" INT((TT /N * 100 + .5) /100);
260 PRINT TAB(50) "$" INT((TT /N * 52 * 100 + .5) /100)

270 PRINT "COST OF MATERIALS ";
280 U$ = "$$#,###.##"
290 PRINT TAB(20) USING U$; TM ;
300 PRINT TAB(33) USING U$; TM /N ;
310 PRINT TAB(48) USING U$; TM /N * 52
320 PRINT "EXPENSES ";
330 PRINT TAB(20) USING U$; TL + TR + TV + TI + TQ ;
340 PRINT TAB(33) USING U$; (TL + TR + TV + TI + TQ) /N;
350 PRINTTAB(48)USINGU$; (TL+TR+TV+TI+TQ)/N*52

360 TE = TL+TR+TV+TI+TQ
370 P = TT - TM - TE
380 PRINT
390 PRINT "PROFIT " ;
400 PRINT TAB(20) USING U$; P ;
410 PRINT TAB(33) USING U$; P /N ;
420 PRINT TAB(48) USING U$; P /N * 52
```

Bugs in this program
You may need to tune the TAB numbers to get the figures in line.
Some BASICs print invisible blanks in front of numbers.

The final W may be odd. It should finish up being the same as N
but some BASICs obey the FOR W = 1 TO N line and then on line
180 obediently give the NEXT W, which will be N + 1.

INT bugs
The machine's own attempt to round up decimals can cause weird
results. At best, a computer is never as accurate as a calculator, and
around figures with six or seven digits there is always an area of
doubt. 19999.99 * 100 /100 should give 19999.99. Does yours
give 20000 ?

Then there is a computer crime called 'rounding up'. A fraction of
a penny syphoned off a multi-million turnover can earn a crooked
operator quite a pleasant income. So watch out!

Even if your turnover isn't in the millions, don't behave as if it does. Never let the computer print out your cheques or a crooked operator could strip your bank account in microseconds. Sign cheques reluctantly with a squeaky pen.

PRINT USING bugs
Are almost always your fault for getting the punctuation wrong.

There are too many versions of PRINT USING. As well as the modern dialect U$ = "###.##" given here there are older BASICs with: / / where the spaces between the slashes indicate the number of digits and ! represents one character. Some have ' to allow words, where 'LL means shuffle all the characters to the left, 'RR means move everything to the right and 'CC means centralise the printout.

The so-called Standard BASIC has <### meaning justify left and >### meaning justify right, and insists on there being a + or − sign in front of the ###.## pattern.

To sum up

You have read how to remove unwanted decimals with INT( ), CINT( ), FIX( ) and how to round up by adding .5 and multiplying and dividing by 100. Read about **DEFINT** in Chapter 20.

You need to check your manual for the acceptable way of writing PRINT USING statements, but in any case they are based on your setting a pattern, a mask, a mould, an image of #,###.##. You may even be able to add extra words or $ symbols to that.

Exercises

1. Rewrite this simple accounts program to work more accurately with your own business expenses. Turn the final printout to LPRINT if you like and certainly cut down on the number of times you type TL+TR+TV, etc.

2. Write a short program that gives answers accurate to one thousandth of an inch (three figures of decimals). Use both INT and PRINT USING.

3. PRINT USING sometimes can handle strings. But the method uses ! and % instead of # and is different with every dialect of

BASIC. Read your manual to see if you can INPUT a name like
JOHN PAUL DEFARGE then have the computer print out J. P.
DEFARGE.

4. In a street, the odd-numbered houses are on the left, the
even-numbered are on the right. But how can the computer tell if a
number is odd or even? Here's a hint . . . is N/2 always the same as
INT(N/2)?

13

DATA

You have put facts into the computer by using the INPUT command
. . . it asks the question, you give the answer.

There are plenty of occasions though when you want to ask the
question and expect it to dig into its store of facts to bring out the
answer. How many things are in stock? Whose turn is it to do
tonight's shift? How many 16-year-olds are on the payroll? What's
Soandso's telephone number?

It is your first disillusionment with the Golden Age of the
Microchip when you realise that before these facts can be pulled
out, somebody has to volunteer to type them in.

Facts go in with DATA statements. The details of your regular
supplier's telephone numbers might be programmed:

    60 DATA "ACME LTD", 12345, "BESTEST CO", 45678, "COLLOS
       INC", 78910, "DOMINANT CO", 98765, "EVERLAST LTD"
    70 DATA 54321, "FANTAST INC", 19283, "GREATEST LTD", 28374,
       "HUGE CO", 91827

Look at the layout. Every data line starts with the word DATA. There
is no comma after it but there is a comma between every other item
of data. There is no comma at the end. Words, strings, come
surrounded by inverted commas. Numbers need no inverted
commas.

These DATA lines can be anywhere in the program. First, last, in
the middle, out of sequence: wherever they are the computer will
find them on the command READ. To read a string you tell it to
READ N$, say. To read a number you tell it to READ PH, say. To
read both:

    20 READ N$, PH

To read the next word and number, you tell it to go back and do it
again:

    50 GOTO 20

The Phone number program, so far, will list:

```
20 READ N$, PH
50 GOTO 20
60 DATA "ACME LTD", 12345, "BESTEST CO", 45678, "COLLOS
   INC", 78910, "DOMINANT CO", 98765, "EVERLAST LTD"
70 DATA 54321, "FANTAST INC", 19283, "GREATEST LTD", 28374,
   "HUGE CO", 91827
```

If you RUN it, there will be a slight pause before the screen shows an error message, OUT OF DATA IN 20.

In slow motion replay, this is what happens: line 20 looks all over for some string data, finds it in line 60, reads ACME LTD and stores ACME LTD in its memory under the label N$. Still in line 20, it looks for more data to fill the PH slot and it finds 12345 where it expected: the next item on the DATA line now that ACME LTD has been dealt with. The 12345 is stored in memory, labelled PH.

If it had found a string in that position instead of a number, if there had been "BIGGEST LTD" instead of 12345, it would have complained. The screen would have shown a TYPE MISMATCH ERROR because you can't store words under PH, or any numeric variable. Not many BASICs are smart enough to let PH ignore strings until it finds the nearest real number.

Line 20 has finished, so on to line 50, which tells it to go back to line 20. Line 20 looks for DATA for the second time. At the top of the list, now that ACME LTD has gone, is BESTEST CO and this is taken away to the memory store. The N$ label is taken off ACME LTD, which is thrown out and forgotten as its place in the N$ slot is taken by BESTEST CO. In the same way, the PH label is tied to 45678 and the old 12345 is driven out of memory.

Line 50 will keep on returning the computer to line 20 and the words and numbers under the N$ and PH variables will change every microsecond.

In passing, notice how EVERLAST LTD is at the end of line 60 yet its telephone number 54321 is at the beginning of line 70. That doesn't matter at all. You could have put the phone number way along on line 2000 and PH would have found it in its search for the next bit of data.

Finally, HUGE CO and 91827 are read and stored as the latest N$ and PH. Yet line 50 still sends the program back to line 20. And 20 still tries to READ more data. But there isn't any more left. It has all been read. Hence the OUT OF DATA IN 20 message.

What's the situation right at this moment? Ask: PRINT N$, PH and you will get:

HUGE CO   91827

What has happened to ACME and COLLOS INC and 54321? All read, stored for a microsecond, then forgotten. To catch one of them, you need to break into the program in that fraction of a second *after* it has been labelled yet *before* the next one takes its place.

Which phone number do you want?

```
10 INPUT "WHO DO YOU WANT "; W$
20 READ N$, PH
```

Is this the one you want?

```
30 IF N$ = W$ THEN PRINT N$, PH : END
```

If it isn't, then have a look at the next phone number:

```
50 GOTO 20
```

Now when you RUN this, the screen will ask, and you will answer, then up will come the result:

```
WHO DO YOU WANT ? COLLOS INC
COLLOS INC              78910
```

and the program will END in accordance with the instruction after the colon in line 30.

You have got to spell the names exactly right because the finicky microchip won't recognise COLLOS LTD as being similar to COLLOS INC. But what happens if you ask for a firm that it has never heard of?

It just keeps on looking until it runs out of data and you get that error message again. There are two cures for this. If you knew how many names you were going to store in the DATA lines, you could tell it to READ for only that number of times:

```
15 FOR R = 1 TO 100
20 READ N$, PH
50 NEXT R
```

for instance, to cover a 100-name phone list.

There are plenty of times when you will use this routine (see the chapter on arrays). In this case though, because you are going to be adding to that list and taking firms out, there will never be a fixed number.

The trick is to type a fake name and phone number at the end of the data. You use something that would never be met in the normal course of events. You could use the word END or something stupid like ZZZ and 999 in the full knowledge that none of the firms you deal with is likely to be called ZZZ or have a 999 number.

Add these to the last DATA line:

70 DATA 54321, "FANTAST INC", 19283, "GREATEST LTD", 28374, "HUGE CO", 91827, "ZZZ", 999

You know then that, if the program gets that far, the genuine phone number that you asked for is not in the list:

40 IF N$ = "ZZZ" THEN PRINT "SORRY, NO IDEA" : END

Here are three runs through the complete program:

```
RUN
WHO DO YOU WANT?   EVERLAST LTD
EVERLAST LTD                54321
READY
RUN
WHO DO YOU WANT?   BUCKINGHAM PALACE
SORRY NO IDEA
READY
RUN
WHO DO YOU WANT?   HUGE CO
HUGE CO                     91827
READY
```

And here is a listing of the complete program:

```
10 INPUT "WHO DO YOU WANT "; W$
20 READ N$, PH
30 IF N$ = W$ THEN PRINT N$, PH : END
40 IF N$ = "ZZZ" THEN PRINT "SORRY, NO IDEA" : END
50 GOTO 20

60 DATA "ACME LTD", 12345, "BESTEST CO", 45678, "COLLOS
   INC", 78910, "DOMINANT CO", 98765, "EVERLAST LTD"
70 DATA 54321, "FANTAST INC", 19283, "GREATEST LTD",
   28374, "HUGE CO", 91827, "ZZZ", 999
```

Data bugs
You know that if you ask for 80 READs then there have to be 80 items of data to read.

90 FOR N = TO 80

You know that if you have a line saying

100 READ G$, Z, C2$, BN$, V, V1, F$

then the data line has to have its strings and numbers in that same pattern

240 DATA "DATSUN", 598, "AXLE", "JOINT", 3455, 344, "BIN NUMBER 23"

You also take care over the commas and the quotation marks.

    250 "TOYOTA", 677, "CARB", "FLOAT CHAMBER", 4747, 269, "BIN
        NUMBER 56"

So why are you getting an OUT OF DATA IN 90 error ?

You can spend hours agonising whether two words like FLOAT CHAMBER count as two items of data. (No they don't, not if they are enclosed in one set of quote marks.) Or if BIN NUMBER 23 should be considered as a numeral. (No, it's a string because it is inside quote marks.) You count and recount to make sure that there are 80 items of data. (There are; we haven't bothered to print them in this book.) What can be wrong with line 90 ?

Nothing. The bug is way down the program in line 250. You have forgotten to write DATA.

When debugging, don't always assume that the error is in line 90 just because the computer says so. It could be somewhere else; making line 90 out to be a liar.

Happily, nobody complains if there is more data than the READ line ask for.

    10 FOR N = 1 TO 5
    20 READ BJ
    30 DATA 3, 5, 9, 7, 1, 8, 6, 2, 4
    40 NEXT N

would work. The last few figures − 8, 6, 2, 4 − just wouldn't get read, that's all.

How many characters does your computer allow in a string? Most allow 255 or 256 characters, which is ample. But others can only handle 18. So in:

    10 READ L$
    20 DATA "THE WORLD'S GREATEST ESTATE AGENTS"
    30 PRINT L$

only

    THE WORLD'S GREATE

would be printed because spaces and punctuation marks count as well. The rest would be ignored.

Arithmetic isn't allowed as data:

    20 DATA 3.14 * R * R

has a bug in it.

RESTORE

To have your Telephone program running continually, the obvious answer would be to add a line that sends it back to the start, ready for your next query. But replacing the commands END in lines 30 and 40 with GOTO 10 isn't enough.

Sure, it would go back to 10 after giving you COLLOS INC's phone number but there wouldn't be the full range of data left for line 20 to read on the second run through. The command RESTORE brings all the forgotten ACMEs and BESTESTs back to be read again. After RESTORE, the READ line starts at the beginning of the DATA again.

To sum up

DATA is a way of putting facts into the working memory. It can go literally anywhere in the program and can be on several lines. Its sister command READ is the one that needs to fit in proper sequence in the program.

Except in a very few BASICs, DATA has to mirror READ with strings and numeric variables coming in the right order. Strings need to be surrounded by quote marks. There isn't a comma after the word DATA nor at the end of the line, but there is a comma between every item.

You keep READ working with a FOR–TO loop. This can have less than the number of data items but not more.

Or you can keep READ working with a GOTO command and stop it with a flag signal like: IF Q = 999 THEN END. You can put the READ back to the beginning of the data with RESTORE, and one or two BASICs allow you to specify a line number to RESTORE to. READ stores, in this chapter, only the last item that it read.

To see how all the data can be labelled with different variable names and recalled, read about **arrays** in Chapter 14.

Exercises

1. Where exactly would you put the command RESTORE in the Telephone program?

2. For your firm's party, screw up the computer with a libellous program that asks WHO'S THIS TALKING TO ME? and if the answer is, say, Diane, the screen shows HELLO DIANE, HAS THE TAXMAN FOUND OUT ABOUT YOUR LITTLE ENTERPRISE YET? or something like that.

3. Cut down on typing invoices to your regular customers. Write a program that will LPRINT the entire address: THE WORKSHOP MANAGER, DYNAMIC TOOLS LTD, 23 ANYSTREET, ANYTOWN whenever you type in just the letters DY.

14

Arrays

Your processing plant is monitored by temperature sensors. Every so often, the operator makes a note of the temperature. Could the results be incorporated into a BASIC program to make a chart, or could they be printed as a graph?

The BASIC is there. The TAB function from Chapter 4 is just one way of making a crude graph. You learned that PRINT TAB(10) would start the printing at the tenth place across the screen. But there is no need to stick with straight numbers: TAB will accept variables and arithmetic expressions. TAB(Z) is valid, so is TAB(Z * 5 + 1).

So taking the temperature as TE, these two lines would print a graph point at the correct distance from the left of the screen:

```
130 TE = 45
230 PRINT TAB(TE); "*"
```

Or, if the temperatures were too big to fit on the screen width, you could scale them down, just as you choose a scale for graph paper:

```
130 TE = 345
230 PRINT TAB(TE/10); "*"
```

These though, are just static numbers: you would have to rewrite the program for every different temperature. An improvement would be to use INPUT:

```
130 INPUT TE
230 PRINT TAB(TE); "*"
```

But this would need to be RUN for every different temperature, unless you added:

```
330 GOTO 10
```

This still makes a scruffy graph if you tried to type it in from the keyboard. The screen then would become:

?40

                                                        *

?44

                                                            *

?35

                                                    *

with your INPUT figures intruding.

So the problem is how to get figures into a graph if you are typing them into the keyboard. One answer is to extend the INPUT command so that all the input is got over with at the start. Then to clear the screen before asking for the TAB graph:

```
130 INPUT TE, TF, TG, TH, TI, TJ, TK, TL
230 CLS
330 PRINT TAB(TE); "*"
430 PRINT TAB(TF); "*"
530 PRINT TAB(TG); "*"
630 PRINT TAB(TH); "*"
730 PRINT TAB . . .
```

By this time you are guessing that there must be an easier way. With this program you are doing more work than the computer – which can't be right.

Arrays – the orderly variables

You have met variables in the forms of F, H$, F9, LK$, TE, G6$ and, if your computer accepts them, TEMPERATURE and CUSTOMER$.

You know that there is no relationship whatever between R, R8, RD, R$, RD$ and RB$. You know too that B need not be bigger than A or K3 come after K2.

Yet these variables, in the attempt to draw a temperature graph, are related in a way. The second TF may not be higher than the first TE but at least it is input to the computer *after* TE. They can be renamed as TE(1), TE(2), TE(3), TE(4) and so on and in this form they are called 'a single subscripted variable', 'a vector' or 'a one-dimensioned array'.

Notice that there is a considerable difference between straight variables like W3 or Z9 and those with subscripts in brackets like W(3) and Z(9). The W3 type have been named arbitrarily; W3 is no closer to W4 than it is to XF. But W(3) has a definite position in life: it is the third variable in the W( ) array; it comes just before you get to W(4). Straight W3 is like the name 'Henry Ford' while W(3) is like 'Henry Ford III', because it's the third in the line of Henry Fords.

Even more useful than numbers, the computer will accept a variable inside that bracket, for example W(A) or EF(ZX) or TE(Q2). It will also accept an arithmetic expression like W(A − 1). Any variable or expression, within reason, that you want.

This widens the possibilities of programs. That Temperature one can be put into a loop with the 'A' increasing every time so that the TE(A) array practically labels itself:

```
110 FOR A = 1 TO 8
130 INPUT TE(A)
140 NEXT A
```

RUN that alone and the computer will collect in its memory banks nine values of TE and label them, not TE(A), but TE(1), TE(2), TE(3), TE(4) and so on.

To bring them out again for the graph:

```
220 FOR C = 1 TO 8
230 PRINT TAB(TE(C) ); "*"
240 NEXT C
```

Notice that you could have used A in the second FOR–TO part of the program or, as in line 220, you can use a different variable. You could also pick out any of the temperatures by asking:

```
PRINT TE(4)
```

Notice too the brackets in line 230. The outer brackets, the first and last ones, belong to the TAB statement. The inner pair, round the C, belong to the TE(C) array.

String arrays
In the same way as numbers, string variables can be given subscripts.

"NUTS", "BOLTS" and "SCREWS" can be listed as P$(1), P$(2) and P$(3). There will be more about string arrays later but, in the meantime, note where the $ sign goes: right after the variable and before the brackets.

DIMensions
Usually you are allowed the first ten items in an array free of charge. But any more and you have to declare them at the start of the program. Some computers don't even allow you ten. The command is DIM, which stands for 'the dimensions of the array'.

If in the Temperature program you had intended to graph a couple of hundred temperatures, one of the lines before you started allocating the array would have had to be:

10 DIM TE(200)

to give the computer chance to clear and label 200 pigeon-holes ready for the coming data.

If you are working with a small computer that is often running out of memory, you can gain a bit of extra space by dimensioning-down the ten free spaces. To graph, say, only 8 temperatures, you would write:

10 DIM TE(8)

Two-dimensional arrays

If you have a mental picture of an array as a neatly numbered shelf with all the data stored on it – numbers, words and even spaces because there is nothing to stop parts of the shelf being empty – then you can extend your vision to imagine several rows of pigeon-holes.

These are labelled like $Z(7,22)$, which indicates 'the 7th pigeon-hole on the 22nd shelf' and they are called 'doubly subscripted variables', 'two-dimensional arrays' or 'a matrix' (plural: matrices).

They too have to be dimensioned. There has first to be a line:

5 DIM Z(20,300)

otherwise the computer throws up the error message: SUBSCRIPT OUT OF RANGE as soon as you try to give $Z(1,1)$ a value. This means that the subscript, the numbers inside the brackets, hasn't had memory space allocated to it.

You can do all your dimensioning in one line:

5 DIM Z(20,300), AB$(4,4), C3(50,10)

but don't become over-enthusiastic and DIM twice, and continue with:

10 DIM SF(5,5), C3(20,200)

or when it comes to C3( ) a second time, the computer will halt with a REDIMENSIONED ARRAY ERROR message.

The MAT option
The beauty of BASIC is that there are several methods of getting round most problems. When dealing with arrays, expensive

computers have a MAT (for matrix) facility. If yours has, then treat the rest of this chapter as an alternative method.

Should there be more about MAT in this book? It was decided no, even though MAT is more economical of space than the array routines. There's a particularly nice line that comes at the beginning of programs when you want to make sure that all your variables are 0 and not some weird number that might be drifting around in memory:

```
MAT A = ZER
```

will start every A(,) array variable to be 0.

Without MAT, and most micros today are without, you need several lines of a loop:

```
FOR Z = 1 TO 100
FOR X = 1 TO 100
A(Z,X) = 0
NEXT X
NEXT Z
```

Two-dimensional arrays at work

You take temperatures of your processing plant at fixed times every day and in pre-computer days, the pencilled notes could look like Fig. 14.1.

This layout of pigeon-holes, this matrix, is better than a straight list of figures. This way you can compare temperatures horizontally . . . do they alter as the day goes on? And vertically . . . why is Monday noon different from Friday noon?

So split the program into sections. First, tell the computer to clear space in its memory for three arrays of these dimensions:

```
10 DIM D$(7), TI$(8), TE(7,8)
```

The seven D$s will be the days. The eight TI$s will be the times when the temperature is taken. The 56 TEs will be the temperatures taken seven days a week, eight times a day.

Now to put names to the variables. No longer do you have to write:

```
D$(1) = "MON"
D$(2) = "TUE"
D$(3) = "WED"
```

Instead you set up a loop and let the computer do its own labelling:

```
20 FOR D = 1 TO 7
30 READ D$(D)
40 DATA "MON", "TUE", "WED", "THU", "FRI", "SAT","SUN"
50 NEXT D
```

Now, as that loop goes round and round seven times, D$(1) will become MON, D$(2) will become TUE and so on.

Why pick D in line 20? No real reason at all. If you want to use B or Z or VW or Q7, then do so, and have line 30 as READ D$(Q7). You develop your own favourite variables and maybe tend to use Ds for dates, Cs for costs, Ns for numbers, Ts for times, even though the computer doesn't give a damn.

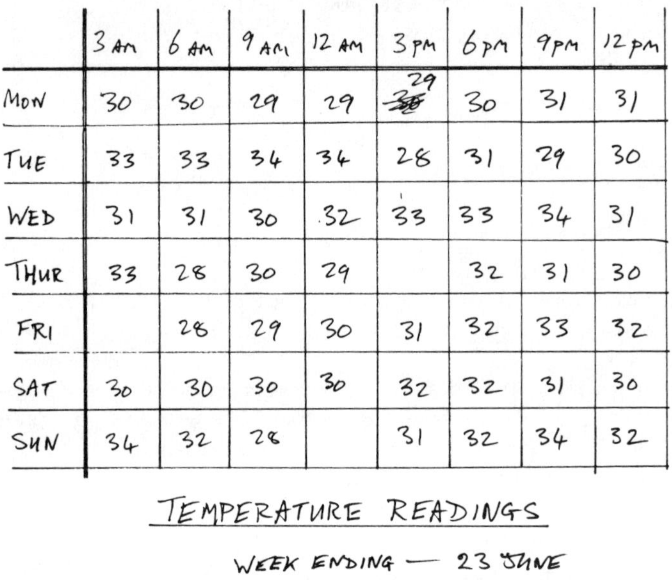

	3 AM	6 AM	9 AM	12 AM	3 PM	6 PM	9 PM	12 PM
MON	30	30	29	29	29 (35 crossed out)	30	31	31
TUE	33	33	34	34	28	31	29	30
WED	31	31	30	32	33	33	34	31
THUR	33	28	30	29		32	31	30
FRI		28	29	30	31	32	33	32
SAT	30	30	30	30	32	32	31	30
SUN	34	32	28		31	32	34	32

TEMPERATURE READINGS

WEEK ENDING — 23 JUNE

Fig. 14.1 Pre-computer, handwritten notes of temperature readings

We can't use T for both Time and Temperature in this problem though, so let's choose TI for Time, TE for Temperature and leave the T for the loop. The Time of course, is a string, so we are talking about TI$:

```
60 FOR T = 1 TO 8
70 READ TI$(T)
80 DATA "3 AM", "6 AM", "9 AM", "12 AM", "3 PM", "6 PM", "9 PM",
   "12 PM"
90 NEXT T
```

Now two of the arrays are filled in. If you ran the program, there would be a slight pause for reading but nothing would appear on screen. The computer would take the attitude: 'You only asked me to read the words, you didn't tell me to write anything anywhere.'

But the details are nicely locked in memory. Without bothering with a line number, you could ask for a couple of the variables at random:

PRINT TI$(3), D$(5)

and be answered on screen with:

9 AM   FRI

For a printout of all of the dates and times, you can set up a PRINT or LPRINT routine later. First comes the collection of temperatures. It is done by loops with an INPUT at the heart of them.

Look again at the chart you are trying to achieve, the one in Fig. 14.1. Point to any one of the temperatures . . . how could it be labelled to distinguish it from any of the others? You could number it. By calling the top left-hand temperature Number One, you could number all 56 of them. So the one you are pointing to would be, what? TE(18)? This is what you would have to do if your computer wasn't smart enough to handle two-dimensional arrays. It would think of TE(18) as being, in this case, 31 degrees.

Your loop would be:

```
FOR N = 1 TO 56
INPUT "WHAT'S THE TEMPERATURE "; TE(N)
NEXT N
```

which is simple enough. The hard work comes when you want to organise the 56 records into a table of temperatures or else you want to find out later what happened, say, on Thursday at 3 p.m.

Method two is to name the temperatures with two subscripts; a bit like a map reference. Point again to the eighteenth temperature in Fig. 14.1, the one that could be labelled TE(18). It is on the third row, the second number. So it can also be called TE(3,2).

And here is how arrays can tie together . . . Your half-completed program already has a D$(3). That's WED. It also has a TI$(2) standing for 6 AM. So your TE(3,2) will be associated with D$(3) and TI$(2). When the time comes to print out a table, your organisation has been done for you.

Labelling the TE(,) array is done with a couple of loops, one for each of the subscripts. As before, the letters in the loops are not important, so, as the start of a general toughening-up process, we won't spoonfeed you with simple As and Bs but use Q1 and Q2:

```
100 FOR Q1 = 1 TO 7          (seven days in the week)
110 FOR Q2 = 1 TO 8          (eight times per day)
120 PRINT "IT IS "; D$(Q1); "AT "; TI$(Q2);
```

This will fish the Date array and the Time array out of memory, one by one, and put them on the screen. As for the semicolons – do you need them? Some computers manage without.

Now the key line, the reason for this program's existence:

```
130 INPUT ". . . WHAT'S THE TEMPERATURE "; TE(Q1,Q2)
```

A definite need for a semicolon here, but no need for a question mark; the INPUT statement will add its own.

Then the routine closing of the loops:

```
140 NEXT Q2
150 NEXT Q1
```

Consider the situation in line 130 after the program has looped backwards and forwards between Q1 and Q2 a few times. Take the time when, say Q1 = 5 and Q2 = 7.That's Friday 9 p.m.

God and the designer alone know what really goes on inside the microchip, but with line 10 it built up that empty two-dimensional array TE and stored it somewhere. With every loop past line 30 it has been filling the shelves. Right now, Friday 9 p.m., it has asked you what the temperature is and it is waiting for you to read the thermometer. As soon as you type in 33 degrees, it is going to whip that 33 away, stick a 'TE(5,7)' tag on it, and store it in the next vacant pigeon-hole.

Even if you don't answer the question, if the thermometer breaks or the operator takes a coffee break, the zero result can be stored. In this imaginary example TE(5,1) and couple of others = " ". If you called them up by asking PRINT TE(5,1) it would look as if the computer did nothing but in fact it would have printed an invisible " ", pronounced 'uh-uh'.

The second half of this program regurgitates the facts from the first half. A loop brings the Time TI$( ) out of memory in the correct order and then, by TABbing them in seven-space intervals across the page, it LPRINTS them out.

```
160 FOR FR = 1 TO 8
170 LPRINT TAB(FR * 7); TI$(FR);
180 NEXT FR
```

The semicolon at the end of line 170 keeps all the Times on the same line. But somehow you have got to stop it or else the Days and Temperatures would run on too. So you slip in:

```
190 LPRINT " "
```

with no semicolon.

Why use FR for the loop? It is to prove that even though lines 60 to 90 created an array called TI$(T), the (T) subscript isn't permanent. Those Times are no longer labelled TI$(T) but are now TI$(1), TI$(2), TI$(3) and so on. So you can call them back by using any variable you like, FR, ZX or S5 . . . and when FR = 3 then it calls up TI$(3). Indeed, you can reuse T and have line 160 reading FOR T = 1 TO 8 if you want.

If you were drawing this table yourself, you would write the top heading of Times then go down the left margin with Days. Not all printers can do that and then backspace to fill in the Monday temperatures. So the D$ ( ) Days and the TE(,) Temperatures need to run on the same lines.

The program needs a double loop plus a bit of juggling with semicolons so that, when Monday is finished, the Tuesday temperatures start on the next line:

```
200 FOR R = 1 TO 7
210 LPRINT D$(R);                          (There goes the Day)
220 FOR C = 1 TO 8
230 LPRINT TAB(C * 7); TE(R,C);
240 NEXT C
```

There go the Temperatures for that day, all spaced out to fit under the Times.

```
250 LPRINT " "
```

No semicolon means a new line for the next Day.

```
260 NEXT R
```

Here comes the next Day.

And here's the completed program, an example of the screen part-way through the RUN, and the final printout.

```
10 DIM D$(7), TI$(8), TE(7,8)

20 FOR D = 1 TO 7
30 READ D$(D)
40 DATA "MON","TUE","WED","THU","FRI","SAT","SUN"
50 NEXT D

60 FOR T = 1 TO 8
70 READ TI$(T)
80 DATA"3 AM","6 AM","9 AM","12 AM","3 PM","6 PM","9 PM","12 PM"
90 NEXT T

100 FOR Q1 = 1 TO 7
110 FOR Q2 = 1 TO 8
120 PRINT "IT IS "; D$(Q1); " AT "; TI$(Q2);
130 INPUT " .... WHAT'S THE TEMPERATURE "; TE(Q1,Q2)
140 NEXT Q2
150 NEXT Q1                                        continued
```

```
160 FOR FR = 1 TO 8
170 LPRINT TAB(FR * 7); TI$(FR);
180 NEXT FR

190 LPRINT " "

200 FOR R = 1 TO 7
210 LPRINT D$(R);

220 FOR C = 1 TO 8
230 LPRINT TAB(C * 7); TE(R,C);
240 NEXT C

250 LPRINT " "

260 NEXT R


READY
>RUN
IT IS MON AT 3 AM .... WHAT'S THE TEMPERATURE ? 30
IT IS MON AT 6 AM .... WHAT'S THE TEMPERATURE ? 30
IT IS MON AT 9 AM .... WHAT'S THE TEMPERATURE ? 29
IT IS MON AT 12 AM .... WHAT'S THE TEMPERATURE ? 29
IT IS MON AT 3 PM .... WHAT'S THE TEMPERATURE ? 29
IT IS MON AT 6 PM .... WHAT'S THE TEMPERATURE ? 30
IT IS MON AT 9 PM .... WHAT'S THE TEMPERATURE ? 31
IT IS MON AT 12 PM .... WHAT'S THE TEMPERATURE ? 31
IT IS TUE AT 3 AM .... WHAT'S THE TEMPERATURE ? 33
IT IS TUE AT 6 AM .... WHAT'S THE TEMPERATURE ? 33
IT IS TUE AT 9 AM .... WHAT'S THE TEMPERATURE ? 34
IT IS TUE AT 12 AM .... WHAT'S THE TEMPERATURE ? 34
IT IS TUE AT 3 PM .... WHAT'S THE TEMPERATURE ? 28
IT IS TUE AT 6 PM .... WHAT'S THE TEMPERATURE ? _
```

	3AM	6AM	9AM	12AM	3PM	6PM	9PM	12PM
MON	30	30	29	29	29	30	31	31
TUE	33	33	34	34	28	31	29	30
WED	31	31	30	32	33	33	34	31
THUR	33	28	30	29		32	31	30
FRI		28	29	30	31	32	33	32
SAT	30	30	30	30	32	32	31	30
SUN	34	32	28		31	32	34	32

Bugs in arrays

The mistake of DIMensioning the same array twice has already been mentioned. There is also a chance that you could skip the DIM line altogether:

```
5 REM *** FOR SOME REASON OR OTHER : GOTO 20
10 DIM D$(7), TI$(8), TE(7,8)
```

Sure: you have written DIM in, but without realising, you have jumped over it. So make sure that a REM is the *last* statement in a multi-statement line; or, better still, keep REMs on separate lines.

It is true that arrays can usually be used wherever an ordinary variable would go. But there are a couple of exceptions. The main one is that they can't be a looped variable. For example,

    FOR A(1,1) = 1 TO 10

is wrong.

If you think about it, A(1,1) will already have a value; it would screw everything up if the loop started to give it more values from 1 to 10.

The second exception is that the function DEF FN(A(1,1)) won't work . . . but more about DEF FN in a later chapter.

It is true that arithmetic can go inside the brackets. In fact, you often want to pick out the variable just before or just after the current one, so you call up P$(F − 1) or P$(F + 1). The bug lurks in division sums. Suppose you set up B$(100/F) and suppose F happened to be 6. That would make the variable B$(16.66666666). That in itself is no problem: the computer ignores the decimals. What is in doubt is: does your computer just chop off the decimals and call it B$(16) or does it go to the nearest whole number and call it B$(17)?

Again, some computers start their arrays at zero, others start at one. Which is the first pigeon-hole in your computer? B$(0) or B$(1)?

Test it. Set up a quick program on the lines of:

```
10 DIM B$(20)
20 FOR F = 0 TO 20
30 READ B$(F)
40 NEXT F
50 DATA "JILL", "FRED", "JO", "SAM"   (and so on)
60 PRINT B$(0): PRINT B$(100/6)
```

to see if it does start arrays at 0 and also what it thinks about the 16.66666 problem.

The cure for the bugs
Avoid putting zero in the brackets. Always start with B$(1) even if it means losing a bit of memory space.

Check and recheck any complicated arithmetic that looks like going into the brackets. Use the INT function. INT means integer, a whole number . . . you've read about it earlier.

To sum up

You have been reminded about the TAB function from Chapter 4 and have used the semicolon in a PRINT command.

You have learned about arrays, which are variables with a bracket (a subscript) to label them. You have used the FOR–TO loop to read DATA into the arrays.

Exercises

1. There are too many loops in the Temperature program. Can you shorten it by incorporating the LPRINT lines into the READ–DATA loops?

2. What's the average temperature every day? Can you get the computer to print that out?

3. Jill, Jo and Jean sell between $1,000 and $4,000 worth of insurance every week. Chart their performances over a four-week period.

15

String sort

A nice thing about computers is that not only can they handle words but they can also sort them out. There is nothing special about a machine recognising that 6 is greater than 4. But to know that COKE comes before PEPSI in the alphabet . . . that's magic.

There is more about this later in the chapter on CHR$, but the secret is that every letter is coded. C is usually 67 and P is 80 so the computer sees that 67 comes before 80. Sorting out words then becomes no more difficult for it than sorting out numbers.

In business you hit a lot of sorting problems. Perhaps you sell video films and, as new titles come on the market, you want to update your sales catalogue by retyping it in alphabetical order. Your salesmen want the list in order of titles while your storemen want it in bin location order. The Personnel department want the salesmen's names in alphabetical order, the Accounts want them with the top bonus earners first while the Pensions department want them in order of age.

BASIC will sort lists in a very primitive, though effective way. It takes one item of the list and compares it with the next item of the list, asking, 'Is ITEM(1) bigger than ITEM(2)?' If it is bigger, then ITEM(1) gets put to one side. Do this a few thousand times and the big items go one way and the small items go the other way.

Lay half a dozen pencils, all of different sizes, on your desk. Shuffle them about and then put them into a random line. Close your eyes. Pick up the first one in your left hand and the second one in your right hand.

By blind touch alone: which is the longer? The one in the right hand? Transfer that one to your left hand, keep it moving and lay it down on the desk. Transfer the second pencil to your left hand and pick up a new pencil with your right hand.

No peeking —which is longer? Lay that one in the newly forming line to the left of your desk, transfer the remaining pencil to your left hand and pick up number four with your right hand. Which is longer? Work through the six pencils – whichever of the two in your hands is the longer will go out to the line on the left; the shorter of the two stays in your hand to be compared with the next pencil you pick up.

At the end of the first run-through, move to the partly sorted line lying on the left, pick up the first pencil in your left hand, the second pencil in your right hand. Put the longer of the pair aside in a new row on the left, transfer the shorter one to your left hand and pick up number three with your right hand.

Repeat these blind comparisons time and time again until you make one pass without needing to swap any pencil from one hand to the other. That means that they are in order.

You can open your eyes. Because that's how computers sort.

The video business

Suppose then that you sell videos of old movies. Clear the screen for printing:

```
10 CLS
```

How many movies titles do you intend to stock? 100? So you need an array of 100 bins in your warehouse to store them. The dimensions of that warehouse will be B(100) with F$(100) films in the bins:

```
20 DIM B(100), F$(100)
```

Now the video films. So far you have only 20 yet you still need that 100-bin warehouse for when business expands. The films with their bin numbers go in data lines, way down at the end of the program. The end of the list of titles is signalled by the trick of using 999, "END" and that is on line 2000 so that there is plenty of room to insert new titles in the future:

```
1000 DATA 7,"MIDNIGHT COWBOY", 8,"THE SERVANT", 14,"THE
     VIKINGS", 9,"SOME LIKE IT HOT", 4,"WHATEVER HAPPENED
     TO BABY JANE?"
1010 DATA 13,"BEN HUR", 20, "THE HUNCHBACK OF NOTRE
     DAME", 19,"ROOM AT THE TOP", 3,"PSYCHO", 1,"CAT ON A
     HOT TIN ROOF", 2,"EXODUS"
1020 DATA 18,"THE APARTMENT", 12,"NEVER ON SUNDAY",
     16,"BREAKFAST AT TIFFANY'S", 6,"THE ENTERTAINER",
     5,"WEST SIDE STORY"
1030 DATA 11,"THE ALAMO", 10,"GIGI", 17,"CASABLANCA",
     15,"GUNSMOKE"
2000 DATA 999,"END"
```

The READ

You need a routine to read and label all those films. It can be done with a little loop that uses N to number them and also looks out for the 999 signal to know when to stop. This will take time so, since inexperienced operators worry if the screen stays blank (they think the computer's broken), line 30 prints a reassuring message:

```
30 PRINT @ 340,"JUST A MINUTE – I'M READING THE LIST"
40 N = 0
50 N = N+ 1
60 READ B(N), F$(N)
70 IF B(N) = 999 THEN 90
80 GOTO 50
```

Line 40 could be missed out and the program would still work. It is just a precaution to make sure that N really does start off at zero.

Don't get confused over what is physically in the bins in your warehouse and what is in the B( ), F$( ) arrays. In Bin number 1 there are copies of 'Cat on a Hot Tin Roof': you can see them, pick them up, post them to your customers.

In the computer memory $B(1) = 7$ and $F\$(1) = $ "Midnight Cowboy". That's how the video business works: next month you might buy in a couple of other titles, 'The Old Man and the Sea' and 'Some Like it Hot'. These wouldn't necessarily go into Bins 21 and 22; one might go into Bin 16 to replace 'Breakfast at Tiffany's', which wasn't selling so well. A later section of the program is going to sort these out into proper order.

The menu

```
90 PRINT : PRINT "O.K. I'VE READ IT"
100 PRINT : PRINT "HOW DO YOU WANT IT SORTED OUT . . .?"
110 PRINT TAB(10) "TYPE 'B' FOR 'BIN NUMBER' "
120 PRINT TAB(10) "TYPE 'T' FOR 'TITLE' "
130 A$ = INKEY$ : IF A$ = "" THEN 130
140 IF A$ = "B" THEN 400
150 IF A$ = "T" THEN 200
160 PRINT "SORRY, YOU MUST ANSWER ONLY B OR T" : GOTO
    100
```

In line 130, INKEY$ has been used for a fast response to the operator's answer. If your computer uses GET or CALL KEY then alter line 130. If it has none of these then use INPUT and have your operator pressing the ENTER key after they answer B or T.

Whatever you use, there will still be a need for line 160 because there are always clowns who refuse to hit the right keys. Notice that line 160 is never reached under normal conditions. As long as your operator hits the correct B or T then the program jumps over the error-trapping line 160. Notice too that there is no need for a line 155 saying IF A$ < > "B" AND A$ < > "T" THEN PRINT "YOU HAVE TO PRESS 'B' OR 'T' ". Because if they haven't answered B or T and the program hasn't jumped to lines 400 or 200 then it is bound to go on to line 160.

The sort

This is the bit where the operator has answered T and the films are going to be sorted into alphabetical order.

The heart of the sort will be in line 240:

```
240 IF F$(C) <= F$(C+1) THEN 290
```

where, just as you did with pencils, the computer will look at two film titles F$(C), and the next one, F$(C+1). If F$(C) is smaller than or the same as F$(C+1) then it will leave them as they are and jump away to line 290. If F$(C) is greater than the next title, if it comes after it in the alphabet, then lines 250, 260 and 270 will do as you did with the pencils and swop them over.

For instance: in the first sweep, F$(8) "Room at the Top" will be held in a temporary variable TE$ while F$(9), which is F$(C+1) "Psycho", becomes F$(8). Then TE$ "Room at the Top" becomes the new F$(9). That's one little progression towards being in alphabetical order: Psycho is now in front of Room at the Top.

It is as if you had stood in front of the real bins and picked up all the Room at the Top films, held them temporarily under one arm while you took all the Psycho films out of Number 9 Bin and loaded them into the Number 8 Bin.

Here is the routine. First it clears the screen and prints a reassuring JUST A MINUTE message:

```
200 CLS : PRINT@ 340, "JUST A MINUTE – I'M SORTING"
210 FOR SW = 1 TO (N–1)
220 JU$ = "NO SWOPS"
230 FOR C = 1 TO (N – SW)
240 IF F$(C) <= F$(C+1) THEN 290
250 TE$ = F$(C) : TE = B(C)
260 F$(C) = F$(C+1) : B(C) = B(C+1)
270 F$(C+1) = TE$ : B(C+1) = TE
280 JU$ = "THERE'S BEEN A SWOP"
290 NEXT C
300 IF JU$ = "NO SWOPS" THEN 320
310 NEXT SW
```

Concentrate on lines 250, 260 and 270. There in line 250 are the temporary variables to hold the film title TE$ and the bin number TE.

In line 260 the second film title F$(C+1) swops over and becomes F$(C) while its associated bin number B(C+1) becomes B(C). In line 270 the old F$(C), which was called TE$ for a fraction of a second, now moves one forward and becomes F$(C+1). That's the sorting mechanism.

But you, when you sorted those pencils, knew when to stop. First when the two pencils in your hand were already right, you didn't bother to swop them over, but picked up the next one from the pile. Secondly, after you found you had done a complete sweep of the whole pile and everything was in order, you knew that there was no need to do another sweep.

Look again at line 240. It says that if the two films are already in the right order then jump all over the swopping lines and go to line 290 NEXT C. It also jumps over line 280 "THERE'S BEEN A SWOP". Quite rightly, if there hasn't been a swop.

When the list of films has been sorted once, with every film moving one place closer to alphabetical order, the program passes to the outside loop of line 210 for another SW sweep.

Before entering the C loop for another look at pairs of films it picks up a flag, JU$, saying "NO SWOPS". This flag is soon knocked down by line 280 if there have been any swops. But suppose, this time, no title needs to be swopped, everything is in order? This is what happens:

210 Another sweep starts
220 The flag says "NO SWOPS"
230 The films are examined two at a time
240 Does Film 1 come before Film 2 in the alphabet? Yes, it does, so 290, jump to the next film.
240 Does Film 2 come before Film 3 in the alphabet? Yes, it does, so 290, jump to the next film.
240 Does Film 3 come before Film 4 in the alphabet? Yes, it does, so jump . . . until all twenty are checked.
300 Does the flag still say "NO SWOPS"? Yes it does, so don't go back to 210 for another complete sweep. Instead go to the printout.

The printout

```
320 CLS : PRINT "FILM TITLE"; : PRINT TAB(50)"BIN NUMBER"
330 PRINT
340 FOR PR = 1 TO N
350 PRINT F$(PR); :PRINT TAB(50) B(PR)
360 NEXT PR
```

This simply loops for as long as you have films, and prints the titles in their new, alphabetical order. Do you want it on paper? Then change these last PRINTs into LPRINT.

You want them in Bin order? You want to know what happens if you operator presses B and wants to go to line 400? That's your problem. It is Exercise 1 at the end of this chapter! Meanwhile, here is a listing of the program so far.

```
10 CLS
20 DIM B(100), F$(100)
30 PRINT@ 340,"JUST A MINUTE - I'M READING THE LIST"
40 N = 0
50 N = N + 1
60 READ B(N), F$(N)
70 IF B(N) = 999 THEN 90
80 GOTO 50

90 PRINT : PRINT "O.K.  I'VE READ IT"
100 PRINT : PRINT "HOW DO YOU WANT IT SORTED OUT ... ?"
110 PRINT TAB(10) "TYPE 'B'  FOR 'BIN NUMBER'"
120 PRINT TAB(10) "TYPE 'T' FOR 'TITLE'"
130 A$ = INKEY$ : IF A$ = "" THEN 130
140 IF A$ = "B" THEN 400
150 IF A$ = "T" THEN 200
160 PRINT "SORRY, YOU MUST ANSWER ONLY  B  OR  T" :
      GOTO 100

200 CLS : PRINT@ 340,"JUST A MINUTE - I'M SORTING"
210 FOR SW = 1 TO (N-1)
220 JU$ = "NO SWOPS"
230 FOR C = 1 TO (N - SW)
240 IF F$(C) <= F$(C+1) THEN 290
250 TE$ = F$(C) : TE = B(C)
260 F$(C) = F$(C+1) : B(C) = B(C+1)
270 F$(C+1) = TE$ : B(C+1) = TE
280 JU$ = "THERE'S BEEN A SWOP"
290 NEXT C
300 IF JU$ = "NO SWOPS" THEN 320
310 NEXT SW

320 CLS : PRINT "FILM TITLE"; : PRINT TAB(50)"BIN NUMBER"
330 PRINT
340 FOR PR = 1 TO N
350 PRINT F$(PR); :PRINT TAB(50) B(PR)
360 NEXT PR

1000 DATA 7,"MIDNIGHT COWBOY",8,"THE SERVANT",14,"THE
       VIKINGS",9,"SOME LIKE IT HOT",4,"WHATEVER HAPPENED TO
       BABY JANE ?"
1010 DATA 13,"BEN HUR",20,"THE HUNCHBACK OF NOTRE DAME",
       19,"ROOM AT THE TOP",3,"PSYCHO",1,"CAT ON A HOT TIN
       ROOF",2,"EXODUS"
1020 DATA 18,"THE APARTMENT",12,"NEVER ON SUNDAY",16,
       "BREAKFAST AT TIFFANY'S",6,"THE ENTERTAINER",5,"WEST
       SIDE STORY"
1030 DATA 11,"THE ALAMO",10,"GIGI",17,"CASABLANCA", 15,
       "GUNSMOKE"
2000 DATA 999,"END"
```

Notice how the titles are not sorted just by their first letter. 'The Alamo' and The Apartment' are in alphabetical order right up to the eighth letter. A computer is a very powerful tool.

Sort bugs

For the first time you have met a delay in a computer's responses. Some machines take almost 14 seconds to sort these 20 titles because they run through more than 200 letter-by-letter comparisons. Double the number of films to 40 and the sorting time increases to over 40 seconds as the comparisons increase to over 800.

Imagine how long it would take if, instead of reading the data into a couple of arrays at the beginning, it had had to jump out of the loops 800 times to READ the next film title from the DATA statement.

Your machine may be faster or slower than this. Time it from the moment you hit T to the start of the printout.

The cures

You can either design a faster method of sorting or else you can make the machine run through the loops faster.

There are faster methods. Some are based on the way that people sort. We don't work through a pile of pencils methodically from left

Fig. 15.1 The Torch micro, with integral screen and built-in disk drives

to right. We take a quick look, grab the big ones and shove the little ones to one side. Only where the sizes are pretty close do we make an exact measurement.

There are whole books written on better sorting methods than this simple program you have written. Yet no matter what method you use, a BASIC program is always going to be slow in sorting large amounts of data. The trouble with BASIC is that, as well as swopping the arrays around, it is also having to translate your programmed instructions into binary code. The best way to sort (and this is a terrible admission in a book about the beauties of BASIC) is to work in machine code.

You can buy machine code sort programs or, if you own one of the latest disk operating systems, there may be a sort routine patched into the BASIC. Since 1981, for instance, with NEWDOS (which runs the Tandy TRS-80) you can set up an array as you did in lines 20 to 50, call up CMD"O" (pronounced Command O) and the array is sorted at electronic speed. Comparisons of the order of 20 minutes for a BASIC sort against 12 seconds for CMD"O" have been quoted.

It is possible to learn how to program in machine code but that needs another book. See USR in a later chapter.

To sum up

To sort, you read an array into memory then run loops that compare the items of data with one another. If they are out of order you put them into temporary variables while they are shuffled into place.

A rough rule is that the easier it is to write the program, the slower it is to run.

Machine code is faster than BASIC. To know more, read about 'binary sorts' and 'tree sorts' in another textbook.

Exercises

1. Complete the subroutine that should start at line 400 and which sorts the films into numerical order by Bin number. Don't renumber the printout in lines 320 to 360 but make that into a separate subroutine.

2. How can you stop the program from printing "END 999" among the film titles?

And, finally, an idea . . . The telephone company issues lists of towns with their dialling codes. But not the other way round: if you see the code 0206 you can't find out which town that is.

Yet the program on page 116 can sort dialling codes into numerical order. Scrap the DATA lines, redimension the arrays (there are about 5000 exchanges in the UK), make lines 10 to 80 accept typed INPUT "TOWN"; F$(N) and INPUT "CODE"; B(N). Then sort it using the BIN NUMBER option, which you will now call DIALLING CODE.

The snags? This sort is very slow; typing the telephone booklet will be very boring; and does your computer have enough memory space for those very large arrays? (See the next chapters for a way round this last snag.)

16

SAVE

This book was written on a battered old computer with only 48K memory. That's enough for no more than a chapter and a half. Yet the entire book is stored on two floppy disks.

Well before the small memory was filled, the morning's typing would be transferred to permanent storage on disk. Every time there was a coffee break, the current chapter, about PRINT @ for instance, was saved as "PRINTATA" or "PRINTATB" and finally as "PRINTAT/BOO" while the program to illustrate it was saved as "PRINTAT/PRG". To the computer these are entirely unrelated names.

After the break it would be LOADed back into the computer and typing would continue. This way, a cheap inadequate computer is transformed into a powerful machine with virtually unlimited memory.

File names

Not everything in a computer is a program. You could put in boring lists of train schedules or warehouse stock. Certainly the words in this book are not a program.

The jargon word is 'file', named after the cardboard-covered files of paper in office filing cabinets. A program is a file but a file isn't necessarily a program.

You are allowed up to 8 or 10 characters for a file name. A few machines, like the IBM, allow any character but usually the first character must be a letter, not a number, and you can't use $ % – ! type symbols. A file name can be as simple as "Z" or as complicated as:

"DOCLIST6/JAN . ABRACADA :2" , A

    1   2   3   4   5

(1) File name. This on its own is enough: 2, 3, 4 and 5 are optional disk directions.

(2) Three-letter extension. In machines using CP/M a dot is used instead of a slash, as DOCLIST6.JAN

(3) Password to prevent unauthorised people using your file. Is the full stop essential? Check your manual. Don't know the password of a store-bought program? There are programs to remove passwords.

Fig. 16.1 The text of this book – hundreds of sheets when printed out – was stored on two floppy disks

(4) Maybe you are working on Disk Drive 1; this tells the computer that DOCLIST6/JAN is for Drive 2. But check your manual about that colon. CP/M will not hunt through disk drives on its own. You send it from the first drive (called A) to the second drive (called B) like this:

A< B: LOAD "DOCLIST6.JAN"

Though it does have a question mark in case you forget the file name: DOC??ST?.JAN might find it. And there's a wild card:

DOCLIST6.* would find all the DOCLIST6s
*.JAN would find all files ending in JAN

(5) Usually, programs are stored in compressed form for speed and space saving. This ,A tells the computer to save it in ASCII coding (more of this in a later chapter). Advantages? The program can be re-read and edited by word processing programs . . . Imagine changing all PRINTs to LPRINTs in one stroke!

DOCLIST6 is different from DOCLIST7, and DOCLIST6/JAN is different from DOCLIST6/FEB. Yet DOCLIST6/JAN :1 is considered to be a different file from DOCLIST6/JAN :2 on Drive 2. But don't bank on this. If you forgot to close the disk drive door, or there was a write-protect tab on the disk, most computers would head for the first usable drive, no matter which it was.

Check if your machine allows two passwords. Does yours consider that DOCLIST6/JAN . ABRACADA and DOCLIST6/JAN . SESAME are the same or different?

What happens if you give a new program the same name as one already stored? If you have physically wound the cassette recorder to a fresh strip of tape, the second program will be SAVEd with no comment. You will have two SAMENAMEs on tape. The confusion comes next day when you try to load one.

With disk, or if you start from the beginning of a tape, and rely on the computer to find its own space the older computers might give a warning but usually they write right over the existing SAMENAME.

Disadvantage? You lose the first file. The advantage? Perhaps you want to deliberately wipe out last week's stocklist when you record the new entries.

SAVE
You have a program on screen and you want to keep it permanently. Run the wire from the computer's socket (the Cassette Port) and plug the other three ends into the REM, MIC and EAR recorder sockets. If you use music tape, fast-wind past the non-magnetic leader strip. Switch to Record, but the recorder shouldn't move: it should be awaiting a computer signal

If you are in a hurry, wind fast-forward, listening to the squeal of earlier recorded programs until silence shows a blank section of tape.

With disk drives, make sure that you are using a disk with its write-protect tab off. Disks are far faster and more automated than tape.

The commands are usually SAVE for disks and CSAVE for cassettes: but check your manual. Type: SAVE "PROGNAME" or whatever, press ENTER and the recorder should turn or the disks whirr.

To bring a program off disk and into the computer, type: LOAD"PROGNAME". For cassette the command is usually CLOAD (pronounced C LOAD) but again: check your manual.

Can your machine do without the second speech marks after the file name? Try SAVE "PROGNAME (with no final quote marks). It saves typing time but notice, with disks, that the final " has to be there before the ,A in the ASCII method of saving.

DIRectory
With a cassette you look at the tape counter then write on the label where programs start and finish. With disks you type DIR or CATALOG and get a screen like this:

SUBROUT/CMD	GOBUG/CMD	PRINTAT/PRG
COMPDATE	SORTB	TABGRAPH/BOO
GOSUB/BOO	USING/PRG	PRILIST/BAS
SORT/PRG	STOCK/DAT	ARRAY/BOO

Not all programs are in BASIC. The arithmetical Visicalc, the word processing Wordstar and even BASIC itself, are not written in BASIC. To call non-BASIC files, you stay in DOS, the disk operating system, and simply type their name with no word LOAD and no inverted commas. In CP/M there is an extension .COM (in other machines /CMD) standing for COMmand File . . . you don't need to type this extension.

Calling a BASIC program from disk needs two stages: (1) bring the BASIC language off the disk. This is a Command File, catalogued as BASIC.COM or BASIC/CMD so it is enough to type BASIC; (2) once BASIC is in the computer you can recall the program needed with LOAD "PAYROLL/BAS

What if you call a BASIC program while still in DOS? You get an error message. Can you call DOS while still in BASIC? See the Exercises at the end of this chapter.

Got a file that will not load either from DOS or from BASIC? It might not be a program but just a list of names and addresses, temperature readings or a parts list. A data file, maybe with the extension .DAT. This will only load when called up by a BASIC program (read how in a later chapter). You can't call it yourself.

RUN
You already use RUN to start off a program. It can also be used straight from disk or tape. Once you have BASIC in the computer, RUN"PROGNAME/BAS" will find PROGNAME/BAS, load it and start it running.

In most disk operating systems, the command AUTO, as in AUTO BASIC, will automatically load BASIC into memory as soon as you switch on. The better DOSs give you two stages: AUTO BASIC RUN"PROGNAME/BAS so that the computer clicks and buzzes into BASIC; and then the program, without any work from you.

Notice how BASIC didn't have inverted commas because it is a DOS Command File, while "PROGNAME/BAS needed at least the first inverted commas because it is in the BASIC language.

AUTO has a different meaning in the BASIC language. Here it will, on most machines, automatically type out the next line number for you after you've pressed ENTER. It goes up in tens, too!

KILL

To all appearances, when you type KILL "FILENAME/DAT" (no inverted commas when in DOS. In CP/M the word is ERA for ERAse) the file is wiped off the disk.

Some machines have a PURGE command to let you wipe out a whole batch of programs. But the trick is that they are still there. All the computer does is to delete their entry in the directory so the disk drive can't find them.

If you KILL by mistake then buy a Monitor program, a toolkit program (it might have 'zap' in its name). These special programs let you look at the contents of a disk and, admittedly with difficulty, you'll find your so-called KILLed program. You may be able to repair the disk and get it back. But hurry: the computer could well write fresh data right over the lost program.

Dedicated keys

SAVE, LOAD and RUN are so frequently used that, if your keyboard has a row of function keys, it pays to program so that commands can be entered with a single keystroke.

Some Sharp computers have a pleasant system. The directory scrolls on-screen, you move an arrow to the program you want then hit the RUN key.

But beware of a KILL key in case your finger slips.

LOAD bugs

These are usually mechanical. Set your cassette recorder's tone control as high as possible and if the volume control isn't graduated then paint numbers on it so that you can make fine adjustments. A cheap transistor standing next to the computer and tuned off-station can pick up the sound of a program being loaded. Learn to distinguish the noise of a good load and adjust the recorder's volume accordingly.

With both tape and disks make frequent backups. Even if you have only half composed a program, SAVE it.

Proprietary programs bought on cassette can be saved on disk and disk programs can be saved on tape. It's a safe way of making backups. They will reLOAD but you can't always RUN them because Disk BASIC is a slightly more complicated language.

Disks are vulnerable to electrical disturbances. The best people to help rescue them are the amateur geniuses in your computer's user group.

If a single program doesn't LOAD, are you calling it up by its right name? Has it a password? Are you calling from DOS when you should be in BASIC?

If a program LOADS but doesn't RUN then LIST through it. Somewhere there might be a little glitch that has corrupted it and way down on line 30500 might be PRICT instead of PRINT.

SAVE bugs
A silly mistake, but disastrous, is to type SAVE instead of LOAD . . . even when you're not in BASIC.

Suppose you are using a word processor and have typed out almost all of this chapter. It is coffee break so you slip in a disk and type SAVE"CHAP16" . . . that's fine.

After coffee, you switch the computer on, load in the word processing program and get a nice clear screen, empty except for the READY prompt. You then carelessly type SAVE"CHAP16" when you mean LOAD. The computer obeys you; it saves the blank screen on disk, wiping out the original words of CHAP16.

To sum up

Programs can be called files and be given names of up to 8 or 10 characters, three-letter extensions, passwords and drive numbers.

The commands are SAVE, LOAD, RUN, KILL and AUTO with little variations between different computers.

Not all files are in BASIC. Some are in the computer's own machine code, some are in other languages and some are mere lists of data. Read about **ASCII** in Chapter 18.

Exercises

1. DIR doesn't show all the files on a disk. So that the screen won't be crowded, it doesn't bother with routines doing the housekeeping chores of disk operation: clock interrupts, keyboard intercept, FORMAT, debug. Find out how to show these invisible files on screen.

2. Good BASICs (and consider this when buying a new computer) can hold the current program in memory while you have a quick visit to DOS, and then carry on with BASIC again. Here is part of a Mailing List program:

```
20030 PRINT "DO YOU WANT TO MAKE A BACKUP COPY?"
20040 W$ = INKEY$ : IF W$ = "" THEN 20040
20050 IF W$ = "N" THEN RETURN
20060 PRINT "PUT THE BACKUP DISK INTO DRIVE 1"
20070 CMD "COPY MAILBOXA:0 TO MAILBOXB:1
20080 PRINT "O.K. THAT'S DONE."
```

Line 20070 starts with CMD (pronounced Command) telling the computer to go to its disk operating system and then to run the COPY facility. It copies the file MAILBOXA on Disk Drive 0 to the backup disk in Drive 1, giving it the new name of MAILBOXB. When finished the computer comes back to BASIC in line 20080.

With this kind of facility you can break into a program and ask FREE to find out how much disk space there is left. Or DIR :1 to see what is on Disk 1. But CMD is not a word used in many machines. Look in your manual to see how your computer jumps to DOS.

17

String handling

You work in an antiquarian bookshop and you are offered an ancient manuscript reading . . . 'Some books are to be tasted, others to be swallowed and some few to be chewed and digested.' Did Shakespeare write it?

Every writer has an individual style. Some use long words, others never begin a sentence with 'And'. Can a computer recognise those subtle patterns?

Word length, for instance: you, personally, would count the letters, count the words then do a division sum. You know that 'Some' is a word, 'books' is a word, 'are' is a word; so there are three. But apart from the odd PRINT and GOTO, words are just strings of electronic impulses to a computer.

But if we redefine a 'word' as a string of characters ending with a space then a computer can recognise spaces and count them:

```
70 IF B$ = " " THEN N = N + 1
```

Now if the machine were to loop through every character in the 'Some books' quotation, every time there was a space (B$) then N would add it up. At the end N would tell us how many spaces there were and, since there isn't a space after the last word of any quotation, N + 1 would be the number of words.

But how many letters are there? You could ask the operator to count them:

```
30 INPUT "WHAT'S THE QUOTATION "; Q$
35 INPUT "HOW MANY LETTERS IS THAT"
```

but if you have to count the letters you might as well do the whole job yourself. So scrap line 35: there must be a better way.

LEN( )
The word is LEN( ), standing for LENgth of the string variable inside those brackets.

```
40 L = LEN(Q$)
```

will tell you how many characters there are in any quotation you input.

And since we need to feed every character through a loop to see if B$ is a space then that loop has to go on for L times.

```
50 FOR W = 1 TO L
```

MID$($,,)

As the quotation is processed through the loop, MID$(Q$,) can pick out any sub-string in the MIDdle of it. The spaces in the brackets are to take numbers to show, first, where the selection is to start, and second, how many characters you want:

```
IF E$ = "FOR EXAMPLE"
MID$(E$,5,4) = EXAM
```

because it starts at position 5 (the space after FOR counts as a character) and picks the next 4 characters.

Machines like the Sinclair use PRINT E$(5 TO 9), meaning print from the fifth to the ninth character, but these are in the minority. This book will use MID$.

We want MID$ to start at the beginning of the 'Some books' quotation and to look at every single character. In line 50, W starts at one and increases until the end of the quote. So:

```
60 B$ = MID$(Q$,W,1)
```

should work its way through the quote.

Here again is the loop which makes the heart of the anti-forgery program:

```
30 INPUT "WHAT'S THE QUOTATION "; Q$
40 L = LEN(Q$)                    :' L is the length
50 FOR W = 1 TO L                 :' loop round every letter
60 B$ = MID$(Q$, W, 1)            :' call every letter B$
70 IF B$ = " " THEN N = N + 1 :' N counts the spaces
80 NEXT W                         :' check the next letter
```

CLEAR

Most BASICs allow about 50 characters free of charge for strings. To clear more shelf-space in the area of memory allocated to strings, you declare at the start of the program how much more you need:

```
CLEAR 3000
```

would let you store 3000 bytes of strings during the program. Enough for a few A$(20,50) type arrays. In this program:

```
10 CLEAR 260
```

will be enough because most BASICs can't handle more than 255 characters in a single string. Some cheap machines can only take 15-character strings.

Elegant programmers take pride in being parsimonious with string space. But if you own plenty of memory and a program halts with OUT OF STRING SPACE, then zip back to the early lines and give yourself a lavish CLEAR 5000.

Some dialects use CLR, but don't confuse this with the CLS used in this book to clear the video screen:

20 CLS : N = 0

will start the program with a blank screen and make sure too that N starts off as zero.

Finally comes the arithmetic of 'letters divided by words = average word length'. The number of letters is the length of the quotation minus the spaces, L − N. The number of words is one greater than the number of spaces, N + 1.

90 PRINT "THE AVERAGE WORD HAS " (L−N) / (N+1) " LETTERS"

When you RUN that 'Some books' through the program, the answer comes:

THE AVERAGE WORD HAS 4 LETTERS

and you look on your chart and find that it isn't Shakespeare. Four letters is the characteristic word length of Francis Bacon.

But of course, this example is statistically ridiculous. There'd have to be a lot more INPUT to get a realistic word average. And that's not the only criterion for judging authorship. See the Exercises at the end of the chapter.

The complete program and the sample RUN are as follows:

```
10 CLEAR 260
20 CLS : N = 0
30 INPUT "WHAT'S THE QUOTATION ";Q$
40 L = LEN(Q$)
50 FOR W = 1 TO L
60 B$ = MID$(Q$,W,1)
70 IF B$ = " " THEN N = N+1
80 NEXT W
90 PRINT "THE AVERAGE WORD CONTAINS " (L−N)/(N+1) " LETTERS"

WHAT'S THE QUOTATION ? SOME BOOKS ARE TO BE TASTED OTHERS TO BE
SWALLOWED AND SOME FEW TO BE CHEWED AND DIGESTED
THE AVERAGE WORD CONTAINS  4  LETTERS
READY
>_
```

INPUT bugs

That comma in the quotation after the word 'tasted,' can cause a bug. Most INPUTs halt at a comma and ignore the rest of the quote. If your machine has LINE INPUT then use that because LINE INPUT realises that commas are a part of speech and accepts them.

   Anyway, it might be better to miss all punctuation out; it would only screw up the letter count.

CLEAR bugs

Remember how in Chapter 14 the A(20,50) style arrays had to be DIMensioned so there was enough memory space allocated for them? Well, CLEAR wipes that out.

```
10 DIM A(50), B$(100)
20 CLEAR 2000
```

gives a mysterious error. You wonder where you've gone wrong. You have to DIMension *after* CLEARing:

```
20 CLEAR 2000
30 DIM A(50), B$(100)
```

LEFT$($,) and RIGHT$($,)

```
IF E$ = "FOR EXAMPLE"
LEFT$(E$,2) = FO
RIGHT$(E$,4) = MPLE
```

There is only one number in these brackets. LEFT$ picks out that number of characters from the left of the string, RIGHT$ picks them from the right.

   You could use MID$(E$,1,2) to pull out 'FO', just as LEFT$ did. But to find the last four characters would need the more complicated MID$(E$,(LEN(E$)−3),4) instead of the simple RIGHT$

   LEFT$ is a useful way out of a programmer's dilemma over 'Yes/No' answers. An experienced operator can spell Y−E−S wrongly or they might type NOT YET instead of NO. Yet if you just ask for the first letter, they don't know what you mean:

   HAVE YOU FINISHED (Y/N)?

confuses them. So ask:

```
1000 INPUT "HAVE YOU FINISHED? YES OR NO "; AN$
1010 IF LEFT$(AN$,1) = "Y" THEN END
```

and it doesn't matter how they spell the rest of the word.

   RIGHT$ can be used to select parts of an address. It could pick out all customers who live in Birmingham, all German firms ending in G.m.b.H., all B.Sc. graduates.

String bugs

These usually come from the brackets. You miss one of the numbers in MID$(Z$,5,7) or get tangled in an A$(2,3) array with LEFT$(A$(N−1) , (N+1)), whatever that might mean.

To sum up

Pronounced 'MID string', 'LEFT string' and 'RIGHT string', these operators can step into a string of characters and pull out the ones you want.

Read Chapter 14 again about arrays, remembering the warning that DIM must come after CLEAR.

Exercises

1. Word length alone is not enough to prove authorship. Add subroutines to the 'Quote' program to check how often words like 'and', 'I' and 'then' crop up. Who uses short sentences? Who uses the most punctuation marks?

2. A clerk types hundreds of 18283926G3b57−style stock numbers and naturally makes mistakes. Yet if the number contains either 344 or 652 it means a Ford component. If it has 345 or 97B somewhere, it's a Datsun part. Write a program that tells if a number is a FORD, DATSUN or NEITHER.

3. How can you make a mailing list, full of FRED SMITH style names, address envelopes with F. SMITH?

4. How can you turn a 01/11/85 date into 1ST NOV. 1985 or, assuming it's in American style, into 11TH JAN. 1985 ?

18

ASCII

Computers think electrically. And electrical switches have only two states: either ON or OFF.

So, while you think of that upside-down vee shape with a line across its middle as the letter A, a computer imagines it as OFF-ON-OFF-OFF-OFF-OFF-OFF-ON. This isn't a new idea. Morse code, using only two signals, represents 'A' as DOT DASH.

When you hit 'A' on the keyboard the computer turns that keystroke into OFF-ON-OFF-OFF-OFF-OFF-OFF-ON and sends the signal to the video screen, which re-translates OFF-ON-OFF-OFF-OFF-OFF-OFF-ON into little lighted dots that form the shape of an A. So BASIC is a slow language.

If you are into mathematics, you know that OFF-ON-OFF etc can be written as 01000001 with '0' for OFF and '1' for ON. That's a binary number valued at 65 in everyday decimal numbers. Letter B is thought of as 01000010, which is 66. This is the ASCII code (see pages 133–137).

ASCII (pronounced 'Askey') stands for American Standard Code for Information Interchange. Not all computers use it. Older mainframes use EBCDIC (Extended Binary-Coded Decimal Interchange Code).

This has a similar principle to ASCII, though using different numbers. Unfortunately for this book, not every microcomputer uses the same numbers to represent the letters.

Find out what yours thinks by asking:

PRINT ASC("FRED")

The odds are that it will answer:

70

because it only gives the code for F, the first letter of the string in the brackets.

TABLE 18.1. The American Standard Code for Information Interchange – ASCII. Most computers and even printers follow the same code. There is still logic to other machines' coding (two typical examples, the Sharp and the ZX81, are given). Codes 127 to 255 are mostly used for graphics characters and video colours; 165 to 255 store BASIC commands in machines like the ZX Spectrum; 192 to 198 are cursor controls in machines like the Sharp; 192 to 255 create a series of blanks in the Tandy TRS-80 and the Video Genie

ASCII code	Usual meaning	Epson printer	Sharp	ZX81	Other machines
0			SPACE		@ Atom, BBC, Commodore
1			A		BREAK Tandy
2			B		
3			C		
4			D		
5			E		
6			F		BELL Atom
7	BELL	BELL	G		
8	BACKSPACE	BACKSPACE	H		
9	TAB	TAB	I		
10	NEW LINE	NEW LINE	J		
11	CURSOR UP	MOVE LINE	K	´	
12	NEW PAGE	NEW PAGE	L	$	CLEAR SCREEN Nascom, BBC
13	ENTER	RETURN	M	:	CURSOR HOME UK101
14	CURSOR ON	BIG LETTERS	N	?	
15	CURSOR OFF	SMALL	O	(	
16			P	)	
17		READY	Q	>	CURSOR DOWN Commodore
18			R	∧	CURSOR FORWARD Nascom
19		NOT READY	S	∨	CURSOR HOME Commodore
20			T	=	CURSOR DOWN Nascom
21			U	+	CURSOR FORWARD Apple
22			V	−	

ASCII code	Usual meaning	Epson printer	Sharp	ZX81	Other machines
23			W	*	BIG LETTERS Tandy
24	BACKSHIFT	ERASE	X	/	
25			Y	:	CURSOR FORWARD Tandy
26			Z	,	CURSOR DOWN Tandy
27	ESCAPE	ESCAPE		.	[Atom
28	CURSOR HOME			0	\ Commodore, Atom
29				1	] Commodore
30	ERASE LINE		↓	2	↑ Commodore
31	CLEAR		0	3	
32	SPACE		1	4	
33	!	SIZE	2	5	
34	"		3	6	
35	#		4	7	
36	$		5	8	
37	%	CHANGE	6	9	
38	&	CHANGE	7	A	
39	'		8	B	
40	(		9	C	
41	)			D	
42	*	DENSITY		E	
43	+		=	F	
44	,		;	G	
45	-			H	
46	.			I	
47	/			J	
48	0	LINE SPACE		K	
49	1	LINE SPACE		L	
50	2	LINE SPACE		M	

ASCII code	Usual meaning	Epson printer	Sharp	ZX81	Other machines
51	3	LINE SPACE		N	
52	4	ITALICS		O	
53	5	NO ITALICS		P	
54	6			Q	
55	7	ASCII ONLY		R	
56	8	BELL OFF		S	
57	9	BELL ON		T	
58	:			U	
59	;			V	
60	<			W	
61	=			X	
62	>			Y	
63	?			Z	
64	@		SPACE		
65	A	LINESPACE			
66	B				
67	C	PAGE			
68	D	TAB			
69	E	EMPHASISE			
70	F				
71	G	DOUBLE			
72	H		~		
73	I				
74	J	LINESPACE			
75	K	DENSITY			
76	L	DENSITY			
77	M	ELITE			
78	N	END PAGE			

ASCII code	Usual meaning	Epson printer	Sharp	ZX81	Other machines
79	O				
80	P	PICA	..		
81	Q		←		
82	R		∨		
83	S	SUBSCRIPT	⌐		
84	T				
85	U		⌐		
86	V				
87	W	ENLARGED	∧		
88	X				
89	Y	FAST	/		
90	Z	DENSE			
91	[				↑ Tandy
92	\				↓ Tandy
93	]				]← Tandy
94	^				π Commodore
95	_	UNDERLINE			← Nascom, BBC
96	`		π		
97	a		-		
98	b		:		
99	c		#		
100	d		$		
101	e		%		
102	f		&		
103	g		`		
104	h		⌣		
105	i		⌢		
106	j	REVERSE	*		

Notice how these are in the same order as the shifted top row of the keyboard

ASCII code	Usual meaning	Epson printer	Sharp	ZX81	Other machines
107	k		+		
108	l	MARGIN			
109	m		` ,			
110	n				
111	o				
112	p			CURSOR UP	
113	q			CURSOR DOWN	
114	r			BACKSPACE	
115	s	SLOW		FORWARD	
116	t				
117	u				
118	v				
119	w		~		
120	x				
121	y				
122	z				
123	{				
124						
125	}				
126	~				

The opposite is CHR$ (pronounced 'character string'). Put a number in a bracket, as in CHR$(65), and most computers will give A.

Here's the program, with a loop that doesn't go higher than 255, the highest ASCII code:

```
10 FOR N = 1 TO 255
20 PRINT N; " = "; CHR$(N),
30 NEXT N
```

Notice semicolons to make the 65 = A print together. Then the comma at the end so that the columns tab across the screen.

On most machines the middle of the printout, from about 32 to 126, will give the alphabet and punctuation marks. Notice how lower-case characters, the small letters, are a regular distance above the capital letters. The ASCII code for 'a' is 32 more than the code for 'A'. So while CHR$(65) gives 'A', CHR$(65+32) gives 'a'.

Your screen shows weird things before and after CHR$ 32 to 126. For instance, there are the graphics. Simple machines stick to mere blocks and squares, others have hearts, diamonds, squiggles and little men.

But what goes on during the CHR$ where nothing comes on screen? Did the computer give a bleep at CHR$(7)? Did the screen jump and scroll with CHR$(10), CHR$(11) and CHR$(12)?

As well as coding letters and shapes, there are codes covering Backspace, Cursor Up, Cursor Down, New Page, Large Letters, Reverse Video, Clear the Screen, Enter, and all the other controls. And while a high percentage of machines use CHR$(65) for A, there isn't much uniformity about these other codes. Perhaps only CHR$(7) to make a bleeping noise and CHR$(27) to ESCape from the computer and control, say, the printer, are commonly used.

Why use CHR$( )?

There's no sense in programming:

```
PRINT CHR$(70); CHR$(82); CHR$(69); CHR$(68)
```

just to spell out FRED.

Some people use the code for a space (CHR$(32) on most machines) or the CHR$ for asterisks and dashes, but it is simpler to write PRINT " ", PRINT "*" or PRINT "———".

There's a STRING$(20, 42) in some dialects that prints 20 asterisks, if CHR$(42) is your code for an asterisk. Yet instead of memorising the ASCII code, you could easily type PRINT "********************".

At most you will use CHR$(34) (if that's the code for quote marks) if you wanted to print on screen:

THE GERMAN FOR "DOG" IS "HUND"

where the quotation marks round "DOG" would confuse the computer into thinking it had come to the end of the quote. So this would be:

PRINT "THE GERMAN FOR "; CHR$(34); "DOG"; CHR$(34); " IS "; CHR$(34); "HUND"; CHR$(34)

The real use of CHR$ comes in making double-sized letters come on screen, in reversing the video to give black letters on a white background, or in clearing the screen. You check with the manual then type:

PRINT CHR$( )

putting the necessary code in the brackets.

Controlling a printer by BASIC is possible. With golfball or daisywheel printers, provided the mechanism is there, you can program them to backspace, move the paper up a line or roll the carriage to the next page.

With a dot matrix printer, the commands are far better. These printers don't have the alphabet fixed on golfballs or daisywheels: they don't have letters at all. They have a row of pins striking through the inked ribbon. For example, the letter E is stamped on the paper as:

11111
10000
10000
11111
10000
10000
11111
00000   (Why the two unused rows at the bottom? To give
00000   room for the tails of g, j, p, q, y.)

with 1s representing when the pin strikes and 0 when it doesn't. There is no reason why E shouldn't be printed as:

1111111111
1111111111
1110000000
1111111111
1110000000
1111111111
1111111111
0000000000
0000000000

to give bigger, bolder letters. And you can program this.

If you can translate binary numbers into decimal, and there are conversion tables to help, you can make every pin strike or not strike and so create you own shapes. You can buy off-the-shelf programs with ready-made Gothic, Italic and 'handwritten' typestyles.

More advanced printers have their own ability to recognise control codes. The usual signal is CHR$(27), which says 'Don't print the following letters but treat them as codes and adjust your print style.'

This would work on an Epson printer:

```
10 LPRINT CHR$(27); "!"; CHR$(62);
20 LPRINT "THESE ARE BOLD, ENLARGED LETTERS"
30 LPRINT CHR$(7);
```

but while line 30 might ring the 'out of paper' bell on other printers, it is unlikely that Epson's "!"; CHR$(62) for bold printing would be understood by other machines. Again . . . check the manual.

You can write in an 'OK, I'm ready' bell. Put LPRINT CHR$(7), if that's your printer's bell code, after giving the computer a long task to do. You can then take a coffee break knowing that when everything is sorted out, the machine will give a little bleep – don't forget to have the printer switched on.

Similar programming will let it bleep if the operator makes a mistake.

Bugs in CHR$ ( )

These happen when the printer's code disagrees with the computer's controls, and where you think you are sending, say, a 'print in italics' signal, the printer thinks you mean 'go to the next page' and spews the paper out. It's not dangerous: you just have to find an alternative signal, like using "i" instead of CHR$(105), or the other way round.

And, don't confuse STR$(A), which means 'turn the value of variable A (which is, maybe, 87.0037) into a string "87.0037" with STRING$(5,32), which means 'put on screen 5 of ASCII character 32' (in this case: 5 blank spaces).

PEEK

Imagine the computer's memory to be thousands of tiny, orderly, labelled pigeon-holes. If you peek into one of those holes (and the command is PEEK (12345) where 12345 is the address of that hole) you might find it, and all its near neighbours, permanently occupied with one of the instructions for doing the chores of operating the computer. Or you might find it empty. Or, if you have a BASIC program running at the time, there might be one bit of program in it. . . a 2 for instance, if you were perhaps multiplying 2001 * 432.

As you switch on, a few thousand of those memory addresses are already filled. As you feed in the BASIC language and before you start typing, a tide of IF, GOTO, ERROR, VAL, INPUT and SAVEs flow into the spaces reserved for them. Your typed program gets stored into a vast empty storage area and any X,Y, A$, B$ variables are stacked in their areas.

This book can't say what will be in the addresses of those memory storage bins because different microchips give them different numbers. Look in your manual for the 'Memory Map'.

Unfortunately this will be vague, giving only general areas rather than naming exactly where specific instructions are stored. So, whenever you read a feature in computing magazines mentioning any PEEK addresses of your machine, make a note. Conversely, if you see a written program that contains the word PEEK or POKE (about which, more in a minute) don't bother to try it on a machine of a different make. It won't work.

The following routines use imaginary addresses, just for illustration; they won't work with any machines.

PEEK at work
You've written a program that adds up the hours everybody has worked, multiplies by the hourly pay, subtracts tax, siphons off the pension scheme and it comes to the lines:

```
2300 LPRINT"NAME  HOURS  RATE  TAX  DEDUCTIONS  PAY"
2310 LPRINT NA$;" ";   H; " "; R; H*R/99;   10.56;   " ";H*R
```

which work beautifully every time you test them.

Then a non-computnik typist tries it for real and the whole machine jams up. The screen goes dead, there's no response from the keyboard, the printer won't work.

What's wrong? They've forgotten to switch the printer on. The poor computer is battering at a closed door, trying to send "NAME HOURS RATE . . ."The technical term is 'locked in deadly embrace', and there is no way it will answer the keyboard short of switching right off and losing the whole morning's work.

The answer is a PEEK. Before sending LPRINT, have a peek at the printer port to see what's in its memory location. Have everything right: paper in, power on, 'on line' switch on, cables plugged in. Then RUN this test, changing the 14312 to suit your machine:

```
10 PRINT PEEK (14312)
20 GOTO 10
```

and a stream of numbers scrolls down the screen (the number 63 maybe) to show all is well.

So from now on, you could preface any LPRINT lines with:

2250 IF PEEK(14312) < > 63 THEN PRINT "THE PRINTER ISN'T READY" : GOTO 2250

and you can elaborate . . . Keep the little program running and take the paper out of the printer so that its 'paper end detector' switch complains. The number flashing along the screen should alter (to 233 maybe). Unplug the printer cable and watch the number alter again. Switch off and on. Switch to 'off line'.

You can now add more lines to help an inexperienced operator in the style of:

2260 IF PEEK(xxxxx) = zz THEN PRINT "THE BLUE CABLE IS UNPLUGGED"

POKE

This command has two numbers:

POKE (12345, 89)

as it goes to location 12345 and puts the value 89 into it.

Why POKE? For speed. There is no translating from BASIC, the instruction gets poked directly into memory. So POKEing is ideal for fast-moving graphics.

There are commands that can't be carried out without POKE. If you want the BREAK key or the LIST command to be disabled so a pirate can't rip off your ideas, then POKE (xxxxx, zzz) — the numbers depend on the make of your machine. You can disable the keyboard so kids can't screw up your program . . . but before you RUN that one, POKE in the correct code to bring the keyboard back because, with the keys out of action, you wouldn't be able to type it in later!

To POKE in a lot of stuff, first look at the memory map for the location of some free space. Then the program goes:

```
100 FOR N = first location TO last location
110 READ A
120 DATA 123, 45, 678, these are poke instructions, 910 etc.
130 POKE (N, A)
140 NEXT N
```

with the suitable numbers in place. It may not look familiar, but that DATA line is the machine code program.

POKE bugs

It is always implied that it is disastrous (that's a word often used) to POKE the wrong number into the wrong address.

There's an odds-against possibility of accidentally setting your disks running, but nobody seems to know anybody who caused permanent damage by wrong POKEs. There are only vague rumours about damage to the video of early PETs. The odds are that if you make a mistake, and it is easy enough to type the wrong number, then you get a screen full of garbage. Which isn't too serious.

However: there's a liability disclaimer at the beginning of this book. So play safe and only have a few gentle POKEs until you know what's what.

USR

To use your system as a word processor, or to sort out hundreds of items quickly . . . then BASIC isn't good enough.

To connect up to a music synthesiser or to transmit to another machine through a telephone modem or to use a plotter or light pen . . . then, if you have a living to earn, you buy machine code programs because writing your own takes up too much of your life. Machine code doesn't mess with the easy-for-humans, laborious-for-computers BASIC commands; it puts the language straight into the memory banks.

From DOS, the disk operating system, you call a machine code program directly by typing its file name:

DISKZAP.COM

That would bring the non-BASIC program DISKZAP if you have a CP/M (Control Program for Microcomputers) machine.

If you are half-way through a BASIC program, you call up a machine code subroutine in several stages:

(1) Compose it with that READ-DATA-POKE routine given earlier.

(2) Note the address in memory where you've POKEd it.

(3) There are two more little pigeon-holes in memory dedicated to storing the above address. You translate the address into hexadecimal, cut the number in half, swap the halves around, change them to decimal (it's all complicated and outside the scope of this book) and POKE the two numbers into the 'address' pigeon-holes.

(4) At the appropriate place in your BASIC program, type:

X = USR(0)

and the program goes to the pigeon-holes, finds the address, goes to that address and finds the machine code routine, which it then runs.

SYSTEM

If you have bought a word processing program on tape or if you have a proprietary program that will pack your long, involved, plenty of REMarks, Accounts program into a small package to fit on the disk . . . then these types of program have built-in instructions to locate themselves automatically in some corner of memory so

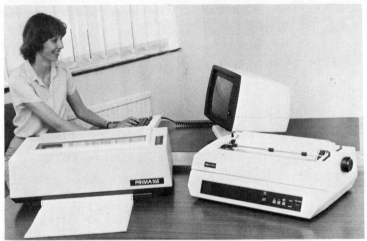

Fig. 18.1 Daisywriter 2000 daisywheel printer and Prima dot matrix printer, offered by CPU Peripherals Ltd

they won't get overwritten by the big surge of BASIC. You won't know they are there. To call them into action, type:

SYSTEM

Depending on your computer, your screen will ask:

*?

You answer, depending on your computer, something like:

/12345   (ENTER)

where 12345 is the address in memory that the program's instruction book told you to call.

This is equivalent to the familiar RUN "PROGRAMN.AME" because, as you hit ENTER, the machine code program will be found and start to run.

Machine code bugs
In BASIC if you type PRIMT instead of PRINT it is easy to spot the bug. Not so in machine code: those rows of numbers can be

mistyped. So work on a backup disk and keep important programs out of harm's way until you get the routine right.

Do you really want to get involved in POKEs and USRs? It's better than crossword puzzles as a hobby. It can be profitable if you invent a saleable Space Invaders game. But if the time taken in learning interferes with business, ask yourself which is the more profitable.

To sum up

Letters, symbols and commands are numbered under the ASCII code. Show this by asking PRINT ASC("Z").

The opposite is PRINT CHR$(90), which puts the character on screen.

LPRINT CHR$(27); CHR$(n) is often used to control printers.

PEEK (12345) looks at location 12345 in memory. POKE (12345, 67) puts 67 into 12345.

USR and SYSTEM are ways of calling faster machine code programs into action.

Exercises

1. Use the CHR$ codes to control your printer. No handbook? Then try first the codes for Line Feed (LF), Form Feed (FF) and Backspace (BKSP).

2. Write a subroutine to check if the printer is ready before an LPRINT. Give it line numbers in the 5000 range so that you can call it up in future with GOSUB 5000.

3. No printer? Then find out how your computer knows that the cassette recorder is switched on.

4. Does your machine have DEBUG or similar command that throws memory blocks up on screen? Do you own a Toolkit, Zap or Monitor program that displays the contents of a disk? With an unimportant program in place, use these facilities to look at how information is stored. If you can't understand it . . . don't worry.

19

Programming style

You own a chain of restaurants and you send your staff to Italy for training. So they have to learn Italian.

```
20 DATA "THE ASHTRAY", "IL PORTACENERE", "THE BEER", "LA
   BIRRA", "THE BILL", "IL CONTO", "THE BOTTLE", "LA BOT-
   TIGLIA"
30 DATA "THE BOWL", "LA SCODELLA", "THE BREAD", "IL PANE",
   "THE BUTTER", "IL BURRO", "THE CARAFE", "LA CARAFFA"
40 DATA "THE CIGARETTES", "LE SIGARETTE", "THE CLOAKROOM",
   "IL GUARDAROBA", "THE COFFEE", "IL CAFFE", "THE CREAM",
   "LA PANNA"
```

These are going to be read into two arrays, English and Italian, so set out the DIMensions of the memory needed to be cleared to hold all these words:

```
10 DIM EN$(20), IT$(20)
```

and when you add to that vocabulary, you DIM more spaces than (20).

Now to READ the DATA. You could set up a FOR N = 1 TO 20 loop if you could be sure that there would always be exactly 20 English and 20 Italian words. It is more convenient to have the computer looking out for a special word like "END" and when it reaches it, to stop reading:

```
50 DATA "END", "FINITO"
```

The computer has to read the words, number them, then store them into English EN$( ) and Italian IT$( ) arrays so that they can be picked out when needed:

```
100 N = 1
110 READ EN$(N), IT$(N)
120 IF EN$(N) = "END" THEN 200
130 N = N + 1
140 GOTO 110
```

Here's an action replay. Line 110 reads the first English word and the first Italian word and labels "THE ASHTRAY" as EN$(1) and "IL PORTACENERE" as IT$(1). Line 120 checks if "THE ASHTRAY" is the same as "END". It isn't, so in line 130, N becomes 2.

The program goes back to line 110 to read the next words and stores them as EN$(2) and IT$(2). Sooner or later, in this example at about the thirteenth loop, EN$(13) becomes "END". So, on the instruction of line 120 the program jumps out of the loop and goes to line 200. Which isn't written yet.

Run the program so far and interesting things would happen inside the computer's brain but nothing would show on screen. Because you've not asked it to PRINT anything.

```
210 PRINT"WHAT IS "; CHR$(34); EN$(R); CHR$(34) " IN ITALIAN";
```

would display:

WHAT IS "THE BILL" IN ITALIAN

with those CHR$(34)s providing the inverted commas. And EN$(R) would be THE BILL if you could make R = 3.

It would be impossible to put R = 3 in line 210 because you'd have to rewrite it with a different number every time the program was RUN. You could ask your students, with: INPUT "THINK OF A NUMBER"; R but they would always key in their favourite number. If you made a FOR R = 1 TO 13 loop, the questions would always come up in the same order and your staff would cheat.

RaNDom

The answer is RND( ), which throws up a random number. Put a figure in those brackets, say RND(99), and the machine will pick any number up to 99. In this Italian test, it has to pick any one of N words:

```
200 R = RND(N)
210 PRINT"WHAT IS "; CHR$(34); EN$(R); CHR$(34) " IN ITALIAN ";
220 INPUT AN$
```

Remember from the chapter on arrays that, although the EN$( )s were read in a loop with an N variable, they were memorised as EN$(1), EN$(2), EN$(3) and so on. It doesn't matter now that you are using R as the variable. If it becomes, say 7, at random, then the computer will print EN$(7), which is THE BUTTER.

Your student now answers AN$ and the program has to see if that's correct. When it printed EN$(7) it also knew that IT$(7) was

"IL BURRO" but it was keeping that secret. Now it compares the
answers:

300 IF AN$ = IT$(R) THEN PRINT "RIGHT": GOTO 200

and asks another question at random.
    But if the answer isn't right:

350 PRINT "OH NO IT ISN'T" : GOTO 210

and ask the same question again.
    Here's the complete program and also a sample RUN.

```
 10 DIM EN$(20), IT$(20)
 20 DATA "THE ASHTRAY", "IL PORTACENERE", "THE BEER",
    "LA BIRRA", "THE BILL", "IL CONTO", "THE BOTTLE", "LA
    BOTTIGLIA"
 30 DATA "THE BOWL", "LA SCODELLA", "THE BREAD", "IL PANE",
    "THE BUTTER", "IL BURRO", "THE CARAFE", "LA CARAFFA"
 40 DATA "THE CIGARETTES", "LE SIGARETTE", "THE CLOAKROOM",
    "IL GUARDAROBA", "THE COFFEE", "IL CAFFE", "THE CREAM",
    "LA PANNA"
 50 DATA "END", "FINITO"
100 N = 1
110 READ EN$(N), IT$(N)
120 IF EN$(N) = "END" THEN 200
130 N = N + 1
140 GOTO 110
200 R = RND(N)
210 PRINT"WHAT IS "; CHR$(34); EN$(R); CHR$(34) " IN
    ITALIAN ";
220 INPUT AN$
300 IF AN$ = IT$(R) THEN PRINT "RIGHT": GOTO 200
350 PRINT "OH NO IT ISN'T" : GOTO 210


RUN
WHAT IS "THE BILL" IN ITALIAN ?   IL CONTO
RIGHT
WHAT IS "THE COFFEE" IN ITALIAN ?   IL CAFFE
RIGHT
WHAT IS "THE ASHTRAY" IN ITALIAN ?   IL PORTANERE
OH NO IT ISN'T
WHAT IS "THE ASHTRAY" IN ITALIAN ?   IL PORTENERE
OH NO IT ISN'T
WHAT IS "THE ASHTRAY" IN ITALIAN ?   -
```

Random bugs
To be pedantic, RND gives only pseudo-random numbers. If you
need to get closer to true randomness, some machines have a
RAND, RANDOM or RANDOMISE command, which is given first
to regenerate a new series of numbers.

Usually the bug comes if you step outside the range needed. In this Italian test, suppose the stop-reading-the-data signal in line 50 had been "ZZZ", "XXX". This would have occasionally been thrown up as a question. The cure would have been to change line 200 to R = RND(N − 1).

Program bugs

Starting from the beginning: there's no title; there are no REMarks to explain what's happening; and though DATA lines can fit anywhere in a program, it is usual to put them at the end so that more data can be added. Yet with The "END" flag in line 50 right next to line 40,

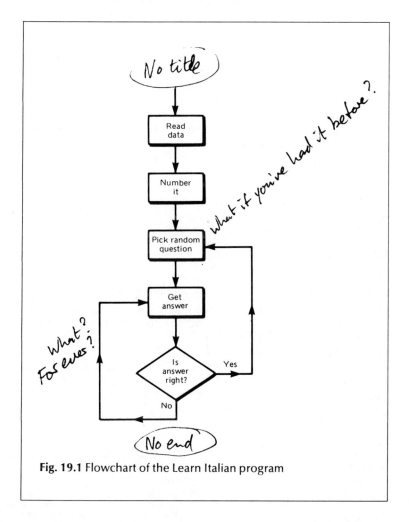

Fig. 19.1 Flowchart of the Learn Italian program

there's not much room for extra words. It would have been better to change line 50 to, say, 90. And suppose somebody can't remember what the Italian for "THE CLOAKROOM" is? Does the program go on for ever?

The classic cure is to draw a flowchart of every program before you lay hands on the keyboard. That's what the schools recommend. It might look like Fig. 19.1.

Whether you flowchart or not depends upon the sort of mind you have. Pedantic programmers admire elegant programs. They call the use of GOTO lines 'spaghetti programming' because the chart goes backwards and forwards on itself. Programs composed straight on the keyboard are hard for a stranger to debug . . . there are plenty of arguments for flowcharts.

Against? Well, flowcharts don't run computers. Once the diagram has been drawn the program still has to be typed in, checked and debugged.

Yet the computer doesn't mind how illiterate your program is: it will still graph your biorhythms, forecast price rises and keep track of your transport costs. Maybe a bit slower; maybe a bit more wasteful of space. My advice is certainly to work in modules and collect a little library of routines for handling the date, printing out titles, calling up data and opening files. Use GOSUBs to call on these.

Flowchart if you wish. Otherwise, bang away at the keyboard but give your first line a highish number to leave space for those dammit-I-forgot items.

Go-faster tricks

1. *Work from memory*
If this Italian program had started around line 200 and had to READ the data every time a new question was asked, it would have been slower. As it is, the questions are snatched from the arrays in memory. If it had to start up a disk drive every time to read the facts off disk, that would really be slow.

The bug? A lot of data takes time to load in. So print a JUST A MINUTE WHILE I GET THE FACTS apology on screen during that time.

2. *Don't repeat yourself*
Time these:

```
10 A = 5                    10 FOR N = TO 1000
20 FOR N = 1 TO 1000        20 A = 5
30 PRINT A + 6              30 PRINT A + 6
40 NEXT N                   40 NEXT N
```

Of course the first one is faster. Both say that A = 5. There is no need to repeat yourself a thousand times as in line 20 of the second program.

3. *Miss out the variable in FOR–NEXT loops*
Remove the N from the last line of the first program:

    40 NEXT

and it should be faster because BASIC doesn't bother to check which variable should be NEXT.

The bug comes in a complex program. Just make sure your computer knows that it needs the NEXT N and not the NEXT Z or any other variable that might be around.

4. *Variables are faster than numbers*
Test:

```
10 T = 1
20 FOR N = 1 TO 1000        20 FOR N = 1 TO 1000
30 A = A + T                30 A = A + 1
40 NEXT                     40 NEXT
```

The explanation is that BASIC takes less time to look up a variable than it does to convert the decimal 1 to the binary 00000001 which it uses in its brain. Certainly, in calculations about circles, always use PI = 3.14159 (if your machine hasn't got PI) instead of using the number throughout.

5. *Add is faster than * 2*

```
10 FOR N = 1 TO 1000        10 FOR N = 1 TO 1000
20 A = N + N                20 A = N * 2
30 NEXT                     30 NEXT
```

Is N+N+N+N+N+N+N+N faster than N * 8 in your machine?

6. *Squares and SQR are very slow*

```
10 FOR N = 1 TO 10000       10 FOR N = 1 TO 1000
20 A = N * N * N * N        20 A = N ↑ 4
30 NEXT                     30 NEXT
```

7. *Put the most popular variables first*
This is too subtle to time with a stopwatch over a small program, but the computer finds them quicker.

8. *Put subroutines first*
This is contrary to the way that orthodox computing is taught in schools, where subroutines are always put at the end. Yet they are found quicker at the beginning of a program.

9. Use GOTO instead of GOSUB
Use GOSUB only for a subroutine that is called several times. Because GOSUBs use memory. If a subroutine is called only once, GOTO uses hardly any memory at all.

10. Remove REMs

```
10 FOR N = 1 TO 1000        10 FOR N = 1 TO 1000
30 NEXT                     20 REM REMOVE THIS
                            30 NEXT
```

REMs are not much used in this book because of clarity but they are essential in your master copy to explain how it works. But save both time and space by deleting REMs from the working copy.

11. Remove spaces

```
10 FORN=1TO1000             10 FOR N = 1 TO 1000
20 A=N+N                    20 A = N + N
30 NEXTN                    30 NEXT N
```

Spaces are used in this book for clarity. Missing them out saves typing time (no need to hit the space bar), saves memory and . . . time it . . . does it save time?

12. Learn to type
Even if you don't own a computer yet, you can make incredible improvements to program running time by becoming a good typist.

13. Fill in idle moments
Arrays take a long time to load and people take a long time to hit the right key. So have the arrays loading while the machine is waiting for the operator:

```
10 PRINT"DO YOU WANT NAMES OR AGES ?"
20 FOR N = 1 TO 5
30 READ A$(N), B(N)
40 DATA "THOMPSON",34,"PATEL",55,"MACKENNA",32,
   "HEINE",44,"BJORGSEN",48
50 NEXT
60 INPUT "ANSWER 'N' FOR NAMES, 'A' FOR AGES "; W$
```

so that the array is being read while the operator is making up his mind.

14. Printers are slower than computers
Computers can zip wodges of information into the printer's buffer, but then they have to wait until the printer slowly processes it. So give the computer some work in between LPRINTs:

```
10 LPRINT" THIS IS THE TITLE."
20 CLEAR 4000
30 LPRINT"     OF A PROGRAM"
40 DIM A(100), B(200), C(50), C$(200)
50 LPRINT" ABOUT SOMETHING OR OTHER."
```

No memory buffer on your printer? Then you'll just have to wait patiently.

15. *Use integers in loops and arrays*
Normally, variables are treated as if they had a decimal point with six or seven figures after it: A$(N) is not a neat A$(6) but A$(6.0000000).

Save time and space by insisting that the variables in loops and the brackets of A$(N) style arrays are integers, whole numbers. Either DEFine them at the start with DEFINT (more in the next chapter) or label them individually with, depending on your machine, the % symbol after the variable:

```
10 FOR N% = 1 TO 1000        10 FOR N = 1 TO 1000
20 A% = N% + N%              20 A = N + N
30 NEXT                      30 NEXT
```

16. *Multi-statement lines save memory*

```
10 FORN=1TO1000:A=N+N:NEXT    10 FORN=1TO10000
                             20 A=N+N
                             30 NEXT
```

because every line number needs memory. Now time these: are multi-statements faster?

Remember in all of the above: what you gain in speed, you lose in readability (speedy bugs?). Look at the unintelligible gabble of that multi-statement line 10 in 16 above.

To sum up

RND( ) throws a near-enough random number, up to the limit of the number inside its bracket.

The program was a mess but it worked. Flowcharts help some people to think through their ideas.

Speed isn't noticed in short routines but there are tricks to use in long programs. The surprising ones are that variables are faster than numbers, + is faster than *2 and exponents (squares, cubes etc.) are very slow.

Exercises

1. Make the Learn Italian program throw 20 questions and then END. Give your staff chances of three mistakes before they are told THE CORRECT ANSWER IS:. Have it count up how many they got right.

Note that it needn't be Italian: you can have questions more suited to training people for your own job.

2. Suppose they make a minor mistake, say they type LA PANE instead of IL PANE, how can the program say PRETTY CLOSE, NICE TRY? A hint . . . use MID$( ) or RIGHT$( ).

20

DEFine FuNctions

You're a motorcycle importer and spend a lot on sales promotion.

Top seller is the Stepthru model. So it should be, because more advertising is spent on it than any other bike. Second is the Moped which comes second in advertising costs. Yet these two models are at the bottom of the PR budget. Number three in advertising, however, the 400 cc Commute machine, only comes sixth in sales. The comparative sales, advertising and PR rankings are shown in Table 20.1.

TABLE 20.1.

	Bikes sold	Sales position	Advertising money		PR money	
Stepthru	9,990	1st	£45,000	1st	£1,000	9th
Moped	9,000	2nd	£40,000	2nd	£500	10th
Learner	6,500	3rd	£20,000	5th	£10,000	7th
Kidbike	5,990	4th	£19,000	6th	£6,000	8th
Trail	5,000	5th	£10,000	9th	£24,000	4th
Commute	3,000	6th	£30,000	3rd	£19,000	6th
Tourer	2,400	7th	£29,000	4th	£35,000	2nd
Replica	2,000	8th	£5,000	8th	£40,000	1st
Racer	700	9th	£2,000	10th	£20,000	5th
Executive	650	10th	£15,000	7th	£25,000	3rd

But how effective is it all? Comparing the money you spend on advertising with the money spent in Public Relations (chiefly in buying expensive lunches for journalists), which is better for pushing up sales?

Not knowing much about statistics, you find 'Spearman's correlation coefficient' in a maths book. It says that, if you take two lists that are in order of rank, their relationship (R) is 1 minus six

times the sum of the squared differences (D) of the lists, divided by
the number of items in a list (N) multiplied by that number squared
minus 1.

$$R = 1 - \frac{6(\Sigma D^2)}{N(N^2 - 1)}$$

Why it works, you don't know . . . you're a dealer not an academic
. . . but the computer can run it.

So clear the screen and clear some memory for strings:

    10 CLS: CLEAR 2000

The heart of the program would be a loop, going round N times
according to the number of types of motorcycle in the list:

    60 INPUT "HOW MANY TYPES OF MOTORCYCLE IN A LIST "; N

No, change that.

This formula should work for any relationships. Are sales of wine
related to the price? Is the yield of corn related to the type of
fertiliser? Do you get fewer complaints from flat dwellers if the
central heating goes up? So make that line:

    60 INPUT "HOW MANY ITEMS IN A LIST "; N

And, to make it a universal program, instead of having L1$ =
"SALES", L2$ = "ADVERTISING", L3$ = "PR" have:

    70 INPUT "WHAT IS THE NAME OF THE FIRST LIST "; L1$
    80 INPUT "WHAT IS THE NAME OF THE SECOND LIST "; L2$
    90 INPUT "WHAT IS THE NAME OF THE THIRD LIST "; L3$

That's still not right. There has to be a way of saving all that typing.

    40 S1$ = "WHAT IS THE NAME OF LIST "
    70 FOR L = 1 TO 3
    80 PRINT S1$; L;
    90 INPUT L$(L)
    100 NEXT

will make line 80 print WHAT IS THE NAME OF LIST 1? with that
question mark belonging to the INPUT statement because of that
semicolon.

You would answer SALES, and that would be L$(1), which is an
array. There's no need to DIMension it because there will only be
three of them.

Now to put in the figures from the Sales tables. Not the number of
bikes sold nor the amount of money spent on them, but their
position, their ranking, in the tables:

    130 FOR P = 1 TO N

In this case N is the 10 kinds of bike.

```
140 PRINT "WHAT DO YOU CALL NUMBER "; P; " IN "; L$(1);
150 INPUT NA$(P)
```

'What do you call number 1 in Sales? Stepthru'. Its position in Sales is 1st:

```
160 P1(P) = P
170 PRINT "WHAT IS ITS POSITION IN "; L$(2);
180 INPUT P2(P)
```

'What is its position in Advertising? 1'. So $P2(1) = 1$.

```
190 PRINT "WHAT IS ITS POSITION IN "; L$(3);
200 INPUT P3(P)
```

'What is its position in the PR budget? 9th'. So $P3(1) = 9$.

But there is something wrong again. You have had to type "WHAT IS ITS POSITION IN" twice. Surely the computer could do something about that? Back to the beginning:

```
50 S2$ = "WHAT IS ITS POSITION IN "
```

then in lines 170 and 190, you can substitute:

```
PRINT S2$
```

Several arrays have been created. In this program N is only 10, but they had better be DIMensioned for future programs:

```
120 DIM NA$(N), P1(N), P2(N), P3(N)
```

The calculations could be complicated: First add the squares of the difference between Sales and Advertising, then between Sales and PR.

```
220 D2 = D2 + (P1(P) − P2(P) ) ↑ 2
230 D3 = D3 + (P1(P) − P3(P) ) ↑ 2
```

This says: 'The new D2 becomes the old D2 plus the square of the difference in positions.'

To fulfil Spearman's Formula, this has to be multiplied by six, divided by $N*$ (N squared $- 1$), and the whole lot taken away from 1.

```
250 R2 = 1 − (6 * D2)/(N * ( N * N − 1) )
260 R3 = 1 − (6 * D3)/(N * (N * N − 1) )
```

And they still have to be processed with

```
INT(10000 * R2 + .5)/100
```

to turn them into percentages. This is the principle of multiplying by 10000, adding a tiny amount of .5 to round off the decimals then bringing it back by dividing by 100. There must be an easier way.

DEF FN

Just as you had S1$ = "WHAT IS THE NAME OF LIST" it would be nice to let a single variable be all that arithmetic. But you can't, because in the middle of line 250 is D2 and in the middle of line 260 is D3 . . . two different numbers.

The answer is to Define the Function, making a pattern of the bits that are always the same:

Line220 was	D2 + (P1(P) − P2(P)) ↑ 2
Line 230 was	D3 + (P1(P) − P3(P)) ↑ 2
They always had	+ (P1(P) −) ↑ 2
Put in dummy variables	X + (P1(P) − Y) ↑ 2

Call it Function D. And DEFine it near the start of the program:

    20 DEF FN D(X,Y) = X + (P1(P) − Y) ↑ 2

Unfortunately there aren't such legible spaces in most BASICs and the start of line 20 becomes DEFFND(X,Y), pronounced 'Define Function D(X,Y)'.

Now, as this FuNction D is substituted in lines 220 and 230, it tells the computer to use the correct D2 and D3 instead of X, and to use P2(P) and P3(P) instead of the Y:

    220 D2 = FND(D2, P2(P))
    230 D3 = FND(D3, P3(P))

The X and Y ? Nothing. They take no part in calculations. Nor are they part of a doubly subscripted array, even though they look like one. In most BASICs you can have, in the rest of the program, real X = 27.004 and Y = A + B style variables that are *entirely different* from the dummies in the DEFFN statement. To avoid the risk of confusing themselves, some programmers use O and I inside DEFFN brackets, knowing that O and I would not be used as ordinary variables in the rest of the program.

The X and Y, or O and I, whatever you choose, are just there temporarily to form the pattern of the function.

Here's another example:

Line 250 was	1 − (6 * D2) / (N * (N * N − 1))
Line 260 was	1 − (6 * D3) / (N * (N * N − 1))
They always had	1 − (6 *) / (N * (N * N − 1))
Put in dummy variables	Z

Call it Function C. You could DEFine it near the start of the program:

    DEF FN C(Z) = 1 − (6 * Z) / (N * (N * N − 1))

Or you could turn it into a percentage first:

    30 DEF FN C(Z) = INT(10000 * (1−(6*Z)/(N*(N*N−1))) +.5)/100

It's complicated, but it's the answer.

You can go straight to the final printout with:

390 PRINT "THE CO-RELATIONSHIP BETWEEN " L$(1) " AND "; L$(2);
    " IS "; FNC(D2)
400 PRINT " BETWEEN " L$(1) " AND "; L$(39; " IS "; FNC(D3)

and right in the middle of that arithmetic, the computer would substitute D2 or D3 for the dummy Z.

Here are the two versions of our program; the first doesn't use DEFFN, the second (page 160) does. At the bottom of page 160 are the answers to the questions posed at the start of the chapter.

```
 10 CLS : CLEAR 2000

 59 REM    ****.......... GET THE TITLES ..........****
 60 INPUT "HOW MANY ITEMS IN A LIST "; N
 70 INPUT "WHAT IS THE NAME OF THE FIRST LIST "; L1$
 80 INPUT "WHAT IS THE NAME OF THE SECOND LIST "; L2$
 90 INPUT "WHAT IS THE NAME OF THE THIRD LIST "; L3$

119 REM    ****....... MAKE SPACE IN MEMORY .......****
120 DIM NA$(N), P1(N), P2(N), P3(N)

129 REM    ****........ ASK FOR THE FIGURES .......****
130 FOR P = 1 TO N
140 PRINT "WHAT DO YOU CALL NUMBER "; P; " IN "; L1$;
150 INPUT NA$(P)
160 P1(P) = P
170 PRINT "WHAT IS ITS POSITION IN "; L2$;
180 INPUT P2(P)
190 PRINT "WHAT IS ITS POSITION IN "; L3$;
200 INPUT P3(P)
219 REM    **** ADD THE SQUARES OF THE DIFFERENCES ****
220 D2 = D2 + (P1(P) - P2(P)) ↑2
230 D3 = D3 + (P1(P) - P3(P)) ↑2
240 NEXT

249 REM    ****.... CALCULATE THE RELATIONSHIPS ...****
250 R2 = 1 - (6 * D2) / (N * (N * N - 1))
260 R3 = 1 - (6 * D3) / (N * (N * N - 1))
269 REM    ****....... MAKE PERCENTAGES ...........****
270 C2 = INT(10000 * R2 + .5) / 100
280 C3 = INT(10000 * R3 + .5) / 100

299 REM    ****...........PRINTOUT ...............****
300 CLS
310 PRINT TAB(15) L1$; TAB(30) L2$; TAB(45) L3$
320 FOR L = 1 TO N
330 PRINT NA$(L); TAB(17) P1(L); TAB(32) P2(L); TAB(47)
    P3(L)
340 NEXT
350 PRINT
390 PRINT "THE CO-RELATIONSHIP BETWEEN "; L1$; " AND ";
    L2$; " IS "; C2; " %"
400 PRINT "                      BETWEEN "; L1$; " AND ";
    L3$; " IS "; C3; " %"
```

```
10 CLS: CLEAR 2000

20 DEFFND(X,Y) = X +(P1(P) - Y)↑2
30 DEFFNC(Z) = INT(10000 * (1 - (6 * Z)/(N * (N * N - 1)))
   + .5) /100
40 S1$ = "WHAT IS THE NAME OF LIST "
50 S2$ = "WHAT'S ITS POSITION IN "

59 REM    ****......... GET THE TITLES ..........****
60 INPUT"HOW MANY ITEMS IN A LIST ";N
70 FOR L = 1 TO 3
80 PRINT S1$ L;
90 INPUT L$(L)
100 NEXT

119 REM   ****....... MAKE SPACE IN MEMORY .......****
120 DIM NA$(N), P1(N), P2(N), P3(N)

129 REM   ****........ ASK FOR THE FIGURES .......****
130 FOR P = 1 TO N
140 PRINT"WHAT DO YOU CALL NUMBER "; P; " IN "; L$(1);
150 INPUT NA$(P)
160 P1(P) = P
170 PRINT S2$ L$(2);
180 INPUT P2(P)
190 PRINT S2$ L$(3);
200 INPUT P3(P)
219 REM   **** ADD THE SQUARE OF THE DIFFERENCES ****
220 D2 = FND(D2,P2(P))
230 D3 = FND(D3,P3(P))
240 NEXT

299 REM   ****.......... PRINTOUT ...............****
300 CLS
310 PRINT TAB(15) L$(1); TAB(30) L$(2); TAB(45) L$(3)
320 FOR L = 1 TO N
330 PRINT NA$(L); TAB(17) P1(L); TAB(32) P2(L); TAB(47)
    P3(L)
340 NEXT
350 PRINT
390 PRINT"THE CO-RELATIONSHIP BETWEEN "; L$(1); " AND ";
    L$(2); " IS "; FNC(D2); " %"
400 PRINT"                        BETWEEN " L$(1); " AND ";
    L$(3); " IS "; FNC(D3); " %"
```

		SALES	ADVERTISING	P.R.
1	STEPTHRU	1	1	9
2	MOPED	2	2	10
3	LEARNER	3	5	7
4	KIDBIKE	4	6	8
5	TRAIL	5	9	4
6	COMMUTE	6	3	6
7	TOURER	7	4	2
8	REPLICA	8	8	1
9	RACER	9	10	5
10	EXECUTIVE	10	7	3

```
THE CO-RELATIONSHIP BETWEEN SALES AND ADVERTISING IS  68.48  %
                        BETWEEN SALES AND P.R. IS -81.82  %
READY
>_
```

It looks as if Advertising could be better. 68.48% isn't a disaster but it ought to be closer to 100% perfection. As for Public Relations, they have a negative effect on sales. At minus 81.82% your business would improve with no PR department at all!

But, just because a computer prints them out, these results shouldn't be taken as gospel. There could be other factors influencing sales. . . . Is there a relationship between engine size and sales? What effect does government legislation have?

More DEF FN
To find, for instance, the area of a circle, you could have:

```
10 DEF FNA(A) = 3.14159 * Q * Q
20 INPUT "WHAT'S THE RADIUS "; R
30 PRINT "AREA IS "; FNA(R)
```

But if the real figure is known beforehand, there is no need for a dummy substitute in the brackets:

```
10 INPUT "WHAT'S THE RADIUS "; R
20 DEF FNA = 3.14159 * R * R
30 PRINT "AREA IS "; FNA
```

pronounced 'Function A'.

String functions
Strings can be defined in the same way:

```
10 DEF FNT$(A$,B$) = "DR. "+ LEFT$(A$,1) +". "+ B$
20 INPUT "CAN I HAVE YOUR FIRST NAME, PLEASE"; F$
30 INPUT "NOW YOUR LAST NAME "; S$
40 PRINT FNT$(F$,S$)
```

this will run

```
CAN I HAVE YOUR FIRST NAME, PLEASE? ELIZABETH
NOW YOUR LAST NAME? BARRATT
```

and the screen prints out:

```
DR. E. BARRATT
```


DEF PROC
In effect, a DEF FN is a miniature subroutine. Most BASICs restrict them to one line in length.

A few allow several lines with FNEND at the end. And some, like the BBC Micro, allow several lines of procedure. This starts with DEF PROC and ends with ENDPROC.

Check your manual: you could build up a useful library of procedures.

DEF bugs

Bugs are hard to find because error messages don't show up on the
DEF FN line but much later when you call them.

Suppose you got lost in the bracket jungle of:

30 DEFFNC(Z)=INT(10000*(1−(6*Z)/(N*(N*N−1)))+.5)/100

(the trick, when baffled, is to chase the brackets in an LLIST 30,
using different coloured pencils) . . . the error would show as:

SYNTAX ERROR IN LINE 390

yet there is nothing wrong with line 390.

Make sure the DEF FN comes before the line in which you need
it. And check that a GOTO line doesn't jump over it and miss it out.

But don't worry about putting variables into DEF FN even though
they won't be given values until later.

DEFINT

Computers work to an accuracy of about six figures but, though
they think it, they don't print 2.000000 + 2.000000 = 4.000000.
They know that you're not interested in zeros so they strip them off
and print 2 + 2 = 4.

This takes time. So if you state that a number is an integer (with
no decimals) the program works faster. This is done either by
marking every integer, often with a % symbol (which doesn't mean
percent in this case):

   A%   B3%   CZ%

Or the whole lot can be DEFined as INTegers at the start:

   10 DEFINT A−C

and every variable starting with A, B or C will have no decimals.
Not only A, B and C but AE, B7 and COST.

DEFDBL

The better BASICs give a chance of 'double precision', an accuracy
of up to 16 figures. Ask for this with (check your manual) a #
symbol:

   A#   DC#   G9#

and you can have pi as 3.141592653589793. Or DEFine DouBle
precision from the start:

   10 DEFDBL A−N

E

Suppose you don't define double precision and the computer meets a number with more than six figures?

Twelve million would be printed as 1.2E+07, which means 1 followed by 7 figures, the first of which would be 2. The E stands for 'exponent'. For the maths-minded, twelve million would be 1.2 * 10^7.

A tiny decimal of 0.000005 would be 5E−06, with the minus sign showing it was less than 1.

DEFSTR

String variables can be defined to save typing that $ sign every time:

    10 DEFSTR A, K, P

would let you write:

    300 P = "JOHN BROWN"

without getting an error. But write P = 34.078 + 2 and there'd be a protest.

To sum up

Functions are like subroutines, stored anywhere earlier in the program and called up when needed. They save typing time.

First you say DEFFNZ (with or without brackets) = A + B + Z or whatever the arithmetic is. Then use FNZ anywhere you'd use an ordinary variable. As in: C = 100 * FNZ(H).

INTegers, StRings and sometimes DouBle precision numbers can be DEFined too.

Exercises

1. A newcomer wouldn't understand the significance of the final percentage of the motorcycle program (100 per cent is a perfect relationship, 80 or so isn't bad, minus is terrible). Add a procedure that checks the results and prints out their meaning.

2. You build thick concrete drainage pipes. Write a program that gives the amount of concrete (break it down to sand and cement quantities if you like) for various lengths, thicknesses and diameters of pipe. Use DEFFN somewhere.

3. What answer does your machine give for 100/6? Get it to give an integer answer with DEFINT then a double-precision answer.

21

File handling

You're a storeman in, say, a pharmaceutical warehouse, and the customer says, 'Have you any Procaine?'

So you look it up on the parts list, walk all the way to the bin, walk back again with a pack and tell them, 'Yes, we've got plenty.'

'How much is it?' You look through the price list, which is hard to read because of all the alterations from the last price increases, and tell them that it's $95.95.

And they say, 'I'm not paying that much!' So you have to walk all the way to the bin again and put the Procaine back.

Or else a truck comes in with a load of new stock, all listed by Part Number. You are walking all over the warehouse, backwards and forwards. Why can't they put the delivery note in bin order, in a picking order?

If anything cries out for computing, it's the stores. At the very least you need to know how much stuff you've got.

But once you've made a program that can handle that, it is not much more work to have it sorting goods out into bin order to save you walking; sending a signal when stock gets low to remind you to re-order; listing the slow-moving stock so you don't buy any more of that; printing sales invoices and simultaneously knocking that amount off your inventory; giving a quick search to tell if a certain item is in stock; listing all outstanding orders; analysing sales and forecasting future demands; working out prices plus tax and prices minus discounts; giving a valuation; and building in all sorts of what programmers call 'bells and whistles'.

Data files

Before computers, a storeman would stand idle until: (1) the customer asked him about Procaine; then (2) he'd go to the filing cabinet for the Stock List, which would be a long list of items. He'd OPEN the file and read through the list until he found 'Procaine'.

He'd CLOSE the file; and (3) he would remember the location and would walk along the shelves muttering to himself, 'Bin number 4'.

The computer works like that: (1) there's a program to make it move; (2) there's a list of stock in a file. The program OPENs it and CLOSEs it; and (3) there's an area of memory to remember things for a short while.

So:

10 PRINT "DO YOU WANT TO CREATE THE STOCKLIST . . .?"

and of course you do, because without the list the storeman wouldn't be able to find anything.

100 CLS   (clear the screen)
110 PRINT"MAKING THE STOCKLIST"

OPEN

Now the computer has to OPEN a file on a new part of the disk or the cassette tape. It has to state whether it intends to OUTPUT to the disk (that means, write on the disk) or to INPUT from the disk (that means, read data from the disk). In this case, you will be OUTPUTting a list of stock to be written on the disk. You can't input from the file because there's nothing in it yet.

Also the computer has to dedicate an area of its memory to temporary storage for the few minutes between your typing, say, BIN NUMBER 4, PROCAINE, 44657 PACKS on the keyboard until the program tells it to write that on the disk or cassette. Your manual may call this a 'buffer', a 'stream' or a 'file location'.

Then it has to give this new file a name. Something like "STOCK/DAT", with the DAT standing for Data.

All these last three paragraphs are done by one line:

120 OPEN "O", 1,"STOCK/DAT"

It may be clearer when written vertically:

120 OPEN	Start the disk drive or cassette recorder motor.
"O",	Get the disk or tape ready for Output from the computer.
1,	Reserve number 1 of the 15 or so areas in memory for this coming work.
"STOCK/DAT"	Give the new file this name. Engrave this name in the disk DIRectory.

Unfortunately, every BASIC dialect gives a different version of this. The BBC Micro says:

120 1 = OPENOUT ("STOCKDAT")

Others make you give the drive or cassette recorder number (2 in this example):

120 OPEN 1, 2, "O", STOCKDAT

You can use variables. For example:

A$ = "STOCK/DAT", B$ = "O", C = 1
OPEN B$,C, A$

should work.

Now comes the chore that computer salesmen never talk about: typing in thousands of stock items:

130 INPUT "WHICH BIN NUMBER ",BN
140 PRINT "BIN NUMBER ";BN;
150 INPUT "WHAT'S IN IT ";ST$
160 IF ST$ = "ZZZ" THEN 210
170 INPUT "HOW MUCH HAVE WE GOT ";AM
200 GOTO 130

and the screen will ask:

WHICH BIN NUMBER?   and you answer: 1
BIN NUMBER 1 WHAT'S IN IT?   NEOMYCIN
HOW MUCH HAVE WE GOT?   8837

You might like to use data from your own firm: or use the word SHELF instead of BIN or whatever you like. Or else you can copy these meaningless figures for an imaginary pharmacy:

```
1    NEOMYCIN 8837 packs
2    CETRIMIDE 6463
3    LIGNOCAINE 344
4    PROCAINE 44657
14   BORIC ACID 5700
10   HYDROCORTISONE 11900
5    HALOTHANE 773
6    DISULFIRAM 23
7    MENTHOL 84854
9    CHLORBUTOL 1123
11   RECORCINOL 0
12   LECITHIN 3566
13   PHENOL 560
8    BEMIGRIDE 9
15   BENZOCAINE 82
16   ZINC OXIDE 0
17   SULFACETAMIDE 990
```

with the first number being the bin the stuff is stacked in and the last number the number of packs you've got.

The program could have had a neat FOR BN = 1 TO 17 or a BN = BN + 1 loop so that the bin numbers would have been produced automatically. But life isn't as orderly as that. In this storeroom, Bins 1, 2, 3 and 4 are in line but Bin 5 is upstairs, so it is handier to check Bins 14 and 10 next.

There already is a loop as line 200 goes back to line 130 and asks the questions again. Line 160 lets you break out of this by typing the word "ZZZ", a string chosen because it is highly unlikely that you'd sell a product called "ZZZ".

PRINT #1,
Engraving these details permanently on disk or tape is done with the command PRINT #1, meaning 'print the memory area number 1'.

Then it gives instructions on how the data should be recorded. Not only does it state the variables but also, by means of significant commas and colons (which mean exactly the same as they do for PRINTing on screen: a comma for tabbing across the page, a semicolon for cramming everything together, colons for new lines), it sets the pattern for the recording:

180 PRINT #1, BN; AM; ST$

will put 1 8837 NEOMYCIN on the disk.

If you had put commas between them, and this doesn't mean that comma after PRINT #1, but:

180 PRINT #1, BN, AM, ST$

then the image would have been:

1   8837   NEOMYCIN

Colons give:

1
8837
NEOMYCIN

which is a waste of recording space. So, apart from the compulsory comma after #1, the memory area indicator, try to use semicolons.

The pattern from line 180 means that after ST$, the name of the chemical, has gone in, that record will be ended and a new one started. So the image on disk will be:

1   NEOMYCIN 8837
2   CETRIMIDE 6463
3   LIGNOCAINE 344
4   PROCAINE 44657
14 BORIC ACID 5700
10 HYDROCORTISONE 11900
5   HALOTHANE 773

and so on, in rows like this.

Of course the words and numbers are not on the disk and tape as such: they are there as electric impulses. When you put your cassette recorder to 'Play' you can hear the squeals as "STOCK/DAT" runs past.

PRINT # bugs

If you were to RUN this program a second time, the screen would obligingly show:

WHICH BIN NUMBER ?   and you would answer   18

and it would PRINT #1, BN; AM; ST$

But when you came to look at "STOCK/DAT", that's all there would be on it. The earlier 17 chemicals would have been wiped off. Because when a new data file, a new program or a new word processor file is given the same name as an existing file, it writes over it.

The cure is to make a backup. It could be optional, with the menu reading:

30 PRINT "DO YOU WANT TO MAKE A BACKUP . . . 2"

but if inexperienced operators will use your program then make it automatic:

30 COPY "STOCK/DAT" TO "LASTOCK/DAT"

Check your manual for the proper punctuation of this. It will copy "STOCK/DAT" before this program runs and alters it. It will give it the new name of "LASTOCK/DAT"; the name isn't important, you could call it "STOCK2/BAK", whatever you liked. And if you can put it on another disk drive, that's even safer.

There can be another minor bug in some BASICs. It is the reason why, after you have inputted BN, ST$ and AM, line 180 says PRINT #1, BN; AM; ST$ in a different order. In the BN, ST$, AM order, sometimes the ST$ grabs hold of the AM, possibly because of the semicolon between them, and the computer considers "NEOMY-CIN 8837" as one string.

This isn't an earthshaking fault, yet you have to remember that disk operating systems and the internal microchips can also have their own bugs.

CLOSE

When you have noted all your stock, when you have typed "ZZZ", then the "STOCK/DAT" file has to be CLOSEd. Until your program is debugged and running, don't key in any more than 17 or 18 trial items in case of error. The line is:

210 CLOSE 1

which means 'close the file on disk and close the memory area #1'.

Like the command NEXT which doesn't always need a variable after it, CLOSE can be on its own. In that case it will close all the files that are open.

The CLOSE bug

The danger comes when you interrupt your program. Maybe, like now, you are creating a program by altering lines and adding bits. You might do test runs and stop them, mid-flight, with the BREAK key. You might decide to have a break yourself, take the disks out and switch off.

If there is a file still OPEN it could be ruined. It could even ruin the disk directory so that you can't run any of the programs on that disk.

Good BASICs automatically close any files when you hit BREAK or when the machine stops itself with an error message. But don't bank on that. If you hit BREAK or the program comes to a stop, type the command CLOSE before doing anything else. There's no need for a line number and if the command is superfluous then nothing will happen.

But if you type this precautionary CLOSE and the disk drive spins then you know that there was a vulnerable file open somewhere and you've just avoided a lot of trouble.

Put a temporary line 9999 CLOSE at the end of any file handling program that you are half-way through composing.

So how does our program look so far?

```
10 PRINT "DO YOU WANT TO CREATE THE STOCKLIST .....   "

100 CLS
110 PRINT"MAKING THE STOCKLIST"
120 OPEN "O", 1,"STOCK/DAT"

130 INPUT "WHICH BIN NUMBER ";BN
140 PRINT "BIN NUMBER ";BN;
150 INPUT "WHAT'S IN IT ";ST$
160 IF ST$ = "ZZZ" THEN 210
170 INPUT "HOW MUCH HAVE WE GOT ";AM

180 PRINT #1, BN; AM; ST$

200 GOTO 130
210 CLOSE 1
```

Playing with the stocklist

The data file now contains details of 17 or so chemicals and it has been closed.

Reading it needs a complete mini-program in itself. It will be done as a subroutine here, starting with line 400, but "STOCK/

DAT" is already capable of being read by another program or, if your computer has saved it in ASCII format, by a word processing program.

This is useful. You could be using the word processor to compose a report to your managers, saying 'As from 23rd July we are out of stock of the following items:'. Then you could load and merge "STOCK/DAT" with your report. Up would come the list of stock and, using the word processor's facilities, you could delete everything except Recorcinol and Zinc Oxide, where there was zero stock. Then you could carry on writing, 'Please re-order these as soon as possible.'

If you decide to change from the full description to a shorter version ("BOR A" for "BORIC ACID" maybe) then either the word processor, or a BASIC program containing LEFT$(ST$,3), would handle that.

Now that "STOCK/DAT" exists as a file, the possibilities are endless.

Reading the stocklist
This is a subroutine, so call it, way back in line 20:

```
10 PRINT "DO YOU WANT TO CREATE THE STOCKIST . . . 1?"
20 PRINT"                          OR LOOK AT IT . . . 2"
```

You could follow this with IF X = 1 THEN GOTO 100 and IF X = 2 THEN 400 but most BASICs have a simpler:

```
40 INPUT W
50 ON W GOTO 100, 400
```

Does yours have that?
Line 400 starts the subroutine like a mini-program:

```
400 CLS                                   (clear the screen)
410 PRINT "LOOKING AT THE STOCK"
420 OPEN "I", 1,"STOCK/DAT"
```

Notice how line 420 OPENs the file just the same as before . . . a book has to be opened before you can read it. The difference is the "I", which means 'get ready to INPUT data, not from the keyboard but from the "STOCK/DAT" file.'

A memory area, a buffer: Number 1, is made ready. So if you like, you could experiment by opening some other buffer: Number 2 perhaps, it won't make any difference.

Check your manual again to see if your dialect demands a number for the disk drive or cassette recorder: OPEN "I", 1, 1, "STOCK/DAT".

```
440 INPUT "WHAT DO YOU WANT TO KNOW "; WH$
```

which expects you to type in MENTHOL or whatever phar-maceutical you are looking for.

    450 INPUT #1, BN, AM, ST$

Look at the format of INPUT #1. This time there are commas between the variables and these commas don't mean 'tab across the screen' but are just simple separators.

After the word INPUT, the microchip must look along its line and if it finds a semicolon (as in line 440 before ;WH$) it knows there will be information coming from the keyboard. If it finds a # hash sign (think of '#' in the American way as 'number') it takes the information out of the OPEN file on disk. And, typically computer, the data will stay invisibly in memory until you ask the machine to do something with it . . . in this case, to look for MENTHOL.

    470 IF ST$ = WH$ THEN PRINT "THERE ARE ";AM;" PACKS OF "
        ST$;" IN BIN "BN: GOTO 510

This should print THERE ARE 84854 PACKS OF MENTHOL IN BIN 7 and then GOTO line 510 which will CLOSE the file. But it won't.

That INPUT # on line 450 only reads the first record, the Neomycin stock. You have to send it back to read the next record, and the next and the next:

    490 GOTO 450

But what if you reach the end of the file without finding what you are looking for? For Hydrogen peroxide for instance?

Then you'd get an error message. Not because Hydrogen peroxide wasn't there – to a microchip, peroxide is just another string – but because line 490 GOTO 450 had ordered it to INPUT more facts and there weren't any left in the file. So you need some way of jumping out of the 'line 490 GObackTO line 450' loop.

And, in beautiful BASIC there are several alternatives:

(1) You could have a FOR L = 1 TO 17 loop if you could guarantee that there were always going to be 17 items in stock.

(2) You could check IF ST$ = "ZZZ" THEN PRINT "SORRY, I CAN'T FIND IT" then GOTO the CLOSE file in line 510.

(3) Or see if your machine can tell when it reaches the End Of a File. The command is:

    480 IF EOF(1) THEN PRINT "SORRY I CAN'T FIND IT": GOTO 510

meaning 'if you reach the End Of File that's inputting into #1 then print Sorry, etc.'

The last line of this program:

510 CLOSE

means 'close all the books'. And here is the complete listing:

```
10 PRINT "DO YOU WANT TO CREATE THE STOCKLIST ..... 1"
20 PRINT "                        OR LOOK AT IT ..... 2"
30 COPY "STOCK/DAT" TO "LASTOCK/DAT"
40 INPUT W
50 ON W GOTO 100,400

100 CLS
110 PRINT"MAKING THE STOCKLIST"
120 OPEN "O", 1,"STOCK/DAT"
130 INPUT "WHICH BIN NUMBER ";BN
140 PRINT "BIN NUMBER ";BN;
150 INPUT "WHAT'S IN IT ";ST$
160 IF ST$ = "ZZZ" THEN 210
170 INPUT "HOW MUCH HAVE WE GOT ";AM
180 PRINT #1, BN; AM; ST$
200 GOTO 130
210 CLOSE 1

400 CLS
410 PRINT "LOOKING AT THE STOCK"
420 OPEN "I", 1,"STOCK/DAT"
440 INPUT "WHAT DO YOU WANT TO KNOW ";WH$
450 INPUT #1, BN, AM, ST$
470 IF ST$ = WH$ THEN PRINT "THERE IS ";AM;" OF "ST$;" IN
    BIN "BN: GOTO 510
480 IF EOF(1)THEN500
490 GOTO 450
500 PRINT "SORRY ... CAN'T FIND IT"
510 CLOSE
```

File handling bugs
Most bugs come from the syntax of the commands. Are you confusing PRINT (meaning print words on the screen) with PRINT #1 (meaning imprint them on disk or tape)? Have you the commas and semicolons right?

And you can't RUN or LOAD a *data* file directly: it has to be read by a program such as this one. If, on the BASIC READY prompt, you were to type RUN"STOCK/DAT" there would be a screenful of garbage because "STOCK/DAT" has no line numbers and no BASIC commands.

You hit this bug while playing with an unfamiliar disk full of unknown program names. When some of them won't load, don't assume that they are faulty programs: they may be data files.

DOS LIST
The good disk operating systems can list data files on to the screen. The command is LIST STOCK/DAT without, in most DOSs, the inverted commas around the filename. Use TYPE in CP/M, provided all entries are in ASCII format.

Go out of BASIC, into DOS and check if yours can do that.

To sum up

This isn't the last word on file handling: there is much more.

You first OPEN a file, allocate it to a buffer in memory, say whether it is for Output or Input, and call it by name.

You write to this file on disk or tape with PRINT # followed by the buffer number, followed by the variables in order. Then it must be CLOSEd.

Before you read from disk the file has to be OPENed again for "I" input, the buffer number and the filename. It can stay open for as long as you like before data is read from it.

The reading command is INPUT # followed by buffer number, sometimes followed by recording device number, followed by the pattern of variables. These variables needn't be the same as before, but they must be in the same order of numerical and string. Then it is CLOSEd.

EOF(5) means the End Of the File allocated to Buffer 5.

Exercises

1. This stocklist program is over-simplified. Make yours record Price, Date, Supplier and a few other details about the stock. When it is input, have the screen warn you if stocks drop below a certain level. And do it properly with plenty of REMarks and neat subroutines.

2. Are you losing orders because a certain item is not in stock? Have the program count how many times customers ask for something you haven't got.

3. You realise, of course, that file handling doesn't only apply to stock control. Rewrite this program either to run an address list, to file titles of newspaper features or to keep a check on hire-car leasings.

And here's an idea. Maybe you could run a computer dating bureau.

Here's how the program could start:

```
10 PRINT TAB(20) "COMPUTER DATING"
20 PRINT
30 PRINT "ANSWER 1, 2, 3 .... UP TO 10, FOR THESE QUESTIONS"
40 PRINT
50 PRINT "FOR INSTANCE, IF YOU ARE ASKED HOW TALL YOU WOULD
   LIKE YOUR PARTNER TO BE"
60 PRINT "AND YOU WOULD FANCY SOMEBODY SMALLER THAN AVERAGE,
   SOMEBODY ABOUT 5 FT 6 INCHES TALL ... THEN ANSWER PERHAPS
70 PRINT "'4' ... BECAUSE '1' IS VERY SMALL, '5' IS AVERAGE AND
   '10' WOULD BE VERY TALL."
80 PRINT
90 PRINT TAB(20) "THE QUESTIONS"
100 PRINT
110 PRINT "HOW TALL WOULD YOU LIKE YOUR PARTNER TO BE ?"
120 PRINT TAB(5) "1 IS VERY SMALL ... 5 IS AVERAGE ... 10 IS
    VERY TALL"
130 INPUT A(1)
140 PRINT "HOW HEAVY WOULD YOU LIKE YOUR PARTNER TO BE ?"
150 PRINT TAB(5) "1 IS VERY LIGHT ... 10 IS VERY HEAVY"
160 INPUT A(2)
```

and so on. You'd have to file the answers, ready to be compared with another applicant's answers.

That's the key to the program: how do you compare? It is certainly not good enough just to add the answers together and to match men and women with the same scores. In these two questions alone, the adding method would couple someone who requested a tall (10) thin (1) partner (10 + 1 = 11) with a short (1) fat (10) partner because 1 + 10 = 11 also. Lines 130 and 160 are setting up an array, so you'd have to compare arrays. But would you prefer to use the MID$ method from Chapter 17 and compare concatenated strings?

It's your business: it's down to you.

22

Faster files

In last chapter's small, seventeen-item demonstration, you were not hitting the two enemies: time and space.

A real warehouse would handle thousands of items: if there were only 17 they wouldn't need a computer, they could count the stuff manually. It is with a massive amount of data that the program starts to creak. The program still works, but the time spent searching through the disk (even worse if it is tape) will run into minutes or hours.

The cure? 'INPUT #' it as an array first thing in the morning then search memory for the rest of the day.

Line 450 would become:

450 INPUT #1, BN, AM(BN), ST$(BN)

with BN, the Bin Number becoming the subscript of the array. And, of course, you would have to CLEAR string space and DIM AM( ), ST$( ) to the appropriate sizes.

There are a lot of advantages to arrays. Memory searches are the fastest of all searches. You can perform quick, machine-code, sorts on arrays faster than the crude BASIC sort listed in Chapter 15, so the lists could be arranged in alphabetical order.

The snag? Memory space.

The problems of cramming data into early computers' limited 4K memories, and on to early 59K floppy disks, are much less now that cheap computers are sold with 48K memories and hard disks with 10,000K storage. Yet professional programmers still seek ingenious ways of saving bytes. This is why manuals on File Handling are difficult to read: you don't understand what they are doing.

But you can still keep a tight control over data . . .

Space-saving tricks

Do you really need to record everything? A company selling a one-off offer by direct mail, for instance, would have thousands of customers but little likelihood of repeat sales, so it wouldn't need to store customers' names.

Could the name, address and telephone number of the regular suppliers be cut down to, maybe, a number? Then after the number has been INPUT #1 from disk, there could be a translation: IF N = 7 THEN SUPPLIER$ = "NADIRCHEM INC. PARETON AVENUE, DOGTON (034 56789)"

Does the date need the year? Then after the number has been INPUT # there could be: DATE$ = DATE$ + "1985"

If you only need to know the date of the last order to find out how fast-moving the stock is, would just recording the month be enough?

How short can the description be? Could HYDROCORTISONE be reduced by LEFT$ and RIGHT$ techniques to something like HYONE before being stored with PRINT #1?

Could 'yes and no' answers (Should this item be run down? Does this computer get a discount? Has this customer's credit been stopped? Does this product need special handling?) be replaced by 1 and 0? Because "DANGEROUS DRUGS LICENCE NEEDED" takes up far more disk space than "1".

Can everything be put into one string? It might be recorded as an incomprehensible 00150082BENINE11062005007 but only the computer would see that. Chapter 17's MID$ technique would break this up to give a sensible printout of:

```
BIN 15   82 PACKS OF   BENZOCAINE   LAST ORDER: 11/06/85
MINIMUM LEVEL 200   * * * REORDER! * * *
MAXIMUM LEVEL 500
SUPPLIER : NADIRCHEM INC.
```

'Random' files

. . . with 'random' in quote marks because there's nothing random about them. It is better to call them *direct access files*.

The stock program in the last chapter created "STOCK/DAT", a *sequential file* with the facts being stored in sequence. Because of the way that cassette tape spools steadily through the recorder, this is the only type of file that can be stored on tape.

Sequential files are simple to write, which is good. But you have to chug through all the earlier stuff before you find the item you want, which is bad. You can beat that by reading the sequential file into an array held in memory and calling up ST$(452) to get the 452nd record. But this is limited by the computer's memory.

Random files, direct access files, get the disk drive to search the disk for things like Record Number 452. So the computer's memory isn't strained, since all the facts remain on disk. It is quite common to find small businesses managing with a 64K computer handling a mass of facts stored on a 10 megabyte hard disk.

The time to access one record out of thousands on a hard disk feels almost as fast as hunting through the computer's memory. The direct access time with floppy disks is about ten times slower, but still acceptable. So direct access files beat the space problem and give a reasonable compromise for time.

How direct access works
When you input a record such as 12 3566 LECITHIN, the computer gives it a number. When you ask for that number, the disk drive spins and finds it.

If you alter part of that record then PUT it back to disk, the computer rewrites just that record and not the entire file as it does with sequential files.

Files, records and fields
A *file* is the whole collection. Example: "PAYROLL/DAT".
A *record* is part of the file. Example: Record Number 88.
A *field* is part of the record. Examples:

MR. J.C. BOROWSKI
83 HOURS WORKED
3 HOURS OVERTIME
90.01 TAX

are four fields from Record 88 in the PAYROLL/DAT file.   Rember these terms because, even if you buy an off-the-shelf data-handling program, the instructions often demand that you first set up the length of the fields before running the program.

Certainly, a lot of BASICs need the size of the fields to be set up. Here it is in a payroll program.

Payroll by direct access
Direct access opens conventionally enough with:

```
10 CLS                              (clear the screen)
20 PRINT"      ******** PAYROLL ********": PRINT
30 CLEAR 5000                       (make space for strings)
```

But then the commands vary with different flavours of BASIC. So, for the coming lines 40, 50, 70 and 400 to 440, check with your computer's manual.

```
40 OPEN "R", 1, "PAYROLL/DAT", 90
```

This is like the OPENing of a sequential file except that "R" stands for Random, meaning that it doesn't matter if you read the file or write to it. There is no more need for "O" – Output and "I" – Input.

The 1 is the buffer number, the file area number, the temporary storage area in memory; then the file name; and the 90 is the intended length of the record. Simple BASICs won't accept this: they insist on making every record 255 characters long. So if you only need 90 characters, a lot of space is wasted unless you perform some programming tricks. Good BASICs don't need the length to be stated: they automatically fill the disk with the minimum of wasted space.

How do you know your Payroll records will be 90 characters long? You count.

Before switching on, have a think about what you want to record. For a payroll, you might need the employee's NAME which you'll call NA$ and, since something like F.B. ROBINSON is 12 characters long, be on the safe side and allow for 16 character names. Then there'd be the ADDRESS, called AD$, another 16 characters. The TOWN, 10 characters.

The pencilled list might be:

NAME	NA$	16	characters
ADDRESS	AD$	16	
TOWN	TW$	10	
HOURS WORKED	HO$	5	to handle decimals
OVERTIME	OV$	4	
BONUS	BO$	6	for 123.45 style money
PAY	PA$	6	
TAX CODE	TC$	1	a single A,B style letter
TAX	TX$	6	figures of money
DEDUCTIONS	DE$	6	
FINAL PAY	FP$	6	
PAY SO FAR	SF$	8	up to 99999.99 of money
These add up to the		90	character length of each record

FIELD

In several BASICs, these different-length variables must be set out in the pattern they are to go on disk. The command starts off as FIELD 1, with 1 being the number of the memory area, the buffer, the stream, the channel, whatever your manual calls it.

Then all the field lengths are listed in the form of 16 AS NA$, meaning 'save 16 spaces as the NAme of the employee $tring'. This goes up to 8 AS SF$, meaning 'save 8 spaces as the Pay-So-Far $tring'. It looks like:

```
50 FIELD 1, 16 AS NA$, 16 AS AD$, 10 AS TW$, 5 AS HO$, 4 AS OV$,
   6 AS BO$, 6 AS PA$, 1 AS TC$, 6 AS TX$, 6 AS DE$, 6 AS FP$, 8 AS
   SF$
```

So imagine the machine allocating 90 characters of memory area Number 1, chopping that area into 16, 16, 10, 5, 4, 6, and so on, and labelling those empty sections as NA$, AD$, TW$, HO$, OV$, BO$ in readiness for data to arrive. Then writing "PAYROLL/DAT" on to the disk's directory, finding some spare space on the disk, and getting ready to accept the record from memory or else to feed a record into memory.

GET

```
60 INPUT"WHICH RECORD NUMBER DO YOU WANT "; RN
70 GET 1, RN
```

This is like having an office boy who asks, 'Which record number do you want?' And you answer, '5: get record 5 and put it into memory area 1.'

GET is the equivalent to the INPUT # of the last chapter. And, typically computer, it stays hidden in memory until you ask for it:

```
80 PRINT "RECORD NUMBER "; RN

90 PRINT  "1 ... NAME          "; NA$

100 PRINT "2 ... ADDRESS       "; AD$

110 PRINT "3 ... TOWN          "; TW$

120 PRINT "4 ... HOURS         "; HO$,

130 PRINT "5 ... OVERTIME      "; OV$

140 PRINT "6 ... BONUS         "; BO$,

150 PRINT "7 ... PAY           "; PA$

160 PRINT "8 ... TAX CODE      "; TC$,

170 PRINT "9 ... TAX           "; TX$

180 PRINT "10 .. DEDUCTIONS    "; DE$

190 PRINT "11 .. FINAL PAY     "; FP$

200 PRINT "12 .. PAY SO FAR    "; SF$
```

None of this is special; it is 13 lines of PRINT-on-screen commands that you read about in Chapter 3. The commas after lines 120, 140 and 160 are just to tab the words across the screen.

When the program is up and running it will show all the details of your employee's last week's wages. Right now, if you were to RUN it (add a precautionary line 999 CLOSE to avoid bugs) the "1 . . . NAME" and "2 . . . ADDRESS" section would print on screen but, since PAYROLL/DAT is empty, the NA$, AD$ variables would come out as blanks.

So to put details of your employees in:

```
210 PRINT TAB(20)"TO ALTER THESE, TYPE THAT NUMBER IN

    FRONT"

220 PRINT TAB(20)"IF YOU DON'T WANT TO ALTER ANYTHING,

    TYPE  0"

230 INPUT AL

240 IF AL = 1 THEN INPUT "NEW NAME "; AN$

250 IF AL = 2 THEN INPUT "NEW ADDRESS "; DA$

260 IF AL = 3 THEN INPUT "NEW TOWN "; WT$

270 IF AL = 4 THEN INPUT "NEW HOURS "; OH$

280 IF AL = 5 THEN INPUT "NEW OVERTIME "; VO$

290 IF AL = 6 THEN INPUT "NEW BONUS "; OB$

300 IF AL = 7 THEN INPUT "NEW PAY "; AP$

310 IF AL = 8 THEN INPUT "NEW TAX CODE "; CT$

320 IF AL = 9 THEN INPUT "NEW TAX "; XT$

330 IF AL = 10 THEN INPUT "NEW DEDUCTIONS "; ED$

340 IF AL = 11 THEN INPUT "NEW FINAL PAY "; PF$

350 IF AL = 12 THEN INPUT "NEW PAY SO FAR "; FS$

360 IF AL = 0 THEN 500

380 INPUT"ARE YOU ALTERING MORE "; Y$

390 IF Y$ = "Y" THEN 80
```

Again this is nothing new. It's the INPUT command from Chapter 7.

The usual procedure will be that last week, a guy worked 45 hours and this week you want to alter that to 51 hours. So you hit Option 4 and line 270 asks: "NEW HOURS?"

Remember that this is just a demonstration program on direct files: in a real Payroll program you shouldn't need to type in the "NEW PAY". That would be done by arithmetic; multiplying the hours worked by the wage per hour. TAX would be calculated and DEDUCTIONS subtracted.

Buffer variables
But look again at the variables:

(a) They are all strings. This is because most machines refuse to accept numbers into direct access files. So you must input them as strings, as in this case, and use VAL(x$) later before you do any arithmetic. Or some BASICs have complicated but space-efficient MKI$(123) 'MaKe Integer into a string' and CVI(x$) 'ConVert string to Integer' commands.

(b) They are not the original NA$, AD$ and TW$: they have changed.

This is because most machines consider buffer variables, the ones you FIELDed in line 50, as being different from everyday variables. There's no problem about bringing them out of memory and PRINTing them as in lines 90 to 200. But don't play with them in the rest of a program or they will be lost.

Any other letters can be used instead, yet most programmers use look-alike combinations to remind themselves. The untouchable field variable for NAME was NA$ so the letters are reversed in line 240 to make AN$. You could have used N2$ or NM$ . . . anything but the original, fielded NA$.

This leads to further manipulation when you want to put them back into the memory store before being written back on to the disk.

LSET and RSET
When the program is first run, you ask for Record Number 1 and get a blank printout because PAYROLL/DAT is empty. You answer line 210 by typing '1' then fill in your first employee's name. Then '2' to fill in his address and so on.

When Record Number 1 is finished it is saved to disk (these program lines haven't been written yet) and you start on Number 2.

The magic about random files is that if you went out of sequence and jumped from Record 1 to Record 88, the computer would hurriedly write 87, ninety-character-long blanks on the disk to make up the space.

When the program has been running for weeks, you'd ask for a Record Number and the printout would show that employee's NAME, ADDRESS, HOURS WORKED and so on. You wouldn't want to alter the NAME so that would stay as the original NA$. Line 240 would hardly ever be used.

You certainly would want to alter the BONUS from last week's figure to this week's bonus. So line 290 would not only alter the bonus figure from, say 10.85 to 14.04 but it would store the new

figure as OB$, not as the original fielded BO$. And the NEW PAY
SO FAR which would be last week's pay plus this week's pay,
would be now stored as FS$.

The problem, in computers where ordinary program variables
can't be stored on disk unless they have been FIELDed and since
FIELDed variables can't be used much in a program, is to change
the BONUS money labelled OB$ into BO$ and the PAY SO FAR
labelled FS$ into SF$.

Machines like the Tandy TRS-80 use the instructions LSET and
RSET, meaning 'set the characters to the left of the field' and 'set
them to the right'.

You are allocated a 16-character space for employees' names
(line 50 FIELD 1, 16 AS NA$, etc.) yet JOE BROWN has only nine.
So LSET NA$ would put on disk:

JOE BROWN . . . .

We've used dots instead of blanks.

And RSET BO$ where the BONUS was only '77' after 6 spaces
had been allocated (50 FIELD 1, etc., 6 AS BO$) would become:

. . . . 77

Secondly, LSET and RSET (pronounced 'Left set' and 'Right set')
take the variables away from the danger of being polluted by the
program and store them back in the buffer area, where they wait to
be written on disk.

The layout of the transfer is:

```
LSET NA$ = AN$
LSET AD$ = DA$
LSET TW$ = WT$
RSET HO$ = OH$
RSET OV$ = VO$
```

meaning that the 'left set' field variable takes the same value as the
program variable. The 'right set' OVERTIME takes the same value as
the inputted line 280 NEW OVERTIME.

Normally, the lines would look like this:

```
392 LSET NA$ = AN$ : LSET AD$ = DA$ : LSET TW$ = WT$
394 RSET HO$ = OH$ : RSET OV$ = VO$ : RSET BO$ = OB$
396 RSET PA$ = AP$ : RSET TC$ = CT$ : RSET TX$ = XT$
398 RSET DE$ = ED$ : RSET FP$ = PF$ : RSET SF$ = FS$
```

. . . multi-statement lines, setting the values of the field variables.

But in this Payroll Program they would create a bug. You don't
want LSET NA$ = AN$ if nothing has been input for AN$ in line
240. LSET NA$ would then become nothing.

The LSET and RSET instructions are best put at the end of lines
240 to 350. Then they will only be obeyed IF the payroll detail is

altered. You read in Chapter 8 that the second part of a multi-statement line is ignored IF the first isn't true. So rewrite these lines as:

```
240 IF AL= 1 THEN INPUT"NEW NAME"; AN$          : LSET NA$ = AN$

250 IF AL= 2 THEN INPUT"NEW ADDRESS"; DA$       : LSET AD$ = DA$

260 IF AL= 3 THEN INPUT"NEW TOWN"; WT$          : LSET TW$ = WT$

270 IF AL= 4 THEN INPUT"NEW HOURS"; OH$         : RSET HO$ = OH$

280 IF AL= 5 THEN INPUT"NEW OVERTIME"; VO$      : RSET OV$ = VO$

290 IF AL= 6 THEN INPUT"NEW BONUS"; OB$         : RSET BO$ = OB$

300 IF AL= 7 THEN INPUT"NEW PAY"; AP$           : RSET PA$ = AP$

310 IF AL= 8 THEN INPUT"NEW TAX CODE"; CT$      : RSET TC$ = CT$

320 IF AL= 9 THEN INPUT"NEW TAX"; XT$           : RSET TX$ = XT$

330 IF AL= 10 THEN INPUT"NEW DEDUCTIONS"; ED$ : RSET DE$ = ED$

340 IF AL= 11 THEN INPUT"NEW FINAL PAY"; PF$  : RSET FP$ = PF$

350 IF AL= 12 THEN INPUT"NEW PAY SO FAR"; FS$ : RSET SF$ = FS$

360 IF AL= 0   THEN 500
```

EDIT
Those spaces before the colons are put in this book for clarity: your LSET additions would run straight on. Check your manual for how to EDIT a line: how to add more to it.

The result of adding the LSETs and RSETs will be that IF part of a record is altered then the buffer variable will alter. Otherwise, it will stay the same.

```
380 INPUT "ARE YOU ALTERING MORE "; Y$
390 IF Y$ = "YES" THEN 80
```

Because every week there might be several items to be altered.

PUT
The command to put the contents of the memory area on to the disk is:

```
400 PUT 1, RN
```

meaning 'Put the contents of memory area 1 into Record Number 88', or whatever RN happens to be. This is the equivalent to sequential files' PRINT # 1, . . . And finally:

```
500 CLOSE
```

Here are the program and a sample screen printout.

```
10 CLS
20 PRINT"         ******** PAYROLL ********": PRINT
30 CLEAR 5000

40 OPEN "R",1,"PAYROLL/DAT",90
50 FIELD 1, 16 AS NA$, 16 AS AD$, 10 AS TW$, 5 AS HO$,
   4 AS OV$, 6 AS BO$, 6 AS PA$, 1 AS TC$, 6 AS TX$,
   6 AS DE$, 6 AS FP$, 8 AS SF$

60 INPUT"WHICH RECORD NUMBER DO YOU WANT ";RN
70 GET 1, RN

80  PRINT "RECORD NUMBER "; RN
90  PRINT "1 ... NAME          "; NA$
100 PRINT "2 ... ADDRESS       "; AD$
110 PRINT "3 ... TOWN          "; TW$
120 PRINT "4 ... HOURS         "; HO$,
130 PRINT "5 ... OVERTIME      "; OV$,
140 PRINT "6 ... BONUS         "; BO$,
150 PRINT "7 ... PAY           "; PA$
160 PRINT "8 ... TAX CODE      "; TC$,
170 PRINT "9 ... TAX           "; TX$
180 PRINT "10 .. DEDUCTIONS    "; DE$
190 PRINT "11 .. FINAL PAY     "; FP$
200 PRINT "12 .. PAY SO FAR    "; SF$

210 PRINT TAB(20)"TO ALTER THESE, TYPE THAT NUMBER IN FRONT"
220 PRINT TAB(20)"IF YOU DON'T WANT TO ALTER ANYTHING, TYPE   0"
230 INPUT AL

240 IF AL = 1  THEN INPUT "NEW NAME "; AN$       : LSET NA$ = AN$
250 IF AL = 2  THEN INPUT "NEW ADDRESS "; DA$    : LSET AD$ = DA$
260 IF AL = 3  THEN INPUT "NEW TOWN "; WT$       : LSET TW$ = WT$
270 IF AL = 4  THEN INPUT "NEW HOURS "; OH$      : RSET HO$ = OH$
280 IF AL = 5  THEN INPUT "NEW OVERTIME "; VO$   : RSET OV$ = VO$
290 IF AL = 6  THEN INPUT "NEW BONUS "; OB$      : RSET BO$ = OB$
300 IF AL = 7  THEN INPUT "NEW PAY "; AP$        : RSET PA$ = AP$
310 IF AL = 8  THEN INPUT "NEW TAX CODE "; CT$   : RSET TC$ = CT$
320 IF AL = 9  THEN INPUT "NEW TAX "; XT$        : RSET TX$ = XT$
330 IF AL = 10 THEN INPUT "NEW DEDUCTIONS "; ED$ : RSET DE$ = ED$
340 IF AL = 11 THEN INPUT "NEW FINAL PAY "; PF$  : RSET FP$ = PF$
350 IF AL = 12 THEN INPUT "NEW PAY SO FAR "; FS$ : RSET SF$ = FS$
360 IF AL = 0 THEN 500

380 INPUT"ARE YOU ALTERING MORE "; Y$
390 IF Y$ = "Y" THEN 80

400 PUT 1, RN
500 CLOSE




WHICH RECORD NUMBER DO YOU WANT ? 88
RECORD NUMBER  88
1 ... NAME          J.H.BEBEHANI
2 ... ADDRESS       39 DOWNS RD
3 ... TOWN          BOSTON
4 ... HOURS              51      5 ... OVERTIME         7
6 ... BONUS           14.04      7 ... PAY         234.56
8 ... TAX CODE       A           9 ... TAX          90.01
10 .. DEDUCTIONS    13.00
11 .. FINAL PAY     131.55
12 .. PAY SO FAR    678.90
                    TO ALTER THESE, TYPE THAT NUMBER IN FRONT
                    IF YOU DON'T WANT TO ALTER ANYTHING, TYPE   0

? -
```

Random file bugs

This program has plenty. What about recording the date for instance? And 10 characters aren't enough for a town called WEST BERGHOLT.

If your initial planning isn't good, then you get problems. Yet if you are over-generous with FIELDs you might run out of record space in the older computers that allow only 255 characters per record.

It would be uneconomic for machines to reserve, maybe, 15 special memory areas for files. It is only in the last couple of chapters you've kept files at all. So many machines expect you to declare, as you go into BASIC, how many buffer areas you are likely to need. If you don't answer they reserve a token number of about three anyway.

The bugs come in the pedantic syntax of that OPEN "R", 2, "FILENAME.EXT", 123 line, which differs in every BASIC by irritating little commas and numbers. So read the manual.

Field instructions can be very sensitive. It is possible to use numeric variables: instead of FIELD 1, 16 AS NA$ you could say:

```
X = 8
FIELD 1, 2 * X AS NA$
```

but this can cause a bug unless brackets are used:

```
FIELD 1, 2 * (X) AS NA$
```

The length of a file on disk is determined by the highest Record Number you have PUT or Got (ask your machine to PRINT LOF(1) to see if it gives the Length Of File). If you own small capacity disks and accidentally command "GET 1, 1000" the computer would process the entire disk and then throw up an error message OUT OF DISK SPACE.

The KILL bug

A major disaster is if you KILL a program while its files are still open. This can ruin the disk directory. So use the word CLOSE first. A minor bug happens because of the nature of KILL.

KILL does no more than take the filename out of the directory: the file itself is still written on the disk (and with Utility Programs you can sometimes recover accidentally killed files). So, if you are using an old disk there can be quite a lot of garbage on it. Nobody worries, the disk drive happily writes new stuff over the rubbish.

But, suppose you have record numbers running out of sequence. In a Payroll Program there could be women on Records 1 to 75, then a gap, then men on Records 100 to 150. In that gap there could be the killed remnants of last month's Space Invaders.

Fig. 22.1 The NEC PC-8000 microcomputer system with a hard disk drive (on top of the desk) and a backup floppy disk drive (beneath the desk)

And if you wrote FOR N = 1 TO 150 : GET 1, N : TOTAL PAY = LAST TOTAL + THIS AMOUNT . . . you might get some weird results.

To sum up

Sequential files	'Random' files
Go on disk or tape	Go on disk only

Files have a name: e.g. "PAYROLL.FEB"
Records are part of a file: e.g. Number 7
Fields are part of a record: e.g. "23 HIGH ST"

Records are in sequence	Can be got directly
OPEN "I" for Input (read)	
OPEN "O" for Output (write)	OPEN "R" for both
Can't "I" and "O" together	

An area in memory holds the data

	FIELD 1,20 AS A$ is needed
Accept numbers and words	Strings only
INPUT #1, A$, B, C	GET 1, RN
PRINT #1, A$, B, C	PUT 1, RN

End with CLOSE

Read in your computer manual how integers save space.

Exercises

1. You'd cause a pay strike if you used this program. Make it work properly. Have built-in arithmetic to work out pay details after you input the hours worked.

2. Keep this program but alter the headings from NAME, ADDRESS, etc. to VEHICLE, MILEAGE, FUEL, etc. and turn it into a Transport Management program. You will have to alter the lengths of FIELD variables.

3. It is unreasonable to expect your operators to remember that Fred Brown's pay is on Record Number 275 or that the Volkswagen truck is on Record 851. If they know the name, how can they get the Record Number? (Half marks for a printed look-up table on the wall. Bonus points for a method that makes the computer give the answer, because this problem has worried a lot of programmers.)

4. LIST (or better, LLIST to a printer) a store-bought data-management program. How do the professionals handle direct access files?

23

Still can't program? Then cheat

So you know enough to be able to PRINT, GOTO and do a few FOR-TO loops? But you can't pronounce VARPTR and wouldn't know how to POKE even if somebody gave you a stick? Don't worry, there's a way to program even if you are stuck on Page 3 of this book. You cheat.

It is possible to turn out programs that are far beyond your normal capabilities. It is possible to get your computer earning its keep instead of churning out those little, ten-line Fahrenheit to Centigrade conversions so common in the elementary textbooks. You just need a minimal grounding in BASIC and a desire to hit the big time.

It may be very noble to spend months studying. But at the end of your education, you realise that there is a far faster sorting routine than the one you have created, that there are better bug-free error traps than yours, and that somebody somewhere has said the same thing in half the number of lines. For a lot of your study time, you have been re-inventing the wheel.

The only thing you can do better than the professionals is to make their store-bought programs more intelligible to the average human being. So here's how you start your apprenticeship.

Make a backup copy of that Stock Control program you bought and run it until the screen baffles you with computspeak like:

INPUT ACC # (MAX 5 CHAR)?

hit the Break key and the screen will show:

BREAK IN 2345

meaning that the cryptic message was on line 2345.

Have a look at the lines on either side of 2345 by commanding: LIST 2330–2360 and there will be the offending line, surrounded by others like:

```
2340 PEEK POKE VARPTR POKE PEEK
2345 INPUT"INPUT ACC # (MAX 5 CHAR)";AC$
2350 POKE PEEK DEFUSR PEEK POKE
```

This shows that, not only can you change line 2345 into reasonable English, but you also have all the space between 2340 and 2350 to do so.

After deleting line 2345, you could rewrite it as line 2342:

```
2342 INPUT "WHAT'S THE ACCOUNT NUMBER ";AC$
```

then there would be plenty of room to take care of that MAX 5 CHAR gibberish, which presumably means that the account number can't have more than 5 characters in it. Like this:

```
2344 IF LEN(AC$) < 6 THEN 2350
```

If the length of the account number is less than 5 then, all right, go on to the rest of the program. Otherwise:

```
2346 PRINT "I THINK YOU'VE GOT THE ACCOUNT NUMBER
     WRONG. IT OUGHT TO BE SMALLER. TRY AGAIN . . ."
2348 GOTO 2342
```

All the time you are asking, 'Could a newcomer understand the screen if the regular operator was off sick?' And out will go INSERT DATA DISK INTO DR 1 to be replaced by PUT THE DISK WITH THE RED LABEL INTO THE BOTTOM SLOT. You will make keying reponses easier by using INKEY$ wherever possible. The date routine will be made to accept DD,MM,YY and DD.MM.YY as well as DD/MM/YY and the screen will prompt YES OR NO? instead of the computspeak (Y/N)?

And you can personalise the program. For instance, if 90 per cent of your sales come from half-a-dozen items then you make the computer write the entire item when your operator keys in the initial letter. If most of your stuff comes from a few wholesalers then, by keying one reference number, the computer throws up the wholesaler's complete address. If all your sales slips start with the same spiel, have that in automatically.

There is an enormous improvement to be made in professional programs because they are written by computing experts, not English specialists.

But even experts have weak spots. Does the program hang up if it is commanded to print when the printer isn't switched on? Then learn how to PEEK at the computer's printer port and insert a line like (it varies with different machines):

```
7890 IF PEEK(14312) < > 63 THEN PRINT "THE PRINTER ISN'T ON"
```

This, though, is only the beginning.

Making Mail Lists into Accounts Ledgers
Now you have proved that store-bought programs are not
sacrosanct, you can create complex programs of your own. There is
no need to be content with improving the occasional screen
printout line: the entire programs can be transformed.

But first you need to find an example of good programming. LIST
through the programs you own to find one that is well
compartmentalised into labelled modules. There will be Remark
lines throughout it, like:

    999 REM ***** CREATE A FILE *****

then more program, followed perhaps by:

    1999 REM ***** SORT ROUTINE *****

and

    4999 REM ***** DISPLAY A RECORD *****
    5999 REM ***** GET ENTIRE FILE *****
    6999 REM ***** SAVE TO DISK *****
    8999 REM ***** PRINT LABELS *****

and so on. The main theme of the program will roll in a steady,
straight line with neat GOSUB diversions to the various sort, save
and recall routines.

Suppose you find this paragon of a program and it is a Mailing List
and you really want, say, an Accounts program: then that's no
problem . . . it is possible to convert a Mailing List into an Accounts
Ledger within a couple of evenings' programming. Both ask you to
type in the date, both ask for data input, both sort and save the
information to disk. All you have to do is change the words that
come on the screen.

The original mailing list might have this:

    1070 INPUT "ENTER NAME   "; NA$
    1080 INPUT "ADDRESS   "; AD$
    1090 INPUT "TOWN   "; TW$
    1100 INPUT "COUNTY   "; CO$
    1110 INPUT "POST CODE   "; PC$
    1120 INPUT "TELEPHONE   "; TE$

Working from a backup copy, it is no great trouble to alter that to:

    1070 INPUT "JOB NAME   "; NA$
    1080 INPUT "FEE   "; AD$
    1090 INPUT "EXPENSES   "; TW$
    . . . and so on.

It may look daft to have a Fee with the variable name AD$ when you would normally have called it something mnemonic like FE. But by keeping the original variables you can continue to use the well-written, bug-free, original routines. Run your new version with just these minor alterations and it will no longer show:

NAME	F SMITH	but	JOB	ALLSTOP LTD
ADDRESS	23 HIGH STREET		FEE	123.45
TOWN	COMPTOWN		EXP	78.90
COUNTY	BUCKS		TOTAL	202.35
P/CODE	CO6 3JS		DATE	12/10/84
PHONE	01 23456		PAID	05/11/84

And as a bonus, just as the original would pick out every address in the county of Bucks, it will still find every total bill of 202.35. It will rearrange all the jobs into alphabetical order just as it used to in the Mailing List. And, provided you change all those string variables into numeric by using VAL(AD$), it will list the fees paid into ascending order.

What it won't do is arithmetic. This, you create yourself.

A handy place for arithmetic is when the stored data is being collected off the disk and before it is printed on to the screen. A mailing list would have a subroutine with the command GET in it. With luck, the menu might point the direction to this subroutine in lines like:

```
500 PRINT@25, "*** MENU ***"
510 PRINT "1 . . .ADD A FILE"
520 PRINT "2 . . .SORT OPTION"
530 PRINT "3 . . .DISPLAY A RECORD"
540 PRINT "4 . . .DISPLAY ENTIRE FILE" – – – – this is it
550 PRINT "5 . . .CHANGE A RECORD"
560 PRINT "6 . . .PRINTOUT"
570 INPUT "TYPE THE CHOICE YOU WANT"; CH
580 ON CH GOTO 1000, 2000, 5000, 6000, 8000, 9000
```

It is the fourth choice you need, and it should start at line 6000.

The programmer will have OPENed the file and used GET, or a similar command in your computer's dialect of BASIC, to shift the data from disk into the computer's memory. As the variables come streaming off, you catch them and add them up with some sort of arithmetic like:

```
AD = VAL(AD$). . . remember, that was the Fee.
TF = TF + AD . . . the Total of Fees = the total a fraction of a second
                   ago + the Fee that is just being read.
```

Similarly, the arithmetic can add up the expenses or allocate them to various jobs or select the fees that have not been paid. You are writing a little program within the main program.

RENUMBER

But where to put the little program? It could go at the end with a line saying: GOSUB 25000. Or it could fit into this thousand line subroutine if only you could find space.

In this imaginary Mailing List, the programmer has filled, perhaps, lines 6000 to 6300 with POKEs and PEEKs and GETs and FIELDs and all the apparatus of bringing the recorded data from the disk. You'd like to fit your arithmetic into line 6310 but you can't: the PRINT section where all the records scroll nicely across the screen, starts there. It runs to, say, line 6750.

Then there is a gap because the programmer had a tidy mind and didn't start his next subroutine until the next round number: line 7000. If those PRINT lines could be moved on a bit, then there would be a gap at line 6310 to take the arithmetic.

The command is RENUMBER. Different BASICs give this different names. In some it is RENUM; in others, for some reason, it is NAME. And you will have to check in your manual for the correct protocol, but by working out how many lines you intend to shift and seeing that they don't bump into line 7000, you might come up with a command saying:

```
RENUM 6550, 10, 6310, 6750
```

which means, in that particular dialect of BASIC, 'Make the new line 6550, go up in 10s, starting with the old 6310, to the old 6570'.

After hitting RETURN (or ENTER or NEWLINE) the subroutine will be renumbered with a useful gap between where the data is read off disk and before it scrolls on screen. That's where you write your arithmetic.

At no stage of the conversion process is the old Mailing List program disabled. It always works even though it prints out Fees and Expenses instead of Names and Addresses. But it may become inefficient in the way it saves to disk. Maybe it allocated enough space on disk to take Addresses of 'Dunromin 123 Magnolia Avenue' length yet you are now writing Fees into the same AD\$ variable of '1234.56' length.

An expert programmer would consider this heresy, but if there is enough disk space to waste then there's no worry. Leave things as they are.

Otherwise you need to learn the minimum BASIC to understand buffers and fields and files and records. Then you look for the original allocation instruction which, depending on the dialect of BASIC, could look like:

7450 FIELD 1, 25 AS AN$, 25 AS DA$, 19 AS WT$ etc.

and alter it to the length of your shorter entries:

7450 FIELD 1, 20 AS AN$, 7 AS DA$, 7 AS WT$ etc.

MERGE

There are more improvements to go into this do-it-yourself program.

Would you prefer the sort of spectacular title that came with that Games disk? For data input, would you like a cursor flashing to show how many characters were allowed, just as in that Stock List? And the 'Help' prompts that come on screen in that Mortgage Calculation program: would they be useful? Could the clever Invoice Printing routine from Sales Ledger be used as well? All of these are possible with a command called MERGE.

Suppose you once bought a Diary program that had an ingenious way of converting 21/01/84 into 'Saturday 21st January 1984' and it gave the number of days between any two dates. That would be useful in your Accounts arithmetic: it could help forecast your income for the whole year. It would be far better than the pedestrian date routine in the old Mailing List.

So LIST this Mailing List that you are now converting to an Accounts program (see page 194). Look for the lines handling the date . . . and there they are between lines 220 and 350, perhaps. Make a note of the variable that comes out of the routine, the date. Maybe it is DT$. Now – and all this is being done on backup copies of the disk – DELETE those lines. Give the program a temporary name, say, ACCOUNT3 and SAVE it.

Clear everything out of the computer's memory and LOAD that store-bought Diary Program. LIST it and look for the smart Date routine . . . and there it is between lines 14700 and 15890. Even after you have deleted all the rest of the Diary before and after these lines, it still looks too big to fit into the date gap of your Accounts program.

But there is no law that says lines have to go up in 10s. Renumber this routine in 1s:

RENUM 220, 1, 14700, 15890

or however your BASIC manual says.

You now have a little program that starts at 220 and runs in 1s to line 339. It will fit. First you save it on disk in a special way. Normally things are saved in a compressed form for the sake of

```
10   PRINT@25, "*** MAILING LIST ***"
20   PRINT@25, "BY PROF. PROGRAMMER"
..............
..............
220 INPUT "DATE"; DT$
.............
350 DATE - ENDS
.............
..............
500 PRINT@25, "*** MENU ***"
510 PRINT "1 ...ADD A FILE"
520 PRINT "2 ...SORT OPTION"
530 PRINT "3 ...DISPLAY A RECORD"
540 PRINT "4 ...DISPLAY ENTIRE FILE"
550 PRINT "5 ...CHANGE A RECORD"
560 PRINT "6 ...PRINTOUT"
570 INPUT "TYPE THE CHOICE YOU WANT"; CH
580 ON CH GOTO 1000, 2000, 5000, 6000, 8000, 9000
.............
.............
999 REM *****  CREATE A FILE  *****
.............
1070 INPUT "ENTER NAME  ";NA$
1080 INPUT "ADDRESS     ";AD$
1090 INPUT "TOWN        ";TW$
1100 INPUT "COUNTY      ";CO$
1110 INPUT "POST CODE   ";PC$
1120 INPUT "TELEPHONE   ";TE$
.............
.............
1999 REM *****  SORT OPTION  *****
.............
.............
4999 REM *****  DISPLAY A RECORD  *****
.............
.............
5999 REM *****  GET ENTIRE FILE  *****
6000 GETTING FILE - STARTS
.............
6300 GETTING FILE - ENDS
6310 PRINTING DETAILS - STARTS
.............
6750 PRINTING DETAILS - ENDS
.............


        NO PROGRAM LINES




.............
6999 REM *****  SAVE TO DISK  *****
.............
7450 FIELD 1, 25 AS AN$, 25 AS DA$, 19 AS WT$
.............
.............
8999 REM *****  PRINTOUT  *****
.............
.............
24000 END
```

```
10   PRINT@25, "*** ACCOUNTS PROGRAM ***"
20   PRINT@25, "BY ME"
..............
220 NEW DATE FROM DIARY PROGRAM
221 MORE NEW DATE
223 MORE DATE
350 DATE - ENDS
.............
.............
500 PRINT@25, "*** MENU ***"
510 PRINT "1 ...ADD A FILE"
520 PRINT "2 ...SORT OPTION"
530 PRINT "3 ...DISPLAY A RECORD"
540 PRINT "4 ...DISPLAY ENTIRE FILE"
550 PRINT "5 ...CHANGE A RECORD"
560 PRINT "6 ...PRINTOUT"
570 INPUT "TYPE THE CHOICE YOU WANT"; CH
580 ON CH GOTO 1000, 2000, 5000, 6000, 8000, 9000
.............
.............
999 REM *****  CREATE A FILE  *****
.............
1070 INPUT "JOB NAME    ";NA$
1080 INPUT "FEE         ";AD$
1090 INPUT "EXPENSES    ";TW$
1100 INPUT "TOTAL       ";CO$
1110 INPUT "DATE SENT   ";PC$
1120 INPUT "DATE PAID   ";TE$
.............
.............
1999 REM *****  SORT OPTION  *****
.............
.............
4999 REM *****  DISPLAY A RECORD  *****
.............
.............
5999 REM *****  GET ENTIRE FILE  *****
6000 GETTING FILE - STARTS
.............
6300 GETTING FILE - ENDS
6310 ARITHMETIC - STARTS
6320 AD = VAL (AD$)
6330 TF = TF + AD
6340 MORE ARITHMETIC
.............
6490 ARITHMETIC ENDS
.............
6550 PRINT ROUTINE IN A NEW PLACE
6560 MORE PRINT
.............
6810 PRINT - ENDS
6999 REM *****  SAVE TO DISK  *****
.............
7450 FIELD 1, 20 AS AN$, 7 AS DA$, 7 AS WT$
.............
.............
8999 REM *****  PRINTOUT  *****
.............
.............
24000 END
```

speed. This one – give it a temporary name of, say, DATE1 – has to be saved in ASCII format. This format is used when programs are to be messed around with; when they are to be included in word processing programs or, as in this case, when they are to be merged.

The command, and again you'll have to check with your manual, is something like:

SAVE "DATE1",A

with the A standing for ASCII.

With that saved on the backup disk, clear the memory and re-LOAD your much modified ACCOUNT3. Now command:

MERGE "DATE1"

and, if you have got the syntax right, the new date routine will be neatly glued into the Accounts program, between lines 220 and 339.

You will need to make its variable back into the original DT$ so that the rest of the program will understand it, and tidy up a few edges. But, with no mental strain, there is now the facility for 'Saturday 21st January' style dates. It is something that might otherwise have taken weeks to compose and debug.

No MERGE in your BASIC? Then look for APPEND. This tacks bits on the end of the program in memory and the method of renumbering, then saving in ASCII, is roughly similar.

Perhaps your conscience troubles you over butchering commercial programs that were once written by authors far more competent than you? Then look at it this way: you paid for those programs, so you can do what you like with them in the privacy of your own home.

Cheat bugs
Never (and how many times has this warning been given in this book?), never work from a valuable program. Always play around with a backup. And even make backups of the backup. If you take a coffee break with a half-finished conversion in the computer, give it a temporary name like PROGB and then SAVE it.

And it is over-optimistic to expect a Mail List to convert into a perfect Accounts Ledger. There are bound to be sections that don't make sense: you just have to steer round those.

Most RENUMBER bugs come from the protocol of commas in the 'new lines, increment, start line, end line' of the command. But once you master that, RENUM is pretty robust. Programs don't suffer by being renumbered. In fact, if you want a quick check on how many lines there are in a program, renumber it in increments of 1, then look at the last line number.

What about GOSUB 1000 and GOTO 560 in renumbered programs? The magic of BASIC renumbers those too.

MERGE goes wrong if the two programs have the same line numbers. The conflicting lines get lost:

Program on disk	Program in memory	Merged program in memory
10 XXXXX	10 YYYYY	10 XXXXX
20 XXXXX	20 YYYYY	20 XXXXX
	30 YYYYY	30 YYYYY
+	40 YYYYY =	40 YYYYY
	50 YYYYY	50 YYYYY
60 XXXXX		60 XXXXX
70 XXXXX		70 XXXXX
80 XXXXX		80 XXXXX

as in lines 10 and 20.

Some computers merge without your knowing. If you have been examining a program in memory and then call up another one from disk or tape with the normal command LOAD, you may find the old program merged with the new. The cure? Type NEW before LOADING.

To sum up

Programs can be tailored by: rewriting the screen printout; merging one program inside another (but first the incoming program has been SAVEd in ASCII); appending one program to the end of another.

Exercises

1. If you have recently graduated from cassette tape into disc, see if you can upgrade a favourite tape program to run on disk. Hint: the big differences are in the PRINT #, INPUT # commands for file handling.

2. No commercial program to play with? Then revamp earlier programs from this book.

3. Machine code programs are far faster than BASIC, hence their use in video games and fast sorts. Find out how to jump out of BASIC, run a machine code routine, and then come back into BASIC.

24

Error messages

In theory, by use of structured programming and by setting out your program in a flowchart beforehand, you should reduce errors. But as an inexperienced programmer, most of your problems come from hitting the wrong keys or from making grammatical (syntax) errors in the language.

If you are already an experienced typist, you will have to cure yourself of hitting the capital letter 'O' instead of zero 0, and not use the small letter 'l' instead of number 1. Unfortunately, plenty of semi-professional programmers like to use the letter I as a variable. You will find yourself copying out a neat little business program from a magazine and having to use a magnifying glass to tell whether the author means variable I or number 1, variable O or zero, variable S or number 5.

After all that, if the program doesn't work, buy the next month's issue of the magazine . . . where they will be apologising for a misprint.

Upper and lower case
Computers traditionally screen the words in capital letters, but it is nice to have the choice of small letters to improve your screen layout.

Ingeniously, the microchip can usually accept 'a' for 'A' and 'b' for 'B' but don't bank on that. Don't bank on it even if your machine only does capital letters. Try this test: ask it what code it is using for, say, the letter A:

?ASC ("A")

Remember that computers think in electricity, not in letters. Depending on your machine, you could get the answer:

65

198

This is a normal decimal number. In hexadecimal, it would be 41. In binary, 01000001. It means that when you type A, it thinks, 'Electricity off, on, off, off, off, off, off, on.' Check the chart in Chapter 18 (Table 18.1) for the character codes given by different computers.

Now repeat the test but hold down the SHIFT key as you type A:

?ASC ("A")

This will look exactly the same on the screen but the SHIFT key works in the opposite way to a typewriter . . . press it and you get small letters . . . so the computer will be looking for its code for 'a':

97

In hexadecimal, 61. On different computers, a different number.

If both tests gave the same number then you are lucky and can forget the chance of this error.

Notice, though, how easy it was to type 'a' instead of 'A'. Already you had your finger on the SHIFT key to do the bracket and you kept it down to do the inverted commas, so it was a natural mistake to keep the SHIFT for the letter A. And you are pushing the chip designer's benevolence a bit too much if you expect the computer to accept a program "FILeNAME/bAS" as being the same as "FILENAME/BAS".

Problems used to arise with the @ symbol in the command PRINT @. Conventional keyboards show the @ with no shift character (not like the 5 which has '%' above it, and the 6 which shifts to '&'); you can press @ and you can press SHIFT–@ and still get the same @ on screen. But, unless the designers have made special provision for this, the two @'s are thought of differently in memory.

Can your computer handle this? Try the test:

10 PRINT@ (50) "IT WORKS"

RUN this then type it again, holding down the SHIFT key for the @. If it works the second time then you are lucky. That's another bug eliminated.

Computers handle syntax errors in their own ways. A few will not accept an incorrect line when you press ENTER. This is good, because otherwise you would incorporate that wrong line into your program and it wouldn't show up until perhaps days later. It is also bad, because these machines rarely tell you what is wrong: they just squat there, refusing the line.

Most computers accept any rubbish and only complain when you try to run the program. Then they display an error code or an error message. Usually this is automatic, but sometimes you have to type HELP.

The code you have to look up in the manual; the messages never have enough memory allocated to them, so they are pretty terse and cryptic. They tell you what's wrong but not what to do about it.

The next four sections show what could be wrong . . .

Possible computer faults

LOST DATA DURING READ
   Computer timing is out. Does tape run at a different speed from disks?
LOST DATA DURING WRITE
   Computer timing is out.
MEMORY FAULT
   Try a memory-testing program.
ATTEMPT TO LOAD ROM
   Clean the contacts.
OVERFLOW
   A number too big to handle.

Possible disk or drive faults

BAD FILE DATA
   Faulty disk, or tape recorder volume setting wrong.
PARITY ERROR DURING HEADER READ
   Can't find the sector header: try another disk. Drive head out of alignment: try another drive.
PARITY ERROR DURING READ
PARITY ERROR DURING WRITE
   Try another disk.
   Try another drive. Then see under 'Bad parity error'.
CRC ERROR
   Means the same as above. The Cyclic Redundancy Check is looking for errors as data go on disk.
BAD PARITY ERROR
   Every bit is correct except one. Look for it with a zap utility program or use the backup disk.
SEEK ERROR DURING WRITE
SEEK ERROR DURING READ
   That track is not on the badly formatted disk. The speed of the drive is too slow.
DATA RECORD NOT FOUND DURING WRITE

DATA RECORD NOT FOUND DURING READ
  Disk is not formatted or you are asking the wrong question.
SECTOR NOT FOUND
  The disk is faulty or not formatted.
NO SYSTEM
  Is there a disk at all in the first drive? Is it blank? Is it formatted
  only; with no 'boot' sector?
DIRECTORY READ ERROR
GAT READ ERROR
HIT READ ERROR
  Damaged disk directory. Use backup disk or repair it with a
  utility program.
DIRECTORY WRITE ERROR
GAT WRITE ERROR
HIT WRITE ERROR
  Damaged disk directory.
  Write-protect tab still on.

Usually your mistake

ATTEMPT TO READ SYSTEM DATA RECORD
  You have asked for a locked or deleted record.
DEVICE NOT AVAILABLE
  The printer etc. not connected. Has the printer run out of paper?
  Is the door of the Disk Drive 2 closed properly?
ILLEGAL FILE NAME
ILLEGAL LOGICAL FILE NUMBER
  Your program has altered the Directory entry code.
  Or an intermittent fault – try the reset button.
FILE NOT IN DIRECTORY
PROGRAM NOT FOUND
  Or spelled wrongly.
ILLEGAL ACCESS TO PROTECTED FILE
FILE ACCESS DENIED
  Give the password or use a utility program to wipe out the
  password.
BAD FILENAME
  Check the manual for the style of naming a file.
DIRECTORY SPACE FULL
DISK SPACE FULL
  Kill unwanted files or use another disk.
ILLEGAL DRIVE NUMBER
  Is the drive door closed properly?

LOAD FILE FORMAT ERROR
  Not a program. Did you call it from DOS when you should have
  gone into BASIC first, or vice versa?
SYNTAX ERROR
  Check spaces, commas, brackets, spelling.
WHAT?
  A syntax error.
TYPE MISMATCH
  You forgot the inverted commas round a string or tried to call it by
  a numeric variable (A instead of A$).
CAN'T CONTINUE
  You commanded CONT when the program had met an END.

Programming mistakes

FILE HAS NOT BEEN OPENED
  You tried to read or write to a file before the command "OPEN".
DIRECT STATEMENT IN FILE
  The program you are trying to save has a line without a number.
  Or a line too long for BASIC. Ignore this: type LIST . . . maybe it
  has loaded.
FIELD OVERFLOW
  More than 255 (check with manual) characters allocated to a
  buffer.
BAD FILE MODE
  Was it opened for Input when you tried to Output to it? Or vice
  versa?
NEXT WITHOUT FOR
RETURN WITHOUT GOSUB
RESUME WITHOUT ERROR
  The program has met a NEXT, RETURN or RESUME before it met
  the matching FOR, GOSUB or ON ERROR GOTO. Have you
  jumped into a loop?
OUT OF DATA
  Not enough data to READ or INPUT #.
ILLEGAL FUNCTION CALL
/ 0
  You tried to divide by zero, get the square root of a negative
  number, or called a machine code routine without POKeing the
  entry point.
UNDEFINED LINE
  You tried to GOTO a line that wasn't there. Was it deleted when
  you deleted the REM statements? Only a few computers will go to
  the nearest line. For the time being, put in the missing line as a
  REMark; with luck the program will now run.

EOF ENCOUNTERED
   End of file encountered. Use this deliberately to find the end of
   sequential files.
REDIMENSIONED ARRAY
   You used, say, DIM A(20) twice.
OUT OF STRING SPACE
   Go back and increase the CLEAR 200 statement.
MISSING OPERAND
   You forgot the + − * or /
HOW ?
   A missing operand.
STRING TOO LONG
   Your computer limits the length of strings to perhaps a maximum
   of 255 characters.
SUBSCRIPT OUT OF RANGE
   You DIMensioned A(20), say, but asked for A(21).
   Or didn't DIM at all.
OUT OF MEMORY
   Is there a massive A$(200,500) array?
RESERVED WORD
   TO, OR, FN, ON being used as variables. FIELD 1, 15ASC$
   looks like ASC and FORND=PUTO3 looks like RaNDom and
   PUT.

Error codes

There is no excuse, now that memories are growing bigger, yet
computers are still designed to throw up unintelligible <ERRCODE
63F> style messages without saying in plain English what they
mean.
   Try to avoid this in your programs. Good BASICs have an ON
ERROR GOTO routine. You put this at the beginning of your
program before any errors have occurred, not before a CLEAR 2000
line though, or it will be wiped out:

   10 ON ERROR GOTO 5000

where, from line 5000 there will be a subroutine that depends on
your dialect of BASIC.
   Some have ERL, pronounced 'error line' which lists the line
where the error was:

   5000 IF ERL 350 THEN PRINT "YOU CAN'T DIVIDE BY ZERO"

because in line 350 there was a division sum.

5010 IF ERL 470 THEN PRINT "DO A NUMBER PLEASE, NOT A WORD"

because in line 470 it said INPUT "AGE "; AG and somebody typed "Twenty" instead of 20.

   5020 RESUME

is the way to get back to the program.

Debugging

If you have the self-discipline to structure your programs with flowcharts, fine. If you type the lines straight on to the keyboard, that works too because BASIC is so accommodating. You will be too ashamed to show anybody your scruffy programs, but they should run. The time you have to use analysis is when they don't run.

Syntax errors
These are the most common, so check spellings and punctuation. Double check the brackets in expressions like:

   LEFT$(A$(3),(LEN(A$(3))−N))

Columns of printed figures all over the place indicate that you have a semicolon or comma wrong. Some BASICs put an invisible line of blanks after INPUT and PRINT@ statements: a neat diagram on the screen could be broken by an INPUT that insists on going in the wrong place. Tame this by putting a semicolon at the end of the line.

   Commas are essential in DATA lines but one at the end can disrupt the program:

   100 DATA 2, 3, 5.6, 78.99, 4   is right.
   100 DATA 2, 3, 5.6, 78.99, 4,   is wrong.

   You will have made sure that inverted commas are correctly closed, but can your computer handle double inverted commas? Test it with:

   10 PRINT "HE SAID, "HELLO." TO ME."

Which is a perfectly normal statement in English, but does your BASIC print it or does it only give:

   HE SAID,

If you must have quotation marks inside inverted commas there are two ways, depending upon your computer:

```
10 PRINT "HE SAID, " " "HELLO." " " TO ME."
```

where the "HELLO." is surrounded by inverted commas.

```
10 PRINT "HE SAID, ";"""";"HELLO.";"""";" TO ME."
```

where the inverted commas are surrounded by inverted commas.

And a third, reliable, way: after looking up what your computer's code is for inverted commas, use it in a CHR$( ) statement:

```
10 PRINT "HE SAID, "; CHR$(34); "HELLO."; CHR$(34) "TO ME."
```


Errors of logic

Consider this attempt to get a daily average:

```
10 INPUT T              (T is the Takings)
20 PRINT AVERAGE = T/D  (D is the Day)
```

Result?

```
'Division by zero' error
```

Why?

First, you forgot the inverted commas round "AVERAGE =" and the computer read just the first two letters AV, looked them up in its list of variables, didn't find any value so it gave AV the value of 0. That's easily fixed. But, more important, the variable D hasn't got a value. Maybe you intended it to be Day 1 but, to the computer, a variable without a value gets called 0. And dividing T by 0 gives an answer of infinity.

So you fix this by:

```
5 D = 1
```

which works.

Now you want the days to increase: 30 D = D + 1. And you want to repeat the calculation: 40 GOTO 5. The program looks like this:

```
5 D = 1
10 INPUT T
20 PRINT "AVERAGE = " T/D
30 D = D + 1
40 GOTO 5
```

But the results are ridiculous. No matter how many days go by, the Average always equals the Takings. Why?

You are increasing D every time the computer runs through line 30 . . . but you are turning D back to 1 every time it loops back to line 5.

The cure in this example is to change line 40 to GOTO 10. In your own programs, BREAK at the right spot and ask the computer what it has in mind for the variables. In this one you would ask:

? D, T

Expect problems if you alter loop variables. Look again at page 66 where there was a schedule, broken down into weeks. You designed a 'FOR 1 TO 30' loop because there are 30 days in the month. Then you added, 'After the 7th weekday, start again at Day 1' . . . and hit a bug:

```
10 FOR D = 1 TO 30
20 IF D = 8 THEN D = 1
30 PRINT "THE DAY IS " D
40 NEXT D
```

Normally the computer would have looped thirty times. But, with that line 20, every time D reached 7 it went back to 1 again. It never reached 30. It would never stop.

Remember the correction on page 67:

```
10 FOR D = 1 TO 30
15 Z = Z + 1
20 IF Z = 8 THEN Z = 1
30 PRINT "THE DAY IS " Z
40 NEXT D
```

Any letter could be used as that seven-day-counting variable, so long as you left the "D" unhindered to get on with its 1 TO 30 loop.

And suppose you jumped into that loop from somewhere else in the program. Suppose you came in at Line 15. The computer would reach Line 40, wanting the NEXT D, and there wouldn't be a D.

Checksums

If you work in a laboratory typing in code numbers or in a stores doing part numbers, you are bound to make mistakes with meaningless groups like 229000394499. How can the computer help?

It could look at it as a string and check the length:

```
IF LEN(N$) < 12 THEN PRINT "YOU'VE MISSED A NUMBER OUT"
IF LEN(N$) > 12 THEN PRINT "THAT'S TOO LONG"
```

Or, strangely enough, it could improve that group by making it longer. It could add up all the components $2+2+9+000+3+9+4+4+9+9$, which comes to 51, and put that 51 at the end. That's called a checksum.

Of course, a code with the same number of 2s, 9s, 3s and 4s yet in a different order would still add up to 51. But this simple checksum would reduce errors.

To make a unique checksum you could multiply each number by its position in the group:

2*1 + 2*2 + 9*3 + 0*4 + 0*5 + 0*6 + 3*7 + 9*8, and so on.

This would be complicated for a human to work out and it takes a lot of program lines, but it's no bother for a microchip.

TRACE ON–TRACE OFF
Usually abbreviated to TRON and TROFF . . . check your manual.

These commands are written outside the program, without a line number. With your program stopped, you type beside the READY prompt:

TRON

then hit ENTER.

Nothing happens until you RUN the program, and then the number of the line that's working flashes on screen. It can be confusing because it happens fast. And with a line that is repeating itself, such as:

250 Y\$ = INKEY\$: IF Y\$ = " " THEN 250

the screen will fill with 250/250/250/250/250/250/ until you hit the reply key.

TRON, meaning TRace ON (stop it by typing TROFF meaning TRace OFF), can help you follow the path the computer is taking through your program. You see a screen readout of 400/410/420/6000 (ah, that's where it jumps to the subroutine) 6010/6020/6030/430 (now it has RETURNed) 440/450/490 (Hey! Why has it jumped 460? That could be the bug.)

Even bugs have bugs
A message OUT OF STRING SPACE IN 460 doesn't mean that the error was in line 460. It was way back in line 10 when you didn't CLEAR enough string space. Similarly, RETURN WITHOUT GOSUB IN 460 or NEXT WITHOUT FOR IN 460 mean that the fault is earlier than line 460.

Tough problems to debug happen when you have a minutely different version of BASIC, written for the same computer but in a different disk operating system. There is nothing at all wrong with the program, it is just that the DOS doesn't understand it.

Scores of computers operate with CP/M (Control Program/Microcomputer) and there are hundreds of software houses writing programs in CP/M BASICs. In theory the programs should be interchangeable yet occasionally they baulk at a certain task. Typical are the BAD FILE MODE and BAD FILE NUMBER messages in the OPEN 1, "FILENAME.DAT", 90 sort of line. The program is perfectly correct but it was written for a computer that insisted that the buffers — those areas in memory where files are stored before they are PUT on disk — were (or were not) told how big the records were going to be. And the program is now being run on a machine that does not (or does) want the size of file records declared.

To sum up

Expect people to hit the wrong keys, to give the wrong answers and to be baffled by instructions. So have error-trapping routines after every INPUT:

> IF X > 100 OR X < 10 THEN PRINT "ARE YOU SURE"
> IF A$ < > "YES" OR A$ < > "NO" THEN PRINT "DO THAT AGAIN"

Have a surplus of REMark lines to remind you what the variables mean, what the subroutine is doing.

Work in modules, subroutines, that can be isolated and separately debugged.

Have your Aunt Ermintrude, somebody who is anti-computer, test your program.

Exercises

1. Find and use your machine's equivalent to TRON.

2. List your machine's Error Codes and translate them into English.

3. Here is the world's worst program. Your job is to debug it.

```
10 DIM A(20)
20 CLEAR 2000
30 FOR I = 20 TO I STEP -1
40 FOR 0 = 1 TO 5
50 0 = A(I)
60 N + 1 = N
70 IF INT(A(I)+1)/2) =  3 THEN PRINT "OK SO  FAR" ELSE  100:
GOTO 90
80 PRIMT "BUG"
90 PRINT GOOD
100 NEXTI
110 NEXTO
120 GOTO 90
130 IF N=100 ORN=101 THEN PRINT "STILL GOOD ELSE PRINT BUG"
140 DIM A$(5), DIM A(5)
150 FOR FN = 1 TO 5
160 FOR A(B) = 1 TO 5
170 PRINT "CONGRATUALTIONS":
180 NEXT A(B)
190 NEXT FN
200 GOTO 145
```

25

The jargon

Algorithm In the junior school, you called it a 'sum'.

Alphanumeric Both letters and numbers, on a keyboard or in a string.

Array Instead of school algebra with simple variables like A and B, imagine arrays to be like racks of storage boxes where A(3,2) is the variable in the third box on the second shelf.

ASCII American Standard Code for Information Interchange. Letters, numbers and symbols like > $ * & but no £ sign. Watch out that the printer you buy can handle the £.

Assembly language A language close to the machine code used by computers.

Backup A copy.

Bar code Lines printed on packets in supermarkets, translated by bar code readers into the name of the goods.

BASIC The most common language for microcomputers. It has words like IF, GO TO, ELSE, RUN. Even commas and colons have exact meanings.

Baud rate The speed at which data is transferred from, say, a tape recorder, into the computer. The faster the better.

Bells and whistles Extra features. Example: 'Among its bells and whistles, this program sorts stock into numeric order and features a reorder flag.'

Benchmark A speed test for computers.

Binary arithmetic We work in decimal because we have ten fingers. Computers work in twos because there are two conditions of electricity – on or off. For example, 6 is 110 binary and 23 is 10111.

Bit A bit of information inside the circuits, asking, 'Is the electricity on or off?'

Buffer An area in memory where data is stored for a while. Also used in: 'I keep money in this old tin as a buffer between paydays.'

Bug A fault.

Bus An electrical connector.

Byte Eight 'bits' make the letters in the ASCII code. 'Off-on-off-off-off-off-off-on' could represent A. And that is a byte. Microcomputers advertised as '4K' have a 4 kilobyte memory and can hold about 4,000 characters, which is about 500 words.

Cassette recorder Type a program to handle, say, price calculations, and you can save it for future use by connecting the computer to the microphone socket of an ordinary cassette recorder. Later you play it back through the earphone socket. The good point is that this is really cheap storage. The bad is it is very slow.

Checksum With part numbers like 2236277, a typist could make a mistake. So add them together and include the sum 29 as a check.

Clobber When a program not only fails but ruins the disk as well.

COBOL Common Business Oriented Language.

cps Characters per second: how fast a printer works. Golfball typewriters work at the speed of a champion typist: 15 characters per second, which is about 110 words per minute . . . and that is slow. Other types of printer can do 120 cps and more.

CP/M Control Program/Microcomputer. A standardised disk operating system. Good point: it brings standardisation so that programs can be swapped from one make of machine to another. Bad point: there are DOSs with better facilities.

CPU Central Processing Unit – the microchip.

Crash When a program fails.

Daisywheel printer An expensive, computer-controlled, typewriter. Its printhead is a little wheel with letters round the edge like the petals of a daisy. It prints beautiful business letters.

Data Information. It could be 'T. Smith, 23 High Street' or £33.45 or $4.98. The computer can store it, recall it, perform arithmetic on it, select bits of it. It could find all customers living in High Street, it could sort stock into first-in-first-out order. But first you have the long chore of typing all that data in.

Deadly embrace When a computer wants to signal to its printer but is waiting for a 'Ready' signal from the printer. At the same time, the printer is waiting to hear from the computer before it sends its signal. They are 'locked in deadly embrace' and everything comes to a halt.

Debugging Looking for faults. Have you typed letter O instead of zero 0? I instead of 1? Tried to divide by zero? Missed out a comma? Asked for the square root of a negative number?

Dedicated microprocessor Dedicated to only one job, like the microchips in pocket calculators, automatic cameras and diagnostic equipment. You can't ask it to do anything else as you can with a computer.

Dialects Different computers speak slightly different dialects of BASIC. You need to rewrite IBM programs to suit, say, an ITT or Sinclair QL.

Disks For recording data. They record and recall data faster than magnetic tape. This speed is essential for business use. Their weakness is that the data can be corrupted by nearby magnetic fields from vacuum-cleaner motors, videos and electric typewriters.

Dollar Words are called 'strings' and the symbol is the $ sign. Computniks may pronounce Z$ = "FRED" as 'Z Dollar becomes FRED'.

Don't care sign Used when you are not sure of the full name. FILE***E.COM will find the program FILENAME.COM in CP/M and *.BAS will find every file ending in .BAS

DOS Disk Operating System. Pronounced 'doss'. You need additional machinery to spin the disks round, usually with its own power supply, extra memory to control this and a program to tell the computer what to do. DOS sometimes refers to the whole system, sometimes to just the program.

Dot matrix A printer that shapes letters with a row of needles hammered against the paper. A 5×7 matrix gives dotty letters; a 9×7 matrix is almost of letter quality.

Edit Cheap computers perform the simple tasks equally well. It is in editing that the best ones show up. They should be able to find an error and tell you the cause, and you should be able to insert or delete sections of a program.

Electronic office Full of VDUs, shared disks, and printers that churn out miles of paper.

EPROM Erasable Programmable Read Only Memory. A microchip that you can program.

Epsilon The mathematical notation for extremely small. So computniks say things like: 'You could buy this for epsilon cost.'

Expansion interface To expand your computer system by adding extra disk drives or printers can't be done by just plugging in. You need to buy an expansion interface to translate the signals from the computer into electrical impulses that the extra equipment understands.

Exponent The power to which a number is raised. For example, 2 × 2 × 2 (two cubed) is 2^3, which is often shown on screen as 2 ↑ 3. The exponent is 3.

Expression An algebraic formula like A + B or P/SIN(R−1).

Extension The (usually) three letters after a filename to say what it is about. For example, /DAT for data in "STOCKFIL/DAT" or .BAS for BASIC in "ADDLIST.BAS". Some extensions like /CMD for 'command file' and .COM in CP/M don't need to be typed; the computer assumes they are there.

File 67 SMITH 33 Hours £66.00
   68 SOUTH 21 Hours £31.50.
Subdivisions like 21 Hours and £66.00 are FIELDS, the lines are RECORDS, and it is all part of a FILE titled "Payroll".

Filename Examples are: "WOMEN26Y/FEB.ABRACAD", which used the full eight letters, plus three letters for the extension and a password; down to "X" which also works. Numbers are allowed in the middle but not at the beginning.

Filter The power spike as a 'fridge or compressor turns off can travel through the mains and wipe out a day's work on the computer. So buy a mains filter (mains suppressor), which contains capacitors to absorb power surges.

Flag A number added to a field, file or record to indicate that it has ended and that the computer can go on to the next job.

Flavour Variety. 'This accounts program comes in various flavours.' The simple, no-frills program is 'vanilla flavour'.

Floppy disks Look like the floppy records given away in sales promotions. They cost from £1.50 each and come in protective sleeves. You slip them into the disk drive and the computer can read programs off their magnetic surface (see **soft sectored** and **hard sectored**).

FORTRAN A science computer language. In some ways it is faster than BASIC.

Freak A term of awe. An expert will admit that 'he knows a bit about computers' but when he too is baffled, he goes to a computer freak . . . an expert among experts.

FRED A test string keyed in to show how a program works. Notice how FRED came into the 'Dollars' example earlier. He is so popular because the letters F-R-E-D are next to one another on the keyboard.

Games Over half the programs advertised are games. There are Adventure games like fairy stories and Arcade games where you shoot down aliens. Pity that such ingenuity hasn't gone into creating cheap business programs.

Garbage collection When running a program with scores of variables, the computer gets indigestion and disappears inside itself. It stops responding to the keyboard and the program halts while it has a clean-out of stale variables.

GIGO Garbage In = Garbage Out. For instance, a program stating:

```
TI = JI+FI+MI
PRINT TI
```

(with JI, FI and MI being Jan, Feb and March invoices) might print out customers' invoices for three months. But suppose they didn't buy anything? Then, unless you filtered out garbage, they would receive invoices for £0,000.00

Golfball Print heads of many electric typewriters look like golfballs with all the letters round them. Conventional typewriters, though, can't be computer controlled: they haven't the correct solenoids in them. You need something like an IBM 735. Advantages of golfballs are that they type neatly and can be bought secondhand. Disadvantages: they are slower and noisier than other printers.

Graphics Pictures on the screen are considered by shops as a big selling point. They may be fine for hobbyists playing games, but don't let them over-influence your decision, even if you want to produce a lot of graphs.

Halt and catch fire Program failure. As in: 'If you input figures to 18 places, it will halt and catch fire.'

Handshake The electrical signals between computer and, say, the printer, to get them synchronised so they can talk seriously.

Hangup Set a computer an impossible task (to print when the printer isn't switched on; to find data that isn't there; to load a faulty tape . . .) and it will keep on trying until the world runs out of electricity. Nor can you break in to tell it to give up, short of switching right off. That is a hangup.

Hard copy See **printout**.

Hard disks Storage capable of recording at least 10 megabytes of data. Faster than floppy disks. (See **Winchester**.)

Hard sectored Floppy disks where the sectors are marked off by holes. (See the more popular **soft sectored**.)

Hardware The machinery. The cliché is, 'anything you can kick.' A computer does not exist on its own, it needs hardware: a mains transformer, video screen, disc drives. (See **software**.)

Hash sign # Used to distinguish INPUT # to disk against INPUT from the keyboard. Often translates into the £ sign when fed to a printer. Used as a pattern as in PRINT USING ###.##. Used as a 'don't care sign' when J##N will find JOAN or JEAN in a list.

IEEE (Pronounced 'eye triple ee') One of the standards in the industry for, among other things, the socket at the back of the Commodore. Since most other makes use a different standard, the RS232, there have to be expensive adaptors to fit other manufacturers' gear to the early Commodores.

Ink jet A fast, quiet printer where jets of ink are squirted at the paper instead of pins being hammered through ribbon, as with a dot matrix printer.

Input Words and numbers put into computers.

Integer A whole number. No decimal point.

Intelligent terminal Some keyboards have all their work done by a main computer in another room or another building. These have only enough brain to send messages. Intelligent terminals, while nowhere near as smart as the big computer, have enough memory to handle the video and do a few calculations on their own.

Interface A connector. But connecting, say, a golfball printer can't be done with a simple wire. The difference between typing 'a' and 'b' is in the distance the golfball rotates. So a £150 interface keeps the next computer signal waiting until the 'b' is printed. Interface is also used as a verb, as in: 'We must interface with our new neighbours.'

Interrupt A program instruction to do something else. Also used in: 'My wife was trying to nag me with a low-priority interrupt about cutting the grass.'

I/O Input/Output. Terminals can take in data, also put it out. But most printers have no hope of outputting messages back to the computer. Any that can will boast 'I/O' in its advertising.

Justify The right-hand side of the rows of print in this book is 'right justified' (made straight) by differing spaces between the words. Computers can print business correspondence just as neatly. Check that you buy one capable of justifying numbers round the decimal point, or the money columns of your accounts will be untidy.

Kilobyte One thousand and twenty-four bytes of memory. Computers are priced by memory . . . 4K, 16K, 32K, 64K. Think of 1K as about 1,000 letters or numbers. Memory for practical business use must be at least 48K. Check too that this is available for programs and that half of it isn't lost operating the BASIC language or disc drives. Kilobyte is also used in job adverts: 'Systems analyst wanted. 15K and car.'

LED (Pronounced 'el-ee-dee'.) Light-emitting diode. The little light that shines when something is switched on.

Letter quality A printer that turns out work as neat as that from a typewriter.

Light pen A cheap little gadget that reads from, or appears to write on, the video screen.

LIST A BASIC and DOS command, meaning 'show all the program'.

Loop A repeated performance. Typical is the FOR–TO loop . . . FOR A= 1 TO 12: B= 7: PRINT A "TIMES SEVEN IS " A*B: NEXT A . . . will print the seven times table.

Lower case Small letters. Upper case is capital letters. Cheap computers transmit capital letters to their video screens, yet somewhere in their circuits are lower case letters. It just needs a bit of soldering to bring them out. Check too, if you buy a cheap printer, that it can handle lower case.

Machine language BASIC looks like English, which is easy for you to understand. But experts program in machine language (it looks like lists of numbers) closer to the code the machine uses. This saves microseconds, so speeding up long programs.

Magic A process too complex to explain to unintelligent laymen. 'Then comes a bit of magic to avoid posting zero invoices.'

Matrix See **array**.

Matrix printer Fires inked needles at paper to produce those characteristic, dotty numbers on computerised invoices. At more than 80 characters per second, dot matrix printers are fast and quiet. Check that the one you buy can do the £ sign.

Megabyte A million bytes. Beware a salesman who is talking in Mega*bits*. These are eight times smaller.

Memory Measured in K (kilobytes), which is about 1,000 characters. The bigger the K, the more you pay. Yet there are tricks to conserve memory: 'IF A = 9 THEN GO TO LINE 200' uses 28 bytes because even the spaces use one byte of memory. So cut this to 'IFA=9GOTO200'.

Menu The list of options. A program that asks: 'Do you want (1) to see the accounts (2) to add an item (3) to delete an item (4) to print ?' is said to be 'menu-driven' and is pleasant to use.

Microcomputers Cost between £30 and £2,000 and have memories up to 64K. Buy them as casually as cameras and expect about the same after-sales service. Mainframe computers stand as big as a deep-freeze and for your money you get staff training and tailored programs. Minicomputers are in between. They cost around £10,000.

Mode The current operating state of the computer. But it comes into conversation as: 'Sorry, I wasn't in input mode,' meaning 'I wasn't listening to what you were saying.' Or 'The VDU is in bananas mode,' meaning that weird pictures are flashing across the screen.

Modem With the telephone handset resting in a modem, your computer can talk to another computer. Telephone authorities are relaxing restrictions on these so expect more home to office link-ups in future.

Modulator Some micros connect to your TV, but not directly; the signal has to go through a £15 modulator first.

Module Part of a program that can almost run on its own. A subroutine that can be used in other programs, e.g. a Date module, a Filing module.

Modulo The arithmetic term for a remainder. For example, $27 \div 4 = 6$ remainder 3 can be stated as '27 modulo $4 = 3$', so computniks use it to mean 'except for' as in: 'The printer works fine now, modulo the upper case bug.'

Monitor TV pictures are not really sharp. Better to buy a purpose-built monitor (video–VDU) that looks like a TV without all the knobs.

Mumble (See **magic**) 'I put in this mumblage to white-out the screen.'

N A numeric variable, as used in 'I've told you for the Nth time, I don't take sugar.'

Nibble Four bits. Half a byte. Geddit?

Number crunching The ability to do arithmetic. And computers are neither as fast nor as accurate as calculators. Before buying, try $0.99 - 0.98$ to see if it comes out correctly as 0.01 or if it shows 0.0099999997.

Numeric pad Computers have typewriter-like keyboards with numbers on the top line. This doesn't make for fast typing if most of your work involves numbers. So a numeric pad is a small, separate keyboard of numbers in a rectangle, as on a calculator.

Output port The multi-pin socket at the back where signals leave to control other machines.

Parallel Computers think of characters not as A, B or C but in a code carrying eight bits of information. From a parallel port runs a ribbon of at least eight wires with the electricity in them, say, off-on-off-off-off-off-on-on. This would be 67, in binary arithmetic 01000011. In computer code it could signal a printer to type the letter C. The eight signals would travel along the wires, in parallel, simultaneously (see **serial**).

Pascal A computer language that is elegant to use but difficult to master.

Patch An improvement to a commercial program by adding extra facilities, usually in machine code.

PC Personal Computer. Used by mainframe manufacturers like Texas Instruments and IBM to indicate their smallest models.

PEEK A BASIC command to look inside the memory.

Peripherals Machines connected to the computer; e.g. printers, disk drives.

Phase of the moon When equipment sometimes works, sometimes doesn't. 'The disk drive is in phase of the moon mode.'

Pin addressable Dot matrix printers don't need to have fixed letters. It is possible to control every one of their nine printhead pins and so form any shape you want. Reproduction of photographs is possible even.

Pixel One of the dots of light on the screen that make up the letters.

POKE A BASIC command to change something in the memory.

Port A multi-pin socket.

Prestel British Telecom's system to link your TV through the telephone to their mainframe computer. The general name for this is Viewdata, while the TV companies call their systems Teletext. The BBC's service is called Ceefax and the IBA's is Oracle.

Printer The varieties, most expensive first, are: ink jet, daisywheel, golfball, dot matrix and thermal printer. Paper can be fed through by friction, as in an office typewriter, or be traction-fed by having sprocket holes along the edges. Before buying, check that the printer is compatible with your system, that it will stand up to hours of use at top speed, that paper costs are reasonable. Expect additional costs to couple it to your computer.

Printout Sometimes called 'hard copy'. The paperwork typed out by a printer.

Processor The computer or its silicon chip. A **word processor** is a different thing; see later.

Program (Note the spelling.) Instructions telling the computer to do something. You can write your own and/or you can buy programs. Because different makes of computers speak different dialects, a program written for one is unlikely to work with another. So before buying a computer compare the quantity and quality of the programs available for it.

Protocol The correct computer signals to operate a machine.

PSU Power Supply Unit. A transformer to make mains voltage low enough and stable enough for the computer. Adverts for cut-price microcomputers conveniently forget to list the extra £15 for the PSU.

Qwerty The first letters of typewriter keyboards. Not the most efficient layout, but typists have got used to it.

RAM Random Access Memory. Advertised as 64K or whatever. This is memory you can use. Buy as much as you can afford.

Random access See **serial access**.

Randomise BASIC has a RND command but this gives 'pseudo-random' numbers because they are based on the same beginning. The command RANDOMISE, or sometimes RANDOM, gives them another start. It is called 're-seeding the random generator' and is used in science or gambling where really random numbers are needed.

Real-time clock Computers contain internal, oscillating, crystal clocks to regulate the milliseconds of their calculations. It is considered a big selling point if hours and minutes can be displayed in real time, on the screen. Yet a £5 wrist watch is more efficient.

Reboot Switch on and the screen shows the manufacturer's name on screen. Work all day and fill screen after screen with data. Then, in another room, perhaps the fridge switches off, a spike of back voltage travels through the mains and the screen blips back to the maker's name. All your day's work is lost. That is a reboot.

ROM Read Only Memory. Routines on how to understand languages, knowing how to multiply, etc. are kept in ROM. If computers were people, RAM would be the brain and able to think; ROM would be instinctive reactions controlling breathing and digestion. Type a command and the microchip tells ROM that you want something. ROM tells the chip to look in RAM to see what you want. The chip looks and sees, perhaps that you want to add $2 + 2$. ROM tells the chip how to do it. Afterwards ROM tells the chip to return to RAM to see how you want the answer. RAM remembers you want it on video. ROM tells the chip how to display the answer. Then it tells the chip to look at the keyboard in case you want anything else.

Routine A part of a program that does a specific job (see **module** and **subroutine**).

RS232 The most widely used standard for plugs and sockets connecting things to computers. The '20mA current loop' is smaller but slower. The IEEE interface does the same job but is designed differently.

Sacred Part of a program dedicated to one job. 'This subroutine is sacred to the address strings.'

Scratchpad A spare disk or an area in memory, used temporarily to do rough calculations.

Serial A letter or number is represented by a code of eight bits of information (see **Parallel**). These can be in parallel, simultaneously down eight wires, or one at a time, in series, down one wire. Serial interfaces are obviously slower but they are cheaper.

Serial access How you find data stored in sequence on a cassette tape; where you have to run through all the earlier stuff before you reach the section you need. Discs go straight to it: that's called random access, though it isn't really random.

Shugart A brand name of a disk drive.

Silicon (With no 'e' at the end.) The element on which the circuitry of the microchip is etched. Silicon Valley is slang for the area between Palo Alto and Sunnyvale or San José, California, where many of the electronic firms live. Silicone Valley? That's Hollywood.

Soft sectored Floppy disks whose different sectors are invisibly distinguished by magnetic marks. The majority of floppies are like this (see **hard sectored**).

Software The programs. Software houses are firms that sell programs. For £10 there are programs to add up your bank account. For £200 there is software to do your annual accounts and payroll, provided you adapt your business methods to fit them. Expect to pay at least £1,000 for a programmer to visit you and write software specially tailored to your own firm.

Sort A program for sorting, say a list of names, into alphabeticat order.

Spreadsheet A program for doing calculations. It sets up an array of columns so big that your video screen seems to be a window on to a three metre square sheet of paper. As you alter one number, the whole column alters in sympathy. Ideal for business projections (see **Visicalc** and **what-if calculations**).

Stack How variables are imagined to be arranged in memory. The next variable comes off the top of the stack.

String A string of letters like JOHN or HIGH STREET. The symbol is $. It can include numbers, as in A$= "23 HIGH ST" and these can be manipulated a little bit. JOHN comes before MARTIN alphabetically, but the square root of 23 HIGH ST is impossible.

Stringy floppy A machine, smaller than cassette recorders, that uses continuous-loop magnetic tape. Getting data off stringies is almost as fast as discs. If they prove reliable they can be an economic way of storing memory.

Subroutine Part of a program that can be reached frequently from other parts of the program (see **module**).

Swell foop Simultaneously. 'It sorts the variables and selects anomalies in one swell foop.'

System All your equipment. Not only the hardware of video screen and disk drives but also the software to operate it. A systems analyst is someone who advises you what to buy and, if he is honest, might well say that you don't need a computer at all.

T A variable often used to indicate time. 'I don't know yet when the booze-up will start but we'll meet outside the pub at T minus 5 minutes.'

Tandy One of America's leading micro manufacturers. Owner of the international chain of Radio Shack stores. The Z80 chip and RS232 interface in the early TRS-80 computers made them easy to expand. There are plenty of programs for Tandy machines. Disadvantages: no different from any other big company.

Terminal A keyboard (for instance, a self-service cash dispenser) wired to a main computer.

Thermal printers Cheap, quiet printers using heat-sensitive paper. However, the paper is expensive and only comes in narrow widths.

Time sharing Renting program time on somebody else's mainframe computer. Or two (or more) terminals that use a central computer's facilities (including files) apparently simultaneously.

Turnkey Pseudo-scientific jargon that salesmen use to describe a system so complete that you just turn the key (that is, plug it in) and it runs.

Uncle Clive Sir Clive Sinclair, brilliant inventor of very cheap computers.

User friendly A system designed to be idiot-proof. It rarely is.

User group A club for fans of one make of computer. Join, and you learn tricks that the manufacturer's manual never dreamed of.

Utilities Programs that help repair other programs. They let you examine the contents of memory, copy other programs, renumber lines, format disks, etc.

Variable In school algebra, if $B + 3 = 9$ then $B = 6$. If $B - 10 = 15$ then $B = 25$. The B varies in different sums. This is a numeric variable. Computers also handle string variables – words. $B\$ =$ "EMPLOYEES" for instance. There is no connection between the variables B (which must be a number) or B(2) or BZ (entirely different numbers) or B$ or BZ$ (which are usually words).

VDU Visual Display Unit – Video. In comparing costs, remember that the VDU is included in the price of some micros but is extra for others.

Visicalc Brand name of the best value-for-money (at about £95) business planning program (see **spreadsheet**).

Volatile memory When switched off, all memory in RAM is lost (see **RAM**). RAM is volatile. Yet ROM is always there. So is some memory in pocket calculators. Modern computers possess more permanent memories.

What-if calculations Computing is so fast that you can project the economics of a proposal by setting up an arithmetical model and then asking: 'What if we increased production by 10%?'

Wild card A symbol, usually *, used when you don't know how to spell a name. For example, FI??NAM* or FI* will find "FILENAME" in CP/M.

Winchester A brand name of a hard disk drive.

Word processor A memory typewriter. This can edit words, shift chunks of text about and transform your correspondence. It cannot compute. Yet computers can be programmed into word processors.

Zap To cure a program fault by altering the main memory or the disk itself. Also used in: 'I zapped my spark plugs and now the car runs OK.'

Zedabetical In reverse order to alphabetical.

Z80 A popular microchip. Now outdated by chips with twice the ability. The Z80 handles eight bits of information at once, whereas machines like the IBM PC can handle 16 bits, and the Sinclair QL has a 32-bit microchip.

26

Different dialects

There is an official, standard BASIC, and the commercially popular Microsoft BASIC is very close to it. So why doesn't everybody use it?

Some computers are too small to hold all the words. The first Sinclair ZX-80 made that into an advertising asset by boasting that it did 'integer arithmetic' and everybody said 'Wow! Integer Arithmetic!' What it really meant was that it wasn't smart enough to do decimals.

So small computers only have room for single-letter variables, they miss out sines and cosines, string manipulation, disk operation and, while they can perform most operations, you have to use BASIC's kindliness and go a long way around.

Modern computers are way ahead of standard BASIC. They offer facilities, and the new words to go with them, that the inventors of BASIC never dreamed of. There are now words like SPOOL (do two things at once), DEVICE (list the machines attached to the computer), VERIFY (double-check a program after saving), BUILD (decide your own format for disks), &H (to convert decimal numbers into hexadecimal) and they give fast sorting routines.

Then there are still manufacturers who perversely choose new words for standard BASIC commands. They have LN instead of LOG for Logarithm, and you never know whether their PRINT means print to the video screen, print to a disk or print on paper.

This book mostly uses the Microsoft version. It breaks away from the norm, mainly with ENTER instead of RETURN for the key you press at the end of every line. RETURN is a relic from typewriter carriage returns (some computers even have a CR key) and it could be confused with the BASIC word RETURN which follows GOSUB. Missing from this book is the MAT series of commands. Arrays are used instead, since they are more common in microcomputers. But it would be nice to have a way of zeroing all variables that is as quick as the traditional MAT ZERO.

Some words like DIR, FORMAT, FREE and MEM should not be thought of as being BASIC: if you want to be pedantic, they are disk operating system commands. But as far as a user is concerned, you type them on the keyboard and they work . . . so it doesn't matter what language they are in.

Some of the words, like KILL, SAVE and LOAD, are in both DOS and BASIC, but there are often minor though essential differences. For instance, KILL"FILENAME", with inverted commas and no space between the words, might erase a file in BASIC yet the same command in DOS might be KILL FILENAME, with no inverted commas but a space. Mix the two up and the worst that could happen would be that the computer would refuse to obey. You can't do any damage: it just puzzles you for a while because you can't see where you have gone wrong.

The hard parts of converting a BASIC program from one dialect to another come when you are trying to control the machinery of the computer. PEEK and POKE, which dig into numbered sections of memory, just cannot work with a different-style memory. The disk drive operating commands, SAVE, LOAD, PUT, GET, PRINT #, INPUT #, differ a lot. And although PRINT is the usual command for putting words on the screen, there is no universal command for putting pictures on screen – not while computers have such varied graphics capabilities.

You won't have the worry of transferring programs. Your only problem is in getting the bastard BASIC used in this book to work on your own computer. It should work but there are bound to be frustrating minor differences.

You will just have to follow the Law of Engineering: 'If all else fails, read the instruction manual.'

DOS and BASIC differences

	Alternatives	Similar look but different meaning	Computers	Page reference
ABS(A)			Most	
The absolute (without minus sign) value of a number				
&H			All	222
Hexadecimal				
AND OR	* +	* + in maths	Most	49
	Not available		Limited BASICS	
Conditions as in "IF A=10 AND B=20 OR C=30"				

	Alternatives	Similar look but different meaning	Computers	Page reference
APPEND "filename"			Tandy	196
	CHAIN		Apple, BBC	
Add one file to the end of another				
Arrays			Most	99, 175
	MAT		Mainframes	222
Numbered variables				
ASC (A$)			Most	132, 198
	CODE(A$)		Sinclair	
	CH(A$)		Atom	
Gives the ASCII code of the first character of a string (but Sinclair machines do not use the ASCII code)				
ASCII			Most	122, 123, 132, 196, 209, 256
A code for characters				
ATN(tan) and (ASN, ACS)			Most	
Gives the angle in radians of a given tangent, sine, cosine				
AUTO line number			Apple, BBC, Tandy	124
		AUTO disk load	Tandy (DOS)	123
	NUMBER		Texas Instruments	
Automatic program line numbering				
BACKUP			Tandy, Sharp, some CP/M	6, 9
	COPY		Most	
	DCOPY		CP/M-86	
	PIP		CP/M	10
Duplicating disks				
BREAK			Most	6, 18, 19, 60, 67, 70
	CTRL BREAK		IBM	
	ESC		Superbrain, North Star	
Stop a program running				
Buffer			All	165, 178, 210
	file location			
	f.a.n			
CALL			Apple, BBC	
	LINK		Atom	
	SYS		PET, VIC	
	USR		Most	143, 257
Calls a machine language subroutine				

	Alternatives	Similar look but different meaning	Computers	Page reference
Checksum Check errors			All	206, 210
CHR$(A) Prints the character given that code number			Most	138, 147, 205
CINT Gives an integer			Most	86
CLEAR(300)			Most	128, 130, 175
	CLR Not needed	Clear the screen	Vic, Sharp, Pet Large memories	
Clear a space for strings. Set variables to zero				
CLOSE	DCLOSE		Most PET	168
Close a disk file				
CLS		CLEAR variables	Tandy, Sinclair	80, 112, 129
	CALL-936 CTRL HOME ESC CTRL CLEAR PRINT CHR$(12)		Apple IBM Atari BBC, Nascom, UK 101	
	PRINT CHR$(198) PRINT CHR$(24)		Sharp Pet	
Clear the screen				
Concatenation A$ + B$ = C$		A + B maths	Most	35, 37
	A$ & B$ = C$ A$,B$ = C$	The PRINT comma	Older machines Older machines	
Joining strings together				
CONT Continue the program after a break			Most	202
COPY	PIP		Most CP/M	9
COS(A) The cosine of an angle			Most	
CP/M A disk operating system			Probably a majority	8, 207, 210
CVI(A$) Convert to integer			Tandy, IBM	181

	Alternatives	Similar look but different meaning	Computers	Page reference
DATA			All	93, 112, 146, 204, 245
A list of information to be read				
DEF FN variable			Most	109, 155
	Not available		Limited BASICS	
Defines an arithmetic function to be used later				
DEFINT			Most	153, 162
Restricts variables to integers				
DEFPROC			BBC	161
Makes a subroutine				
DEFSTR			Tandy, others	163
Restricts variables to strings				
DELETE	D line number		Apple, Tandy	17
	Line number only		Most	
	RUBOUT key		Older machines	
Deletes a program line				
DEVICE			Modern BASICs	222
Refers to a peripheral				
DIM A(10)			Most	101, 112
	Not needed		Large memories	
(Dimension) Allocates enough space for arrays				
DIM A$(5,10)			Most micro-computers	102, 146, 157
	One dimension only		Limited BASICS	
	No string arrays		Atari 400, others	
	MAT		Sol, Most main-frames	102, 215, 222
Two-dimensional arrays				
DIR			Most	8, 123, 223
	Files		IBM	
	CAT, CATALOG		Sharp, Apple	123
Lists the contents (directory) of a disk				
DRAW			BBC, others	80
Draws a line				
Drive number 1, 2, 3, 4			Sharp, others	11, 121
	0, 1, 2, 3		Tandy, others	
	A, B, C, D		CP/M	
The names of the first, second, etc, disk drives				

	Alternatives	Similar look but different meaning	Computers	Page reference
E Exponent	↑			163
EDIT line number			Tandy, Sinclair	27, 183
	COPY key	COPY files	BBC	
	Check manual		Others	
To alter parts of program lines				
END			Most	75, 95
End the program, return to the READY prompt				
ENTER key			Tandy, Sirius, Texas	9 onwards
	RETURN key	GOSUB-RETURN	Most	
	NEW LINE key		Sinclair, Merlin, Video Genie	
	CR key		Sharp	
Pressed to enter information into the computer				
EOF End of file			Most	171, 203
Error messages			All	198
ERR			Most	
	ERL			203
Gives the error				
EXP(A) Gives the 'natural exponential' of a number (the inverse of LOG)			Most	
FIELD 1, 16 AS A$			Varies	178, 193
		Record field		177
Sets out disk variables				
FILENAME/CMD			Varies	120, 165, 199, 212
	FILENAME.COM		CP/M	
The style of writing a file name				
FIX(A) Chops off decimals			Tandy, others	86
FOR A=B TO C			Most	58, 90 101, 151, 206
FOR A=B TO C STEP D			Most	61
	No STEP		Limited BASICs	
Repeats a sequence of lines				

	Alternatives	Similar look but different meaning	Computers	Page reference
FORMAT			Most	10, 11, 26, 223
	BUILD		Modern BASICs	222
To prepare a blank disk for use				
FRE(A\$)			Apple, Atari, Nascom, Tandy	
	See manual		Most	
Shows the amount of string space left				
FREE			Most	223
	STAT		CP/M	
Shows the amount of disk space left				
GET record number		See INKEY\$	Atari, Pet, BBC	
GET (random access only)			Tandy	179, 191
	INPUT #		BBC, Sharp, Tandy	
	BGET		BBC	
To read from disk or tape				
GOSUB line number			Most	70, 83, 152
Branch to another line then RETURN				
GOTO line number			Most	18, 64, 70, 73, 93, 152, 197
Branch to another line				
HELP			A few	199
Explains the mistake				
IF true **THEN** do			Most	46, 71, 95, 171, 183
IF THEN ELSE			Most	48, 75
	No ELSE		Limited BASICs	
	REPEAT UNTIL		BBC, others	
	DO UNTIL		Special BASICs	
As in IF B=5 THEN GOSUB2000 ELSE END				
INKEY\$			IBM, Tandy, Sinclair	42, 113, 189
	GET A\$	GET file	Most	
	CALL KEY		Texas Instruments	
	Not available		Limited, older BASICs	
Immediate response to a key				
INPUT A		INPUT # data	Most	39, 100

	Alternatives	Similar look but different meaning	Computers	Page reference
INPUT"question";A			Apple, Pet, Tandy, others	39, 46, 62, 63, 72, 130
	10 PRINT"question" } 20 INPUT A }		Atari, Nascom, older machines	
Asks for information to be put in				
INPUT @			Advanced BASICs	83
The INPUT question on a special place on the screen				
INPUT #			Most	171, 175, 257
Input data from a disk				
INSTR(A$)			Most	248
Finds a string inside another string				
INT(A)			Most	85, 109, 153, 157
	%(A) Rounds up numbers		Atom Apple, Pet	
(Integer) Whole numbers, no decimals				
KILL "filename"			Most	124, 185, 223
	ERA		CP/M	
		ERASE (array)	IBM	
	UNSAVE		Older machines	
	DESTROY		Older machines	
	PURGE many files		Special BASICs	124
Deletes files from the disk				
LEFT$(A$,3)			Most	130, 176
	A$(1, 3)	A$(1,3) arrays	Older machines	
The left part of a string				
LEN(A$)			Most	127, 189, 206, 250
The length of a string				
LET A=3			Mostly optional	33
	Not essential		Most	
	Essential		Sinclair, old machines	
Gives a value to a variable				
LINE INPUT			Advanced BASICs	130
Allows commas to be input				

	Alternatives	Similar look but different meaning	Computers	Page reference
LIST			Most	17, 19, 60, 173, 215
Lists a program on to the screen				
LLIST			Tandy, Sinclair	187
	PRINT filename	PRINT to screen	Tandy, others	
	LIST "P"		Apple, Atari	
	LIST/P		Sharp	
	CTRL B LIST		BBC	
	CMD3:LIST		Vic	
	CMD4:LIST		Pet	
	Check manual		Most	
Lists a program on a printer				
LOAD "filename"				121, 123, 223
LOAD from disk			Tandy, Sharp, others	257
	BLOAD		Pet	
LOAD from tape			Pet, Sinclair, older machines	
	CLOAD		Tandy, Oric, others	123, 257
	OLD		Older machines	
	Check with manual		Most	
Loading a stored file into memory				
LOF			Advanced BASICs	185
Length of file				
LOG(A)			Most	
	LN(A)		BBC, Sharp, Sinclair	
Gives the natural logarithm				
LPRINT			Sinclair, Tandy, others	25, 63, 106, 116, 140, 141
	PRINT/P	PRINT to disk	Sharp	
	Check manual		Others	
Instructs the printer				
LSET RSET			Tandy, others	181
Tidies strings to left or right				
MAT			Sol, most main-frames	102, 222
	Arrays		Most micro-computers	99
Matrix arithmetic				

	Alternatives	Similar look but different meaning	Computers	Page reference
? MEM Asks how much memory is left	? M Check manual		Tandy, others Others	223
Menu A choice of actions			All	191, 215
MERGE Joins program	CHAIN		Most	72, 193
MID$(A$,3,2) Gives the middle characters of a string	 PRINT A$(3TO5) A$(3,2)	 A$(3,2) arrays	Modern BASICs Sinclair Older machines, Atari	128, 176, 251, 256 128
MKI$(A) Make integers into (disk) strings			Tandy, IBM, others	181
Multi-statement lines A=B : C=D Several statements on one line	 A=B / C=D A=B ; C=D No multistatement	 / division sign ; print command	 Most Older machines Older machines Sinclair, others	 20, 24, 47, 74, 153
Multiple assignment A = B = C No multiple assignments Giving several variables the same value in one line			 Special BASICs Most	
NEW Deletes the current program from memory			Most	16, 19
NOT(A=B) Not available A > < B Answers 0 if true, −1 if false			Extended BASICs Limited BASICs Most	
OLD filename LOAD Call up an existing file			Older machines Most	121, 223
ON ERROR GOTO line number TRAP Not available Prevents the program stopping due to an error			Apple, BBC, Tandy Atari Limited BASICs	203

	Alternatives	Similar look but different meaning	Computers	Page reference
ON A GOSUB or **GOTO** line number			Most	74, 170
	ON–THEN line number		Most	
	ON–GOTO only		UK 101	
	Not available		Limited BASICs	
Given a choice of answers, GO TO different lines				
OPEN file specification			Apple, Pet, Nascom, Tandy	165, 177
	OPENIN OPENOUT		Atom, BBC	
	ROPEN WOPEN		Sharp	
	Check manual		Others	
Opens a file in memory				
OUT port, byte			Nascom, Tandy, Sinclair	
	PUT /	PUT to file	Atari	
	POKE( )		Oric, others	
	Check manual	Most		
Sends a signal to an output port				
PEEK memory address			Most	140, 189, 217, 257
	PRINT ?( )		BBC	
Look (peek) at a memory address				
PLOT			Newer machines	
Controls graphics				
POKE address,byte			Most	142, 217, 257
	byte = ?address		Acorn, BBC	
Write a character into a memory address				
PRINT			Most	15, 20, 39
	?		A common abbreviation	
		? peek ?	BBC	
	DISP		Sharp	
Print on the screen				
PRINT# file specification			Atari, Pet, Tandy, others	167, 257
	PRINT	PRINT to screen	Sharp, Nascom, UK 101	
	Check manual		Most	
Writes data on to a disk				

	Alternatives	Similar look but different meaning	Computers	Page reference
PRINT @ 130			Tandy, others	
	PRINT AT(130)		Most	80, 85, 199, 204,
	SCREEN		Nascom	81, 83
	Check manual		Others	
Prints at a specified place on the screen				
PRINT TAB(10)			Most	22, 80
	Not available		Limited BASICs	
Prints at a specified place on the line				
PRINT USING ##.##			Tandy, others	86, 91
	Check manual		Most	
Prints numbers in a specified layout				
PROC			BBC, others	161, 253
Procedure, a subroutine				
PUT buffer			Tandy, IBM, others	183
		PUT(graphics)	IBM	
	BPUT		BBC	
	Check manual		Most	
Writes data to a disk				
RANDOM			Most mainframes	148
	RANDOMISE		Mainframes	
	RAND		Sinclair	
	RND(−1)		Others	
Resets the random number generator				
RND(A)			Most microcomputers	147
	RND * A		Sirius	
	Check manual		Oric, others	
Gives an almost random number				
Random files			Disk, fast tape, only	176
	Direct access			
Files with accessible records				
READ A$,B			Most	93, 113, 146, 150
Reads a list of data				
Record			All	177
Part of a file				

	Alternatives	Similar look but different meaning	Computers	Page reference
REM			Most	76, 108, 152, 190
			A common abbreviation	
	!		A common abbreviation	
(Remark) A comment that the computer ignores				
RENAME"filename"**TO**"newname"			Tandy, others	
	REN	/	CP/M	
	Check manual		Most	
Renames a program on disk				
RENUM	RENUMBER		Most	192
	RESEQUENCE		Texas Instruments	
	NAME	RENAME file	Some Tandys	
Alter program line numbers				
Reset button			Most	12, 18, 67
Switches off program but not the machine				
RESTORE			Most	97, 244
Start reading data again from the beginning				
RESUME			Those with 'ON ERROR'	202, 204
Return after an error				
RETURN		RETURN key	Most	73, 75
Return after a GOSUB				
RIGHT$(A$,3)			Most	130, 176, 250
	A$(3)	A$(3) array	Atari, older machines	
Gives the right-hand part of a string				
RUN (RUN 50)			Most	15, 123, 255
Starts the program running (at line 50)				
SAVE "filename" (to disk)			Most	120, 257
	SAVE (to cassette)		Pet, Sinclair, older machines	
	BSAVE (to disk)		Pet	
CSAVE (to cassette)			Most	122
	CSAVE (compressed)		Atari	
Write the file on to disk or tape				
Sequential files			All	176
	Serial access			219
Files on tape and disk				

	Alternatives	Similar look but different meaning	Computers	Page reference
SGN(A) +1 if the number is positive, 0 if 0, −1 if negative			Most	
SIN(A) Gives the sine of the angle	Not available		Most Limited BASICs	
Sort Sorting lists into order			All	111
SOUND Makes a sound			Newer machines	
Spaces A+B=C (no spaces) No spaces in BASIC, some spaces in DOS commands	A + B = C spaced		Most Texas, others	33, 152
Squares and powers Methods of showing powers, exponentiation	5 ** 5 = 25 5 ↑ 2 = 25 5 ^ 2 = 25		Sinclair, others Tandy, others Most	151, 157
SQR(A) The square root of the number			Most	151
STOP Stop program, return to BASIC READY command	Not available		Most BBC, others	75
STRING$(10,46) Prints a string of characters	Not available	STR$(A)	BBC, Tandy Most	138, 140
STR$(A) Turns a number into a string			Most	140
Syntax errors Grammatical mistakes			All	204
SYSGEN Writes instructions to disk			CP/M	10
SYSTEM End BASIC, go to operating system	BYE Check manual		Tandy Atari, Sharp, others Most	144
TAB( ) Print inwards a few spaces			Most	22, 80, 89, 99

	Alternatives	Similar look but different meaning	Computers	Page reference
TAN(A)			Most	
The tangent of an angle				
TRACE ON TRACE OFF			Sharp, others	207
	TRON TROFF		A common abreviation	
	TRACE NOTRACE		Apple, others	
Shows line numbers as the program runs				
UNTIL			Newer machines	65
	FOR TO		Most	
Part of the DO UNTIL loop				
USR(A)			Most	143
	LINK address		Atom	
Calls up a machine code subroutine				
VAL(A$)			Most	36, 41, 191
Gives a numeric value for a string				
Variables				
AC = 3 (two letters)			Most	29, 151, 205, 220
	ACCOUNTS = 3 (full words)		BBC, advanced BASICs	
	A = 3 (single letter only)		Limited BASICs	
Ways of naming variables				
VERIFY			Usually automatic	222
Checks a program				
WAIT			Apple, Pet Nascom, UK101	
	PAUSE		Sinclair, others	
	FOR TO NEXT		Most	
Delay the program for a time				
WHILE–WEND			Microsoft	
	REPEAT UNTIL		BBC, Oric	
	FOR–TO		Others	
Loops as long as the expression is true				
WIDTH			Acorn, Sharp, Nascom	
	POKE		Most	
Sets printer or screen width				
WRITE "filename"			Apple, others	
	PRINT #		Most	167
Writes data to disk or tape				

Answers to exercises

Chapter 3

Question 1
The computer hasn't been told to PRINT. It needs:

    20 PRINT X

Chapter 4

Question 1
```
10 LPRINT "-----------------------------------------------------
------"
20 LPRINT TAB(12)"!   LAST YEARS   ! THIS YEARS   !   FORECAST FOR"
30 LPRINT TAB(12)"!    RESULTS     !   RESULTS     !    FUTURE"
40 LPRINT TAB(12)"!                !              !    TRADING"
50 LPRINT "-----------------------------------------------------
------"
60 LPRINT TAB(12)"!";TAB(27)"!";TAB(41)"!"
70 LPRINT TAB(12)"!";TAB(27)"!";TAB(41)"!"
```

Question 2
```
10 LPRINT "-----------------------------------------------------
------"
20 LPRINT TAB(10) "WORK SCHEDULE FOR WEEK"
30 LPRINT ".............................................
...."
40 LPRINT TAB(10) "MAINTENANCE    ! PAINTWORK    !   OTHER WORK"
50 LPRINT ".............................................
...."
60 LPRINT " "
70 LPRINT"MON";TAB(8)"!";TAB(24)"!";TAB(39)"!"
80 LPRINT ".............................................
...."
90 LPRINT
100 LPRINT"TUE";TAB(8)"!";TAB(24)"!";TAB(39)"!"
110 LPRINT ".............................................
...."
```

(Notice the alternative ways of printing a blank row in lines 60 and 90.)

Chapter 5

Question 3
The first mistake is in line 20. The multiplication sign * is missing. It should read HJ = 2 * (GF + 1)

The second mistake is in line 30. The variable OT has come from nowhere so it has a value of zero and so makes HJ become zero too. If you want OT to be 12, which is the current value of HJ, then line 30 should be: OT = HJ

Chapter 6

Question 1
TO is a 'reserved word', part of the BASIC language like ON, AND, OR, COS, etc., and can't be used as a variable.

Question 2
FRED, BOEING 747 and 12/04/84 can be called A1$, C3$, D2$ or E$ but not A1, C3, D2 or E. 34 and 12.0484 can be given to any of the variables already mentioned but, if you want to treat them as arithmetical numbers, use A1, C3, D2 or E. The two wrong variables are 2B and 2B$; they can't be used because they don't start with a letter.

Chapter 7

Question 2
As it is, the INPUT question mark goes on the next screen line. With a semicolon, it will come right after the question, thus:

WHAT IS THE TEMPERATURE IN CENTIGRADE ? ?

so you could miss the ? out of line 10

Question 3
Add:

50 GOTO 10

Chapter 8

Question 2
```
10 INPUT "WHAT'S THE STUDENT'S NAME "; N$
20 H$ = "WHAT PERCENTAGE MARKS DID THEY GET IN "
30 PRINT H$; "COMPUTING ";
40 INPUT C
50 PRINT H$; "MATHEMATICS ";
60 INPUT M
```

```
70 PRINT H$; "PROGRAMMING ";
80 INPUT P
90 PRINT H$; "ENGLISH ";
100 INPUT E
110 R$ = " FAIL"
120 IF C > = 60 AND (M > = 60 OR P > = 60) THEN R$ = " PASS"
140 IF M > = 60 AND (C > = 60 OR P > = 60) THEN R$ = " PASS"
150 IF E < = 50 THEN R$ = " FAIL"
160 LPRINT N$; R$
170 GOTO 10
```

Question 3

```
10 INPUT "WHAT'S THE FIRST WORD "; W1$
20 INPUT "WHAT'S THE SECOND WORD "; W2$
30 IF W1$ > W2$ THEN 60
40 PRINT W2$; " COMES AFTER "; W1$; " IN THE DICTIONARY."
50 GOTO 10
60 PRINT W1$; " COMES AFTER "; W2$; " IN THE DICTIONARY."
70 GOTO 10
```

Chapter 9

Question 1

```
10 N$ = "YOUR NAME"
20 A$ = "YOUR ADDRESS"
30 T$ = "YOUR TOWN"
40 P$ = "POST CODE"
50 FOR L = 1 TO 25
60 LPRINT N$; TAB(20) N$; TAB(40) N$; TAB(60) N$
70 LPRINT A$; TAB(20) A$; TAB(40) A$; TAB(60) A$
80 LPRINT T$; TAB(20) T$; TAB(40) T$; TAB(60) T$
90 LPRINT P$; TAB(20) P$; TAB(40) P$; TAB(60) P$
100 FOR S = 1 TO 4
110 LPRINT
120 NEXT S
130 NEXT L
```

This prints 4 lots of labels across the full width of 9½ inch wide
paper.

Question 2

```
10 S = 280
20 FOR P = 10 TO 0 STEP -1
30 PRINT P
40 FOR D = 1 TO S: NEXT D
50 NEXT P
```

The value of S in line 10 depends on the computer.

Chapter 10

Questions 1 and 2

```
10 BN$ = "BABY'S NAME"
20 LW$ = "LAST WEIGHT"
30 TW$ = "TODAY'S WEIGHT"
39 REM *************   GET THE FACTS   **************
40 PRINT BN$; : INPUT N$
50 PRINT LW$; : INPUT LW
```

```
60 GOSUB 1000
70 PRINT TW$; : INPUT TW
80 GOSUB 1010
90 GL = TW - LW
91 REM              GAIN = TODAY'S WEIGHT - LAST WEIGHT
100 GOSUB 2000
110 NB = NB + 1
111 REM            NB = NUMBER OF BABIES
120 LG = LG + GL
121 REM            LG = TOTAL GAINS
130 WT = WT + TW
131 REM            WT = TOTAL WEIGHTS
140 GOSUB 3000
498 REM
499 REM ************** PRINTOUT SECTION **************
500 LPRINT BN$, N$
510 LPRINT LW$, LW
520 LPRINT TW$, TW
530 LPRINT "GAIN OR LOSS", GL, EX$
531 REM            EX$ IS EITHER BLANK OR EXCLAMATION MARKS
540 LPRINT "AVERAGE GAIN OF ALL"; NB " BABIES TODAY "; AG$
550 FOR R = 1 TO 6: LPRINT: NEXT R
551 REM            MOVING THE PAPER UP
598 REM
599 REM ************** TO START AGAIN    **************
600 PRINT "ANY MORE ?   ... ANSWER 'Y' OR 'N'
610 A$ = INKEY$: IF A$ = "" THEN 610
620 IF A$ = "Y" THEN 40 ELSE END
998 REM
999 REM ************** TO CHECK TYPING ERRORS  **************
1000 IF LW < 17 THEN RETURN ELSE 1020
1010 IF TW < 17 THEN RETURN
1020 PRINT "IS THAT RIGHT ?   .... ANSWER 'Y' OR 'N'"
1030 AN$ = INKEY$: IF AN$ = "" THEN 1030
1040 IF AN$ = "Y" THEN RETURN
1050 PRINT "O.K.   WE'LL TRY AGAIN": PRINT: GOTO 50
1998 REM
1999 REM ************** LOOKING FOR A WEIGHT LOSS  **************
2000 EX$ = ""
2010 IF GL < 0 THEN EX$ = "! ! ! LOSS ! ! !"
2020 RETURN
2998 REM
2999 REM ************** CALCULATE AVERAGE WEIGHT  **************
3000 AG = LG/WT * 100
3010 AG$ = STR$(AG)+" %"
3020 RETURN
```

Chapter 11

Questions 1 and 2
This printout will be different from yours, but it doesn't matter so
long as yours works. The original tiny program is now in the
subroutine from 1000. The flashing symbol routines are in lines
1080, 1140 and 2180 with added bells and whistles between lines
2050 to 2110.

Program lines go up in tens, REMarks are on odd numbered lines.
If you can't understand INT on line 500, all is explained in Chapter
12.

```
10 CLS: PRINT TAB(20) "WALL COVER ESTIMATE": PRINT
20 PRINT "YOU ARE GOING TO BE ASKED FOR THE HEIGHT AND LENGTH"
30 PRINT "OF EVERY WALL, OF EVERY EXTENSION."
40 PRINT "DON'T BOTHER ABOUT THE TRIANGULAR BITS TO THE ROOFS
YET"
50 PRINT "NOR THE DOORS AND WINDOWS. THOSE WILL BE DONE LATER."
60 PRINT:PRINT "WHEN YOU HAVE MEASURED EVERY WALL. ANSWER '0'"
70 PRINT "WHEN ASKED FOR THE 'HEIGHT'": PRINT: PRINT
80 PRINT: PRINT "PRESS ANY KEY WHEN YOU ARE READY...."
90 OK$ = INKEY$: IF OK$ = "" THEN 90
100 GOSUB 1000
101 REM            TO DO THE WALLS
110 GOSUB 2000
111 REM            TO DO THE ROOF TRIANGLES
120 CLS
130 PRINT "DO YOU WANT TO SUBTRACT WINDOWS AND DOORS ?;
140 PRINT "ANSWER 'Y' OR 'N' ....."
150 DW$ = INKEY$: IF DW$ = "" THEN 150
160 IF DW$ = "Y" THEN GOSUB 1000
161 REM                TO SUBTRACT THE WINDOWS
498 REM
499 REM ************* FINAL ANSWER ******************
500 C = INT(TA/15) + 1
510 REM    ONE CAN COVERS 15 SQUARE FEET + AN EXTRA CAN FOR LUCK
510 CLS: PRINT@ 662, "YOU NEED " C "CANS"
520 END
521 REM        THE END OF A PROGRAM CAN BE IN THE MIDDLE !
998 REM
999 REM ************* WALLS AND WINDOWS *************
1000 CLS
1010 PRINT TAB(20) "!--------------------!"
1020 PRINT TAB(20) "!"; : PRINT TAB(40) "!"
1030 PRINT TAB(20) "!"; : PRINT TAB(40) "!"
1040 PRINT TAB(20) "!"; : PRINT TAB(40) "!"
1050 PRINT TAB(20) "!--------------------!"
1060 PRINT : PRINT "HOW HIGH IS THE SIDE 'H' ?"
1070 PRINT@ 600, "TO QUIT,    ANSWER '0'"
1080 FOR F = 1 TO 50: PRINT@ 170, " ";
1090 PRINT@ 170, "H";
1100 NEXT F
1101 REM        THE FLASHING 'H'
1110 INPUT H
1120 IF H = 0 THEN RETURN
1121 REM        H = 0 MEANS - THAT'S THE LAST WALL
1130 PRINT@ 384, "HOW LONG IS THE SIDE 'L' ?"
1140 FOR F = 1 TO 50: PRINT@ 348, " ";
1150 PRINT@ 348, "L";
1160 NEXT F
1161 REM        THE FLASHING 'L'
1170 INPUT L
1180 AR = L * H
1181 REM        AREA = LENGTH * HEIGHT
1190 IF DW$ = "Y" THEN AR = -AR
1191 REM     IF THESE ARE DOORS AND WINDOWS: SUBTRACT THE AREA
1200 TA = TA + AR
1201 REM    TOTAL AREA = LAST TOTAL + (OR MINUS) CURRENT AREA
1210 GOTO1000
1998 REM
1999 REM ************* THE BITS TOWARDS THE ROOF **************
2000 CLS : PRINT TAB(20) "THE ROOF TRIANGLES"
2001 REM            MAKING THE DIAGRAM
2010 PRINT TAB(30) "."
2020 FOR R = 1 TO 6
2030 PRINT TAB(30-3*R) "/"; TAB(30+3*R) ":"
2031 REM            THE SLOPING SIDES
```

```
2040 NEXT R
2050 FOR D = 94 TO 512 STEP 64
2051 REM    THIS DROPS SIX DOTS STRAIGHT DOWN FROM POSITION
2052 REM    '94' TO POSITION '512'.   IT IS FOR A 64 CHARACTER
2053 REM    SCREEN, HENCE THE 'STEP 64'
2060 FOR P = 1 TO 50
2070 PRINT@ 352, " ";: PRINT@ 352, "H";
2071 REM    THIS GIVES A FLASHING 'H' AND ALSO DELAYS THE DOTS
2080 NEXT F
2090 PRINT@ D, ".";
2100 NEXT D
2110 PRINT@ 353, " ";: INPUT H
2111 REM    THE 'PRINT@ 353, " "' IS TO PLACE THE INPUT ?
2120 IF H = 0 THEN RETURN
2121 REM            WHEN YOU FINISH THE ROOF BITS
2130 PRINT@576, " ";
2140 FOR B = 521 TO 562
2150 PRINT@ B, "-";
2151 REM            DRAWS THE BASE OF THE TRIANGLE
2160 NEXT B
2170 FOR F = 1 TO 50
2180 PRINT@ 605, " ";: PRINT@ 605, "L"
2181 REM            THE FLASHING 'L'
2190 NEXT F
2200 PRINT@ 606, " ";: INPUT L
2210 AR = L/2 * H
2211 REM            AREA = HALF BASE * HEIGHT
2220 TA = TA + AR
2221 REM            ADD THE TRIANGLES TO THE REST OF THE WALLS
2230 GOTO 2000
2231 REM            DO ANOTHER ONE UNTIL TOLD TO STOP
2232 REM            THIS ISN'T THE END - SEE LINE 520
```

Chapter 12

Question 2
The textbook answer is:

```
10 INPUT N
20 TH = INT(N * 1000 + .005) /1000
30 PRINT TH
40 PRINT USING "####,###.###"; N
```

and it works fine with numbers like 234.5678. But try it with 999.9999 and you might get 999.999 for TH, the INT calculation, and 1,000.000 for the PRINT USING. Even worse: with N = 999.9899, TH becomes a close 999.989 while PRINT USING gives 999.990 which is very inaccurate.

If this happens, check your machine with this extra line:

```
15 PRINT N
```

and it should faithfully reproduce the number you have typed in. But if you input 999.9999 does it round it up to 1000? And if you input 999.9899 does the computer decide that 999.99 is near enough?

Question 3
Different machines speak in different BASICs. Here is a program for one that says '!' means 'use only the first letter' and '!!' means 'use the first letter of the first string, then a space, the first letter of another string, then another space'.

It also says that '% %' means 'use as much of the string as will fit in the space between the % signs'.

```
10 PRINT "ONE AT A TIME, TYPE YOUR FIRST NAME, SECOND
   NAME"
20 PRINT "AND LAST NAME . . . HITTING 'ENTER' AFTER EVERY
   ONE"
30 INPUT F$, SN$, LN$
40 PRINT USING "! ! "; F$, SN$;
50 PRINT USING "% %";LN$
```

Question 4

```
10 INPUT "WHAT'S THE HOUSE NUMBER "; N
20 IF INT(N/2) = N/2 THEN PRINT N " IS ON THE RIGHT": GOTO 10
30 PRINT N " IS ON THE LEFT": GOTO 10
```

Chapter 13

Question 1
If line 40 has GOTO instead of END, the RESTORE should happen before reaching line 20 again. Line 40 could have: RESTORE: GOTO 10 or line 40 could have: GOTO 5 with line 5 being RESTORE. Or, before line 20 there could be a line 15 RESTORE.

Question 2
Your program will be different. Here is one that gives random, unpredictable answers that make non-computniks think that a computer is more than a machine:

```
10 INPUT "WHO'S THIS TALKING TO ME "; N$
20 FOR R = 1 TO RND(10)
30 READ A$
40 NEXT R
50 PRINT "HELLO " N$; A$
60 DATA " RUDE REMARK", " JOKE", "LIBELLOUS STATEMENT", "
   NASTY CRACK", " SOMETHING CRUEL", " SCANDAL", " CRUDE
   SAYING"
70 DATA " SOMETHING IN BAD TASTE", " CRAZY WORDS", "
   GOSSIP", " FOUL CALUMNY"
```

Question 3
Your program will be different. Look at the two ideas in this one.
(a) The same READ lines are used both to screen-print a list of
abbreviations and also to LPRINT the full addresses. (b) The signal
for the end of data need not be XXX or 999. In this case it is "−−",
which later becomes a way of ruling off the screen.

```
10 CLS
20 GOSUB 3000
30 INPUT "WHICH DO YOU WANT "; W$
40 GOSUB 3000
50 END
998 REM
999 REM ***************** THE DATA LIST ********************
1000 DATA "DY","THE WORKSHOP MANAGER","DYANAMIC TOOLS LTD","23
     ANYSTREET, ANYTOWN","GI","MR DONNELL","GIGANTIC PLC","GAS
     ALLEY, BORGANVILLE"
1010 DATA "AL","ARNOLD HANDLEY","ALLSTOP GARAGE","LANGHAM,
     COLCHESTER","HU","THE CHAIRMAN","HUGE CO.","LONDON"
1020 DATA "BI","JOE BIGGS","THE BIGGEST CO","LIBERT SQ.
     PARIS","WO","THE MANAGING DIRECTOR","WONDERFUL INC.","112
     KHARTOUM ST. BOSTON"
2000 DATA "--","--","---------------------------------- ----
     --","--"
2998 REM
2999 REM *************** READ THE DATA ********************
3000 READ AB$, PE$, CO$, AD$
3001 REM AB$= ABbreviation, PE$= PErson, CO$= COmpany
3002 REM AD$= ADdress
3009 REM ************** THE PRINTOUT ********************
3010 IF W$ <> "" THEN 3030
3011 REM when Line 30 asks 'Which do you want ?' jump Line 3020
3012 REM and don't print the summary again.
3020 PRINT AB$; " ---- "; CO$,
3021 REM print a summary of abbreviations.
3030 IF AB$ = W$ THEN LPRINT PE$: LPRINT CO$: LPRINT AD$
3031 REM if you find the name then LPRINT the address.
3040 IF AB$ <> "--" THEN 3000
3041 REM if you don't reach the end of the data, keep reading.
3050 RESTORE : RETURN
3051 REM return first to Line 30, finally to Line 50 - END
```

Chapter 14

Question 1
Because most printers can't scroll backwards, only the '3 AM 6 AM
etc.' title can be moved. Put it into line 81 and delete lines 160 to
190. The run-on caused by the end semicolon is stopped by line 91.

Question 2
It's not good enough to count the number of readings with
something like NR = NR + 1 and then to divide the total
temperature TT by this NR. For various reasons, your operator may

not take a temperature reading and the computer will take this as zero degrees and so screw the average up. Only if a real reading is taken should the number be counted.

So line 132 says IF TE(Q1,Q2) > 0 THEN NR = NR + 1

Here is the program again, with asterisks against the altered lines:

```
*   10 DIM D$(7), TI$(9), TE(7,8), AV(7)
    20 FOR D = 1 TO 7
    30 READ D$(D)
    40 DATA "MON", "TUE", "WED", "THU", "FRI", "SAT", "SUN"
    50 NEXT D
*   60 FOR T = 1 TO 9
    70 READ TI$(T)
*   80 DATA "3 AM", "6 AM", "9 AM", "12 AM", "3 PM", "6 PM",
       "9 PM", "12 PM","AVERAGE"
*   81 LPRINT TAB(T * 7); TI$(T);
    90 NEXT T
*   91 LPRINT " "
   100 FOR Q1 = 1 TO 7
   110 FOR Q2 = 1 TO 8
   120 PRINT "IT IS "; D$(Q1); " AT "; TI$(Q2);
   130 INPUT " .... WHAT'S THE TEMPERATURE "; TE(Q1,Q2)
*  132 IF TE(Q1,Q2) > 0 THEN NR = NR + 1
*  134 TT = TT + TE(Q1,Q2)
   140 NEXT Q2
*  142 AV(Q1) = TT/NR
*  144 NR = 0: TT = 0
   150 NEXT Q1
- - - - - - - - - 160 to 190 deleted - - - - -
   200 FOR R = 1 TO 7
   210 LPRINT D$(R);
   220 FOR C = 1 TO 8
   230 LPRINT TAB(C * 7); TE(R,C);
   240 NEXT C
*  250 LPRINT TAB(63); AV(R)
   260 NEXT R
*  270 REM    D$ = DAte,  TI$ = TIme of day, TE = TEmperature
*  280 REM    NR = Number of Readings, TT = Total Temperature
*  290 REM    AV = AVerage
*  300 REM    Loop variables that become subscripts are ...
*  310 REM    D (Date), T (Time), R (Row), C (Column)
*  320 REM    Q1 (Day One), Q2 (Time Two)
```

Question 3

Similar averaging techniques are used in this program, except that zero sales are counted. Notice how, in the last few lines, reversing the subscripts gives an average for the columns instead of the rows across.

```
10 DIM N$(4), J(5,3)
11 REM   N$ = Names,  J = sales
20 LPRINT "WEEK",
21 REM  the comma is used to tab across the page
30 FOR R = 1 TO 4
40 READ N$(R)
50 LPRINT N$(R),
60 NEXT R
70 DATA "JILL","JO","JEAN","AVERAGE"
80 LPRINT ""
90 FOR W = 1 TO 4
```

```
100 LPRINT W,
101 REM    W = week number
110 FOR R = 1 TO 3
120 PRINT "WEEK " W " HOW MUCH DID " N$(R) " SELL ";
130 INPUT J(W,R)
140 LPRINT J(W,R),
150 TS = TS + J(W,R)
160 AV(R) = TS/3
170 NEXT R
180 TS = 0
190 LPRINT AV(R-1)
191 REM    print the average.   (R-1) because Line 170 has
191 REM    already moved to the next row
200 NEXT W
210 LPRINT
"_____"
219 REM ********** INDIVIDUAL'S AVERAGES ******************
220 LPRINT N$(4),
230 FOR R = 1 TO 3
240 FOR W = 1 TO 4
250 PS = PS + J(W,R)
260 AP(W) = PS/4
270 NEXT W
280 PS = 0
290 LPRINT AP(W-1),
300 NEXT R
```

This still needs to trap errors when the sales are INPUTted. If sales
are below $1,000 or above $4,000 the program should query it.

Chapter 15

Question 1
(a) The subroutine from line 400 for sorting into Bin number is
almost exactly the same as that from lines 200 to 300. The only
alteration is to line 240 (which becomes line 440) – substitute B for
F$

    440 IF B(C) <= B(C+1) THEN 490

Everything else is the same.
(b) To reuse the printout section in lines 320 to 360, it isn't enough
to write GOSUB 320 on line 300. If you do this, the RETURN (this
will be on a new line 370) will return you to the NEXT SW loop on
line 310.

    Instead, line 300 has to throw you permanently out of the loop to
a separate line saying GOSUB. Then there has to be an END line to
stop the program from crashing through into the subroutine time
and time again:

    300 IF JU$ ="NO SWAPS" THEN 312
    310 NEXT SW
    312 GOSUB 320
    314 END
    320 CLS: PRINT "FILM TITLE" etc., etc., etc.
    370 RETURN

Your added Bin sort routine from line 400 will also finish with a GOSUB 320.

Question 2
There are several ways: don't have "END 999" but "————————————————" in the data statement. Or have, before the printout:

IF B(PR) = 999 THEN F$ = " "

or:

IF B(PR) = 999 THEN jump over the print line

Or make the loop one less than the number of data items.

Chapter 17

Question 1
You can have answers with IF B$ = " AND " to count the frequency of given words, but here is an idea that is well worth saving in your collection of useful subroutines:

```
10 . . . . . . . . . . . . . . . . . . . . . . . . .
20 . . . . . . . . . . . . . . . . . . . . . . . .
30 INPUT "WHAT'S THE QUOTATION "; Q$
40 L = LEN(Q$)
50 . . . . . . . . . . . . . .
60 . . . . . . . . . . . . . . . .        (This was the program in this chapter)
70 . . . . . . . . . . . . . . . . . . . . . . .
80 . . . . . .
90 . . . . .
100 INPUT "WHAT ARE YOU SEARCHING FOR ";S$
110 LS = LEN(S$)
120 FOR W = 1 TO L − LS + 1
130 IF S$ = MID$(Q$,W,LS) THEN C = C + 1
140 NEXT W
150 PRINT S$ " APPEARS " C " TIMES"
```

Line 110 measures the length of the 'and', 'then' or whatever you want. Line 120 sets the program looping through almost the length of the main quotation (L = LEN(Q$)). Line 130 is looking for the three or four (LS) characters somewhere in the middle of Q$ and counting (C=C+1) how often they appear.

Does your machine have INSTR(Q$,word)? This is even more efficient. Check your manual.

Question 2
```
10 INPUT "WHAT'S THE PART NUMBER "; N$
20 L = LEN(N$)
30 FOR W = 1 TO L
40 P$ = MID$(N$,W,3)
```

```
50 IF P$ = "344" AND P$ = "652" THEN PRINT "FORD": END
60 IF P$ = "345" AND P$ = "97B" THEN PRINT "DATSUN": END
70 NEXT W
80 PRINT "NEITHER"
```

Question 3
(a) Try PRINTUSING if yours can handle strings.
(b) If the first name is input separately, use LEFT$(N$,1) + "."
(c) If the whole name is input together, search for the space between the names using the IF B$ = " " technique, then use LEFT$(N$,1) for the initial and RIGHT$(N$, X) for the surname, where X is the position of the space.

Question 4
```
10 REM ********** AN ARRAY OF MONTHS ***************
20 DIM M$(12)
30 FOR R = 1 TO 12: READ M$(R): NEXT R
40 DATA "JAN.","FEB.","MAR.","APL.","MAY.","JUN.","JLY.",
   "AUG.","SEP.","OCT.","NOV.","DEC."
48 REM
49 REM ********** GET THE DATE *********************
50 PRINT "WHAT'S THE DATE ?"
60 PRINT "YOU CAN WRITE IT AS 01/11/85 OR 01.11.85 OR 01:11:85"
70 INPUT "..... THE DATE "; D$
80 IF LEN(D$) <> 8 THEN PRINT "THAT DOESN'T LOOK RIGHT": PRINT:
GOTO 60
81 REM    a rough check for errors
90 PRINT "IS THAT AMERICAN STYLE WITH THE MONTH FIRST ?    TYPE
... A"
100 INPUT "OR BRITISH WITH THE MONTH IN THE MIDDLE ?        TYPE
... B"; S$
110 IF S$<>"A" AND S$<>"B" THEN PRINT"SORRY, IT HAS TO BE 'A'
OR 'B'": GOTO 90
118 REM
119 REM ********** AMERICAN OR BRITISH ? *********************
120 IF S$ = "A" THEN NM = VAL(LEFT$(D$,2)): DD$ = MID$(D$,4,2)
130 IF S$ = "B" THEN NM = VAL(MID$(D$,4,2)): DD$ = LEFT$(D$,2)
131 REM    NM = number of the month, DD$ = day
140 IF NM >12 THEN PRINT "YOU'VE GOT THE MONTH WRONG": GOTO 70
150 IF VAL(DD$) >31 THEN PRINT "YOU'VE GOT THE DAY WRONG": GOTO
70
151 REM    a rough check for errors. You could also check that
152 REM    February didn't get more than 28 or 29 days.
160 IF LEFT$(DD$,1) = "0" THEN DD$ = RIGHT$(DD$,1)
161 REM    removing the 0 in dates like 03
170 DE$ = "TH "
171 REM    most days end in TH ( 12th, 25th, 30th etc.)
172 REM    except ....
180 IF DD$ = "1" OR DD$ = "21" OR DD$ = "31" THEN DE$ = "ST "
190 IF DD$ = "2" OR DD$ = "22" THEN DE$ = "ND "
200 IF DD$ = "3" THEN DE$ = "RD "
201 REM    notice the space left after "TH ", "ND " etc.
209 REM ************** FINAL PRINTOUT ********************
210 PRINT: PRINT
220 PRINT "THE DATE IS " DD$; DE$; M$(NM); " 19";RIGHT$(D$,2)
221 REM    The day + TH, the month, 19 + last two figures.
```

Chapter 19

Question 1
The Italian program needs a FOR L = 1 TO 20 loop starting just
before line 200 and with the NEXT L after line 350. The end of line
300 will need to be altered to GOTO 360 (the NEXT L line).

To ask a question three times, put a counter of C = C+1 at the
end of line 350 in place of the GOTO 210. Then insert a line 352
saying IF C < 3 THEN 210.

Question 2
If a common mistake is to get the gender, the IL, LA and LE, of the
Italian words wrong, you ask the computer to ignore the first three
characters (remember that the space after IL is a character) and just
compare the rest of the answer:

```
220 LI = LEN(IT$(R) )
230 LA = LEN(AN$)
```

meaning that LI is the length of the Italian phrase and LA is the
length of the answer.

```
250 IF RIGHT$(AN$, (LA−3) ) = RIGHT$(IT$(R), (LI−3) ) THEN PRINT
    "YOU'VE GOT THE WORD RIGHT BUT THE GENDER WRONG":
    GOTO XXX
```

which means: if the right-hand side of the answer, all except the
first three characters, is the same as the right-hand side of the
Italian, except its first three characters, then print "You've got the
word right etc." and GOTO whatever line says "Ask another
question."

But there is more to making reasonably close comparisons . . .
You must have discovered that a computer can be *too* accurate. It
won't accept IL CAFE for IL CAFFE for instance, even though an
Italian would know what you meant.

This can be a drawback when, in other programs, you are
searching for, you can't quite remember, is it GEOFF SMITH or JEFF
SMITH . . . 123 HIGH ST or 321 HIGH ST . . . ASPIRIN or
ASPERIN . . . PART NUMBER 887786 or 878786?

The technique, a variation of what is called 'fuzzy matching' is so
useful that it is shown here as a separate example. The variable IT$
still means the Italian word but it is no longer random. AN$ is still
the answer so you can test the technique by giving various wrong
answers:

```
10 IT$ = "IL PANE"
20 INPUT "IL PANE . . . ."; AN$
30 PRINT " ","ITALIAN","ANSWER","MATCHES"
```

There's the Italian. Try inputting something like IL PONE. The next
lines are going to break the two strings into their individual letters

and compare them. Line 30 tabs out the title and line 70 lists the comparison.

```
40 FOR Y = 1 TO LEN(IT$)
50 PT$(Y) = MID$(IT$,Y,1)
60 PA$(Y) = MID$(AN$,Y,1)
70 PRINT Y,PT$(Y),PA$(Y),
```

Translated, that means:

40 Loop for the length of the Italian phrase
50 Take the Italian, one letter at a time and call that letter PT$(Y)
60 Take the answer, one letter at a time and call that letter PA$(Y)
70 Print Y, print a letter of Italian, print a letter of the answer. The comma at the end is to include M, the number of matches, which comes later in line 120

Continuing

```
100 IF PA$(Y) = PT$(Y) THEN M = M + 1
120 PRINT M
130 NEXT Y
150 IF M > LEN(IT$)/2 THEN PRINT "PRETTY CLOSE" ELSE PRINT "NOWHERE NEAR"
```

which means:

100 If the first letter of the answer matches the first letter of the Italian, that's one match. M = M + 1
120 Print the score in the columns
150 If the number of matches M is more than half the number of letters in the Italian, then "Pretty close"

This works fine. But what happens if you miss a letter out and answer "I PANE" for instance? Most people would agree that was pretty close. Not the computer: it would be comparing your " " with the Italian "L", your "P" with the Italian " ", your "A" with "P" and every one would be wrong.

Yet if the Italian were broken into groups of three . . . "IL " (the space counts as a character) "L P", " PA", "PAN", "ANE", "NE " and "E   " . . . then you could check if any letter of your answer matched either the letter before, or the corresponding letter, or the letter after, in the Italian. This way I PANE would be pretty close to IL PANE.

Then alter line 50 so that it grabs three Italian letters:

```
50 PT$(Y) = MID$(IT$,Y,3)
```

with a 3 inside the brackets this time.

Now PT$(Y) is a three-letter string. And you examine every letter with a little three-times loop:

```
90 FOR C = 1 TO 3
100 IF PA$(Y) = MID$(PT$(Y),C,1) THEN M = M + 1
110 NEXT C
```

Line 100 means: if one letter of your answer matches any one of the three nearby Italian letters, then that counts.

This works better. But there is a bug. When the Italian is being broken into groups of three, the last letters have spaces with them: "NE " of "IL PANE" has one space and "E " has two spaces.

Unfortunately, if your keyboard operator inputs a short answer, like "PAN", that FOR Y loop at line 40 keeps on adding spaces until "PAN" is as long as LEN(IT$). The computer compares these added spaces with the spaces in "NE " and "E " and sure enough, they match. So your operator gets an artificially high score.

You have to tell the machine that if the answer has spaces in it, they are not really spaces at all:

```
80 IF PA$(Y) = "" THEN PA$(Y)="*"
```

Then what if your operator keys in too long an answer? IL PANORAMA is nowhere near the correct IL PANE yet it would score a good 6 out of 7 matches. So run a penalty line saying that IF the LENgth of the ANswer is bigger than the LENgth of the ITalian THEN subtract the extra from the number of Matches:

```
140 IF LEN(AN$) > LEN(IT$) THEN M = M - (LEN(AN$)-LEN(IT$))
```

Here is the 'fuzzy matching' routine again, together with two sample printouts:

```
10 IT$ = "IL PANE"
20 INPUT "IL PANE ..."; AN$
30 PRINT " ","ITALIAN","ANSWER","MATCHES"
40 FOR Y = 1 TO LEN(IT$)
50 PT$(Y) = MID$(IT$,Y,3)
60 PA$(Y) = MID$(AN$,Y,1)
70 PRINT Y, PT$(Y), PA$(Y),
80 IF PA$(Y) = "" THEN PA$(Y)="*"
90 FOR C = 1 TO 3
100 IF PA$(Y) = MID$(PT$(Y),C,1) THEN M = M + 1
110 NEXT C
120 PRINT M
130 NEXT Y
140 IF LEN(AN$) > LEN(IT$) THEN M = M - (LEN(AN$)-LEN(IT$))
150 IF M > LEN(IT$)/2 THEN PRINT "FAIRLY CLOSE" ELSE PRINT
    "NOWHERE NEAR"


Screen printout when PT$(Y) = MID$(IT$,Y,1)

IL PANE ...? IL PONI
             ITALIAN          ANSWER          MATCHES
 1           I                I               1
 2           L                L               2
 3                                            3
 4           P                P               4
 5           A                O               4
 6           N                N               5
 7           E                I               5

FAIRLY CLOSE
```

```
Screen printout when PT$(Y) = MID$(IT$,Y,3)
```

IL PANE ...? I PENO

	ITALIAN	ANSWER	MATCHES
1	IL	I	1
2	L P		2
3	PA	P	3
4	PAN	E	3
5	ANE	N	4
6	NE	O	4
7	E		4

FAIRLY CLOSE

And remember: we are not just talking about an Italian examination. Loose matching techniques are needed in stocktaking, in hunting for references, in data handling.

If you are thinking about buying a proprietary database or mailing list program, first check to see if it will handle *inaccurate* queries. Because your memory isn't all that good. You need a program that, if it can't find what you asked for, will give you instead a pretty reasonable guess.

Chapter 20

Question 1
A machine like the BBC Micro with a PROC function needs something like:

```
392 PROCexplanation(Result)
410 PROCexplanation(Result)

1000 DEF PROCexplanation(Result)
1010 IF Result < 0 THEN Explain$ =" A VERY BAD"
1020 IF Result > 0 THEN Explain$ =" NOT A SPECIAL"
1030 IF Result > 50 THEN Explain$ =" A REASONABLE"
1040 IF Result > 70 THEN Explain$ =" A GOOD"
1050 IF Result > 95 THEN Explain$ =" A PERFECT"
1060 PRINT "That indicates ; EX$; " relationship between
     them"
1070 ENDPROC
```

Other machines could have:

```
390 PRINT"THE CO-RELATIONSHIP BETWEEN "; L$(1); " AND ";
    L$(2); " IS "; FNC(D2); " %"
392 RE = FNC(D2)
394 GOSUB 1000
400 PRINT"                       BETWEEN " L$(1); " AND ";
    L$(3); " IS "; FNC(D3); " %"
402 RE = FNC(D3)
404 GOSUB 1000
500 END
1000 IF RE < 0 THEN EX$ =" A VERY BAD"
1010 IF RE > 0 THEN EX$ =" NOT A SPECIAL"
```

```
1020 IF RE > 50 THEN EX$ =" A REASONABLE"
1030 IF RE > 70 THEN EX$ =" A GOOD"
1040 IF RE > 95 THEN EX$ =" A PERFECT"
1050 PRINT "THAT INDICATES"; EX$; " RELATIONSHIP BETWEEN
     THEM"
1060 RETURN
```

Question 2
```
10 DEFFNA(L,OD,ID) = 3.1416 * L * ((OD/2)↑2 - (ID/2)↑2)
11 REM The formula is ₦ * radius² * length. of outside
12 REM minus the empty inside.
20 INPUT "HOW LONG IS THE PIPE "; LE
30 INPUT "WHAT'S THE OUTSIDE DIAMETER "; OU
40 INPUT "WHAT'S THE INSIDE DIAMETER "; IN
50 INPUT "ARE YOU MEASURING IN FEET, METRES OR WHAT "; ME$
60 VO = FNA(LE,OU,IN)
70 PRINT "THE VOLUME OF CONCRETE IS " VO " CUBIC "ME$
```

Chapter 21

Question 1
Between lines 170 and 180 have more INPUTs about price, date,
supplier and, to answer the second part of this question, minimum
stock level. Include these extra variables in line 180 and, for when
they are to be recalled, in line 450.

Then you can give a warning about low stock levels with:

472 IF ST$ = WH$ AND AM < MS (that's the minimum stock amount)
    THEN PRINT "LOW STOCK LEVEL !"

Question 2
The simplest way of counting lost sales is to see how often the
program goes to line 500. Either just before it or just after it, have:

502 LS = LS + 1

LS being the Lost Sales variable.

504 PRINT "THAT'S " LS " SALES YOU'VE LOST."

But that would only count the number of abortive queries since the
computer was switched on that morning. Nor would it list the
chemicals by name.

Chapter 22 might suggest to you a better way of settling this
problem, but in the meantime, try this:

502 LS$ = LS$ + " " + WH$

which will record the names of the chemicals.

To get the computer to remember what customers have asked for
earlier in the month, you need to open a new file. First it has to

input into memory the list of chemicals asked for on earlier occasions:

```
412 OPEN "I",2, "LOSTSALE/DAT"
414 INPUT #2, LS$
416 CLOSE 2
```

So when someone asks for, say, CHLOROFORM in line 440 and you haven't got it, LS$ in line 502 will already have ETHER VALIUM ALUDROX in it. Line 502 will add CHLOROFORM and then LS$ can be saved in a little file called LOSTSALE/DAT that contains nothing but LS$:

```
600 OPEN "O",2, "LOSTSALE/DAT"
610 PRINT #2, LS$
620 CLOSE 2
```

The bug? The first time you run the program, LOSTSALE/DAT will not exist so you can't input from it in lines 412 and 414.

The cure is to command RUN 600 and the program will start at line 600, create an empty LOSTSALE/DAT file and then close it again. Now you can do a normal RUN.

Chapter 22

Question 1
Once the NEW HOURS have been input, a lot of the following lines become automatic. PAY for instance is HOURS multiplied by the hourly RATE. So a new line for the RATE has to be included:

```
262 PRINT "THE RATE PER HOUR IS "; RA$
264 INPUT "IS THAT STILL THE SAME "; Y$
266 IF Y$ = "Y" THEN RA = VAL(RA$): GOTO 270
268 INPUT "WHAT'S THE NEW RATE "; RA
270 INPUT "NEW HOURS "; OH
```

for simplicity, the strings have been turned into numeric variables.

OVERTIME comes after 40 hours have been worked and it is paid at 'time and a half', i.e. RATE * 1.5.

```
272 VO = OH − 40
280 PRINT "NEW OVERTIME "; VO
290 INPUT "NEW BONUS "; OB
292 AP = (40 * RA) + (VO * 1.5 * RA) + OB
300 PRINT "NEW PAY "; AP
```

Tax in many countries stays the same, year after year. The only thing that governments alter is your tax coding, which entitles you to so much money tax-free every year. In Britain, if a married man is allowed £2795 before tax, he gets a coding of 279H and his employer is supposed to ignore 2795/52 every week of his pay before slamming the 30 per cent tax on the remainder.

If the week number is given the variable WE, and the tax-free-so-far is FT, the lines are:

```
312 PRINT "ANNUAL TAX-FREE PAY "; TF
314 FT = TF/52 * WE
```

So the tax deducted (ED) will be PAY SO FAR minus TAX-FREE SO FAR multiplied by .30

```
328 ED = ( (VAL(SF$) + AP) − FT) * .30
```

This large amount is deducted from the total pay received up to week WE:

```
340 PRINT "NEW PAY SO FAR "; VAL(SF$) + AP
350 PRINT "NEW FINAL PAY "; (VAL(SF$) + AP) − ED
```

meaning the pay so far plus this week's pay minus tax.

Then all this has to be stored on disk in place of the last week's pay record.

Question 3

Remembering a Record Number when you only know a name is tricky.

The angle is that direct access files do not need to be recorded in any order. Indeed, you can have blank records. So the Record Number can be arithmetically linked to the name.

It can't be purely on length, because LEN("FRED") is 4, the same as LEN("KATE"). But it could be based on the ASCII coding of the letters, with FRED being $70 + 82 + 69 + 68 = 289$ and KATE being $75 + 65 + 84 + 69 = 293$. The bug is that anagrams would give the same result: TAKE would add up to the same as KATE.

Beat this by multiplying every letter by its position in the word. KATE would become $75*1 + 65*2 + 84*3 + 69*4$. Don't bother to work that out, but it looks big: too big to be a reasonable Record Number. The next lines divide it by 100 then crudely chop away the decimals by FIX:

```
10 INPUT "NAME "; N$
20 FOR S = 1 TO LEN(N$)
30 RN = FIX(RN + ASC(MID$(N$,S,1)) * S /100)
40 NEXT S
```

Now you can call Fred's record from disk with:

```
50 OPEN "R", 1, "FILENAME/BAS"
60 GET 1, RN
```

because earlier you would have used the routine on line 30 to PUT it there.

Chapter 23

Question 1

The simplest way to put a cassette program on to disk is just to do it, then fix the bugs afterwards!

Start off in disk mode to get into BASIC. Connect up the cassette recorder and load the program from cassette into the computer's memory. A good DOS will look at the disk, see that the program isn't there, so it will automatically load from the tape. Other machines may need their special cassette version of the load command – CLOAD for instance. With a few, you may need a command to alter the computer's internal reading speed because tape is read slower than disk.

Once the program is in memory, don't attempt to RUN it. Unplug the cassette recorder. Command SAVE "PROGNAME" giving it whatever name you like and using the disk command for save. It should go easily on to disk. The bugs might show when you load it back from disk and attempt to run it.

Most ex-tape programs should run well. But if it called up files, then LIST or LLIST to a printer and edit the PRINT # and INPUT # lines into the way that disk BASIC likes them. If the program used machine code then it may not run because that code is bumping into disk routines that are now in memory. Read the manual to find out how to relocate the program.

Question 3

The commands are CALL, USR, POKE and PEEK which are not covered in this book because they vary so much with different machines. You will have to puzzle out your manual.

In business use you will often need to jump out of BASIC into DOS in order to ask how much free space is left on the disk, what programs there are in the directory or to copy programs. Certainly you can get to DOS by hitting the RESET button but there should be a way of getting back to your BASIC program without loss. If this isn't explained in the manual, ask the dealer who sold you the system.

Chapter 24

Question 3

```
10 CLEAR 2000
20 DIM  A(20)
30 FOR I = 20 TO 1 STEP -1
40 FOR O = 1 TO 5
50 A(I) = O
60 N = N + 1
```

```
70 IF INT((A(I)+1)/2) =  3 THEN PRINT "OK SO  FAR" :GOTO  90
ELSE 100
80 PRINT "BUG"
90 PRINT "GOOD"
100 NEXT O
110 NEXT I
120 REM DELETE 120
130 IF  N =  100 OR  N  = 101  THEN PRINT "STILL  GOOD" ELSE
PRINT "BUG"
140 DIM A$(5)
150 FOR B = 1 TO 5
160 FOR A = 1 TO 5
170 PRINT "CONGRATUALTIONS"
180 NEXT A
190 NEXT B
200 REM LINE 145 DOES NOT EXIST
210 PRINT"BAD NEWS ... THERE'S STILL A BUG IN THIS"
```

Index